DATE DUE

			PRINTED IN U.S.A.

ENCYCLOPEDIA OF LANGUAGE AND EDUCATION

Encyclopedia of Language and Education

VOLUME 8: RESEARCH METHODS IN LANGUAGE AND EDUCATION

The titles published in this encyclopedia are listed at the end of this volume.

Encyclopedia of Language and Education

Volume 8

RESEARCH METHODS IN LANGUAGE
AND EDUCATION

Edited by

NANCY H. HORNBERGER

Graduate School of Education
University of Pennsylvania
Philadelphia, USA

and

DAVID CORSON

The Ontario Institute for Studies in Education
University of Toronto
Canada

KLUWER ACADEMIC PUBLISHERS

DORDRECHT / BOSTON / LONDON

blication Data

....J education / edited by Nancy H.
Hornberger and David Corson.
      p.   cm. -- (Encyclopedia of language and education ; v. 8)
   Includes bibliographical referencesand index.
   ISBN 0-7923-4642-4 (alk. paper). -- ISBN 0-7923-4596-7 (set : alk.
paper)
   1. Language and education--Research--Methodology.   I. Hornberger,
Nancy H. II. Corson, David. III. Series.
P40.8.R47 1997
407'.2--dc21   97-30206

ISBN 0-7923-4642-4
ISBN 0-7923-4596-7 (SET)

Published by Kluwer Academic Publishers,
P.O. Box 17, 3300 AA Dordrecht, The Netherlands

Sold and distributed in the U.S.A. and Canada
by Kluwer Academic Publishers,
101 Philip Drive, Norwell, MA 02061, U.S.A.

In all other countries, sold and distributed
by Kluwer Academic Publishers Group,
P.O. Box 322, 3300 AH Dordrecht, The Netherlands

Printed in the Netherlands (on acid-free paper)

TABLE OF CONTENTS

VOLUME 8: RESEARCH METHODS IN LANGUAGE AND EDUCATION

Section 3: Language, Culture, and Education: Recent Advances in Approaches, Methods, and Topics

Section 4: Language, Interaction, and Education: Recent Advances in Approaches, Methods, and Topics

GENERAL EDITOR'S INTRODUCTION

ENCYCLOPEDIA OF LANGUAGE AND EDUCATION

This is one of eight volumes of the Encyclopedia of Language and Education published by Kluwer Academic. The publication of this work signals the maturity of the field of 'language and education' as an international and interdisciplinary field of significance and cohesion. These volumes confirm that 'language and education' is much more than the preserve of any single discipline. In designing these volumes, we have tried to recognise the diversity of the field in our selection of contributors and in our choice of topics. The contributors come from every continent and from more than 40 countries. Their reviews discuss language and education issues affecting every country in the world.

We have also tried to recognise the diverse interdisciplinary nature of 'language and education' in the selection of the editorial personnel themselves. The major academic interests of the volume editors confirm this. As principal volume editor for Volume 1, Ruth Wodak has interests in critical linguistics, sociology of language, and language policy. For Volume 2, Viv Edwards has interests in policy and practice in multilingual classrooms and the sociology of language. For Volume 3, Bronwyn Davies has interests in the social psychology of language, the sociology of language, and interdisciplinary studies. For Volume 4, Richard Tucker has interests in language theory, applied linguistics, and the implementation and evaluation of innovative language education programs. For Volume 5, Jim Cummins has interests in the psychology of language and in critical linguistics. For Volume 6, Leo van Lier has interests in applied linguistics and in language theory. For Volume 7, Caroline Clapham has interests in research into second language acquisition and language measurement. And for Volume 8, Nancy Hornberger has interests in anthropological linguistics and in language policy. Finally, as general editor, I have interests in the philosophy and sociology of language, language policy, critical linguistics, and interdisciplinary studies. But the thing that unites us all, including all the contributors to this work, is an interest in the practice and theory of education itself.

People working in the applied and theoretical areas of education and language are often asked questions like the following: 'what is the latest research on such and such a problem?' or 'what do we know about such and such an issue?' Questions like these are asked by many people: by policy makers and practitioners in education; by novice researchers; by publishers trying to relate to an issue; and above all by undergraduate and postgraduate students in the language disciplines. Each of the reviews that appears in this volume tries to anticipate and answer some of the more commonly asked questions about language and education. Taken together, the eight volumes of this Encyclopedia provide answers to more than 200 major questions of this type, and hundreds of subsidiary questions as well.

Each volume of the Encyclopedia of Language and Education deals with a single, substantial subject in the language and education field. The volume titles and their contents appear elsewhere in the pages of this work. Each book-length volume provides more than 20 state-of-the-art topical reviews of the literature. Taken together, these reviews attempt a complete coverage of the subject of the volume. Each review is written by one or more experts in the topic, or in a few cases by teams assembled by experts. As a collection, the Encyclopedia spans the range of subjects and topics normally falling within the scope of 'language and education'. Each volume, edited by an international expert in the subject of the volume, was designed and developed in close collaboration with the general editor of the Encyclopedia, who is a co-editor of each volume as well as general editor of the whole work.

The Encyclopedia has been planned as a necessary reference set for any university or college library that serves a faculty or school of education. Libraries serving academic departments in any of the language disciplines, especially applied linguistics, would also find this a valuable resource. It also seems very relevant to the needs of educational bureaucracies, policy agencies, and public libraries, particularly those serving multicultural or multilingual communities.

The Encyclopedia aims to speak to a prospective readership that is multinational, and to do so as unambiguously as possible. Because each book-size volume deals with a discrete and important subject in language and education, these state-of-the-art volumes also offer authoritative course textbooks in the areas suggested by their titles. This means that libraries will also catalogue these book-size individual volumes in relevant sections of their general collections. To meet this range of uses, the Encyclopedia is published in a hardback edition offering the durability needed for reference collections, and in a future student edition. The hardback edition is also available for single-volume purchase.

Each state-of-the-art review has about 3000 words of text and most follow a similar structure. A list of references to key works cited in each review supplements the information and authoritative opinion that the review contains. Many contributors survey early developments in their topic, major contributions, work in progress, problems and difficulties, and future directions for research and practice. The aim of the reviews, and of the Encyclopedia as a whole, is to give readers access to the international literature and research on each topic.

David Corson
General Editor Encyclopedia of Language and Education
Ontario Institute for Studies in Education of the University of Toronto
Canada

INTRODUCTION

As the final volume in the Encyclopedia of Language and Education, this volume seeks to complement the topical focus of the previous volumes with a comprehensive look at research methods. The volume is intended to provide an overview and starting point for further exploration of the breadth and depth of approaches, methods, and topics in research on language and education. Seeking to ensure breadth of coverage, the volume is organized in four sections, focusing on language and education in relation to society, variation, culture, and interaction, in turn. This organizing frame is borrowed from my four quadrant typology of sociolinguistics, in which two axes defined by micro/macro and linguistic/social levels of analysis yield up four quadrants corresponding to four broad research perspectives (Hornberger, 1989; McKay & Hornberger, 1996).

A major assumption of the four quadrant typology, and of the organizational frame for this volume, is that both micro and macro perspectives and both social and linguistic levels of analysis are critical for an understanding of the interaction between language and education. That is, it is as important for us to understand, for example, the impact of national language policy on classroom medium of instruction as it is to explore the role of teacher-student and student-student interaction in classroom language learning. And it is as revealing to analyze, for example, phonetic and intonational variation in learners' language as it is to study the introduction of pedagogical innovation in one particular multilingual classroom context. The present volume seeks to enable language and education practitioners, researchers and interested lay readers alike to get a sense of the range of issues being pursued in language and education research and the array of methods employed to do so.

Within the Encyclopedia's overall focus on language and education, then, this volume focuses on research methods; and within that focus on research methods, each section of the volume has a particular focus, i.e. society in section one, variation in section two. culture in section three, and interaction in section four. Within each section, in turn, there is a sequence of reviews representing different aspects of that focus: the first two or three reviews take up research approaches that might be considered sub-fields within sociolinguistic and/or educational research; then follow two reviews on specific methods of research which complement these approaches; and in closing, one or two reviews take a more topical perspective, exploring the application of approaches and methods to the study of a particular topic.

N.H. Hornberger and D. Corson (eds), Encyclopedia of Language and Education,
Volume 8: Research Methods in Language and Education, xi–xvi.
© *1997 Kluwer Academic Publishers. Printed in the Netherlands.*

While boundaries and limits between what exactly constitutes a topic vs. a method vs. an approach are not always as clearcut as the above scheme suggests, keeping these various frames and focuses in mind may help the reader to balance across related or overlapping contributions within or across parts of this volume and the Encyclopedia as a whole; ample cross-referencing and indexing in the volume (and in the Encyclopedia) also seek to achieve this purpose.

Section One opens with reviews of two research approaches which adopt a primarily macrolevel perspective on language, society, and education: Su-chiao Chen writes on the sociology of language and Seran Doğançay-Aktuna on language planning. Chen notes that issues commonly addressed in the sociology of language in relation to advances in language education include language contact and spread, multilingualism, language maintenance and language shift, and language planning. Language planning, says Doğançay-Aktuna, refers to activities that attempt to bring about changes in the structure and functions of language or language varieties in order to deal with linguistic or extra-linguistic problems at the national, international, or community level.

Robert Young follows with an overview of the role of social science theory in researching language and education, while Colin Baker summarizes the use of survey methods, often (but not exclusively) associated with large-scale studies. Young asserts that it is useful to identify a small number of relatively systematic hermeneutic positions – conservative and empiricist, Marxist, moderate, critical-pragmatist, and postmodern or radical; and that each of these positions has different implications for theorising and conducting research on language, education, and their conjunction. Surveys, notes Baker, are not synonymous with a particular technique of collecting information, but can occur via questionnaires, structured and in-depth interviews, structured or systematic observation, and content analysis of documents.

The final review in this first section is Rebecca Freeman's look at approaches and methods of research on the role of one social variable, gender, in language and education. Freeman suggests that recent ethnographic and discourse analytic research in a wide range of educational and non-educational contexts has begun to illustrate that gender (and other social) identities are largely discursively constituted and to demonstrate how our language use can reproduce, resist, or transform dominant gender (and other social) practices.

Moving to a more micro focus on language, while retaining the macro-social perspective, Section Two begins with reviews of two research approaches which are interested in the ways that variation in language use interacts with other social processes to reproduce – and contest – social inequalities and ethnic prejudices in educational settings: Stella Maris Bortoni-Ricardo reviews variationist sociolinguistics and Tara Goldstein reviews critical pedagogy. Variationist sociolinguistics, says Bortoni-Ricardo, is premised on the notions of cultural relativism and orderly linguistic heterogeneity, wherein no dialect (variety) of a language is considered inherently superior to another as concerns its structure even though functional distinctions among varieties might be acknowledged. Goldstein describes critical pedagogy as an approach involving working with educators to enable students to analyze the ways they experience oppression and take steps to redress conditions that perpetuate discrimination; specifically, in the case of language and education research, focusing on the ways language use and language learning reproduce or redress those conditions.

Exploring some of the methods commonly used to study relationships between macrosocial and microlinguistic variables in language and education, Ludo Verhoeven presents an overview of experimental design and methods of analysis and Teresa Pica follows with a review of the eclectic and innovative methods used in second language acquisition research. Verhoeven notes that one idea implicit to experimental research is that it is possible to make valid claims from the particular to the general and that new knowledge becomes available from processes of inductive inference. Second language acquisition research design, Pica asserts, can be theory-driven and hypothesis-testing, or data-driven, through pattern identification and analysis.

Two topical research reviews conclude this section: Birgit Harley on (methods and approaches in) the study of age and John Baugh on (methods and approaches in) the study of race and social class as variables affecting language acquisition and use. The role of age in language learning has remained controversial despite an impressive number of studies, Harley says, largely because chronological age though easy to measure reflects life experience as well as biologically determined maturation and is therefore difficult to interpret consistently. Baugh traces development of attention to the relationship between language and race in linguistic research and its application to education, citing the Ebonics controversy which emerged in Oakland, California early in 1997 as one among many cases worldwide where a legacy of racial bigotry, language acquisition, and educational policies coincide.

Section Three exchanges micro for macrolinguistic, and macro for microsocial perspectives, with opening reviews of two research approaches that focus on the mutual relationships between language, culture, and education, as reflected at the microsocial level of peoples' behavior, activities, interaction and discourse in school, classroom, and community settings: Iffat Farah reviews the ethnography of communication and Karen Ann Watson-Gegeo reviews classroom ethnography. The ethnography of communication, notes Farah, is an approach which has its origin in the development of a view in anthropology that culture is to a large extent expressed through language and of the view in linguistics that language is a system of cultural behaviors. Classroom ethnography, in contrast to quantitative approaches to classroom research, says Watson-Gegeo, emphasizes the sociocultural nature of teaching and learning processes, incorporates participants' perspectives on their own behavior, and offers a holistic analysis sensitive to levels of context in which interactions and classrooms are situated.

With regard to specific methods of research which may be employed within an overall ethnographical approach (although not exclusively so), Christian Faltis and Olga Rubio explore case study methods and ethnographic interview methods in their respective reviews. A feature common to case study methods since their introduction into social science research in the 1940s, says Faltis, is that they examine a specific phenomenon as a bounded system. Ethnographic interviews, Rubio asserts, are used by social scientists and educators to get the informant's or interviewee's perspective on their beliefs, values, and understandings of life and other topics or cultural events.

Two topical research reviews, one by Sarah Norgate on blind children and the other by Jan Branson and Don Miller on the signing deaf, provide insight into the methodological challenges and advances in approaches to research on language and education within these cultural groups. Norgate notes that recent research into language development in blind children has raised concern over the extent to which it is appropriate to include a sighted control group or to rely on research strategies which borrow from approaches commonly used with sighted children; once research strategies take into account the different perceptual information available to blind children, their language development is viewed more positively. Similarly, Branson and Miller suggest that the development of research methods for the study of sign languages has been particularly influenced by the unwritten nature of sign language and by its mode of conveying meaning not by sound but rather by a range of conventions based on handshapes, the use of space, the face and body.

In Section Four, the focus moves to the microlevel of linguistic as well as social analysis, beginning with three reviews on research approaches which aim at describing and understanding the role of language in the construction of social relationships in face-to-face interaction in specific educational settings, and ultimately aim also at subverting the reproduction of inequitable relations of power in those settings: Pedro Garcez writes on microethnography, Stephen May on critical ethnography, and Bonny Norton on critical discourse research, all as they relate to language and education. Microethnography, notes Garcez, offers a methodology for the investigation of face-to-face interaction and a particular point of view which stresses that the social and cultural organization of human communicative action involves conversationalists contained in physical bodies, occupying space in simultaneously constraining and enabling social situations, who must reflexively make sense of each others' actions as they act. Critical discourse researchers in education, Norton suggests, are interested in the way language constructs and is constructed by complex and unequal sets of social relationships, and how participants in different educational activities contribute through their discursive practices to the reproduction of hegemonic relations, or contest the legitimacy of those practices. Critical ethnography, says May, highlights the role of ideology in sustaining and perpetuating inequality within particular settings, and aims not simply to describe but to change those settings for the better.

Threads of the microlevel focus and/or critical intent of these approaches are taken up in the following two reviews of specific research methods: James Heap reviews conversation analysis, and Teresa McCarty reviews teacher research. The methods and methodology of conversation analysis, Heap says, have been used by researchers on language and education to advance understanding of classroom talk as a variant of naturally occurring conversation. McCarty notes that all recent teacher research utilizes a qualitative, case study, or ethnographic approach; primary participants are K-12 teachers working individually or collaboratively with other teachers and university-based researchers to address questions of deep personal significance with an eye toward systemic change.

The final two topical reviews of the volume consider some of the above research approaches and methods as used in the study of two special cases of language use in classrooms: Ilana Snyder writes on the use of computers and Marilyn Martin-Jones on bilingual classroom discourse. Snyder's review notes that different methods for investigating computers in literacy contexts include academics working in universities, researchers and practitioners forming partnerships, teacher-led research, and small-scale classroom studies based on teachers' experience and their informal observations. Martin-Jones notes that during the last twenty years or so, increasing diversification of sites and an increasingly interactional bent in approaches to classroom-based research in bilingual or multilingual settings have resulted in the development of powerful analytical tools and a much better understanding of the range and complexity of the cultural and communicative processes at work in bilingual classrooms.

The scholars contributing to this volume hail from five continents and nine countries; they represent a great diversity of linguistic, cultural, and disciplinary traditions. For all that, what is most impressive about the contributions gathered here is the unity of purpose and outlook they express with regard to the central role of language as both vehicle and mediator of educational processes and to the need for continued and deepening research into the limits and possibilities that implies.

REFERENCES

Hornberger, N.H.: 1989, 'Continua of biliteracy', *Review of Educational Research* 59(3), 271–296.
McKay, S.L. & Hornberger, N.H. (eds.): 1996, *Sociolinguistics and Language Teaching*, Cambridge University Press, Cambridge.

Section 1

**Language, Society, and Education:
Recent Advances in Approaches, Methods, and Topics**

SU-CHIAO CHEN

SOCIOLOGY OF LANGUAGE

The sociology of language is the study of the relationship between language and society. It 'focuses upon the entire gamut of topics related to the social organization of language behavior, including not only language usage per se but also language attitudes and overt behaviors toward language and toward language users' (Fishman, 1971, p. 217). The field begins from the assumption that language is a social value, and pursues research on language in contact among social groups, especially phenomena such as language conflict and multilingualism. While Fishman tends to characterize the study at two levels: descriptive sociology of language, describing 'who speaks what language to whom and when', and dynamic sociology of language, explaining the different rates of change of language behavior in different groups, his definition is far from clear in terms of levels of analysis. This gap was bridged by McKay & Hornberger (1996, p. x), who have established a distinctive four-level model for approaching the study of language and society. The scope of this essay falls within the macro – macro level in their model, i.e. the area of sociolinguistics dealing with the relationship between the larger social and political contexts and language use at a macro level. The aim of the essay is to provide an overview of the theoretical and methodological models in this field and to indicate how it has advanced in the field of language education (also see reviews by Fettes and by Schroeder in Volume 1).

EARLY DEVELOPMENTS

Joyce Hertzler's two publications: 'Toward a sociology of language' (1953), and 'The sociology of language' (1965), along with a 1966 sociolinguistics conference in California, were catalysts for intense and sustained research efforts beginning in the late 1960s. Sociologists and educationalists eagerly sought to understand the relationship between language and social disadvantage, linguists eagerly sought to define the notion of communicative competence in a speech community, and anthropologists eagerly sought to investigate the relationship between language and culture.

The explosion of this research interest began with early scholars largely from sociology and anthropological linguistics, who applied their methodologies and theories to the description of the contextual correlates of the use of linguistic varieties. Some scholars (e.g. Haugen, 1966; Gumperz,

N.H. Hornberger and D. Corson (eds), Encyclopedia of Language and Education,
Volume 8: Research Methods in Language and Education, 1–13.
© *1997 Kluwer Academic Publishers. Printed in the Netherlands.*

1968) identified concepts (e.g. dialect; speech community) of fundamental importance; others (e.g. Ferguson, 1966; Stewart, 1968; Kloss, 1968), based on census and language surveys, established formulas and typologies for description and comparison of sociolingusitic situations. Their purpose was to describe a nation's language use by a language profile method. These early scholars of the sociology of language commonly used a demographic approach to the quantitative study of speech communities. A nation's population was categorized in terms of a language criterion (e.g. mother tongue), and the verbal repertoire of a speech community was profiled into 'major' and 'minor' languages, with dimensions including number and function of languages; number and distribution of language users.

While the 'static' approach of the language profile did not interpret the dynamic process of language use and change, it catalogued the diversity and inequality of sociolinguistic situations. Subsequent scholars have advanced this line of research, in which linguistic differences and educational and social disadvantages of minority language groups have become one of the major concerns. Another foundational work, Labov's (1969) exposition on the logic of nonstandard English, played a central role in clarifying that language differences become deficits through popular convention and prejudice (on the standard/non-standard issue see reviews by Corson in Volumes 1 and 6). The confluence of social, cultural and linguistic factors contributing to these inequalities and how they affect the domain of language education have become widely researched topics thereafter.

MAJOR CONTRIBUTIONS

The scope and depth of research has been expanded since the mid-1970s. Investigation of many 'macro-issues', such as language contact and spread, societal multilingualism, diglossia, language policy and language planning, language maintenance and shift, and language attitude, has produced a substantial body of literature. The study of those topics springs from the core sociolinguistic concern, i.e. 'the description and analysis of the organization and change of verbal repertoires in relation to the main processes of societal evolution' (Hymes, 1984, p. 44). Specifically, the work in developed nations mainly focuses on language policies and immigrant language maintenance and shift, while that in developing nations focuses on national language policies and language policies in education. Despite differences in dimensions and in national-type contexts, issues of language education are directly relevant to those sociolinguistic concerns, because educational choices being made can have a direct impact on the opportunities of minority speakers. Issues commonly addressed in the sociology of language in relation to advances in language education include language contact and spread, multilingualism, language maintenance and language shift, and language planning, which will be discussed in the following sections of this review.

Language Contact and Spread

Languages are in contact because of migration and conquest. Although language contact is as old as Babel's confusion of tongues, its study dates back to the early 1950s when Weinreich (1953) began his empirical field research. Work on language contact originated with research of interlingual character (e.g. interference) and has now expanded towards the study of inter-ethnic contacts which in most cases contribute to language conflict. This conflict results from the forces of contact circumstances that cause 'big' languages to spread.

Language spread is defined 'as an increase, over time, in the proportion of a communication network that adopts a given language or language variety for a certain communication function' (Cooper, 1982, p. 6). In early research on language spread, one group of researchers (e.g. Bailey & Gorlach, 1982), used a purely descriptive approach to depict the linguistic ecology of an individual geographical area or nation. Another group of researchers, however, sought to abstract factors and construct a theoretical model to predict the extent of language spread. For example, Fishman, Cooper & Rosenbaum (1977) hypothesized and tested the proposition that in addition to the variables isolated by Brosnahan (1963) – military imposition, duration of authority, linguistic diversity, and material advantages, the five variables of urbanization, economic development, educational development, religious composition and political bloc affiliation, are related to the spread of English in the Third World. Wardhaugh (1987) employed the same approach to the study of language in competition. This approach tends to be restricted to typologies of variables and sees linguistic competition in contact situations as a free market and language spread as a matter of rational choice. Both the purely descriptive and the typological approaches mentioned above rely upon quantification and statistical analyses, but strip social phenomena of all their actualities and complexities. They cannot be used to interpret the dynamics of language spread in different societies.

However, another group of researchers (e.g. Weinstein, 1983), using a socio-political approach, have discovered that language spread always involves the intricacies of political maneuvers and power struggles. Examples include the spread of English in the Third World in which a network of intra-state and inter-state power arrangements are disguised in the pragmatic use of and prestigious attitudes toward English in the world. Recently, McConnell (1990) goes further than describing or providing an account of language spread to propose three theoretical constructs for measuring language spread, namely, formulas, typologies, and a form-function model of language vitality.

These various approaches to the study of language spread have brought to light an understanding of, in general, the societal patterns of language use and change in that use, and, in particular, the spread of World Englishes as natural, neutral and beneficial. Such study of language spread reveals community members' participation in educational opportunities and addresses the concerns for L1 and L2 language education, particularly ESL/EFL, in global and national contexts.

Societal Multilingualism

Societal multilingualism (interchangeably with bilingualism) is defined as the knowledge or use of more than one language by a community. Communicative competence in multilingual contexts refers to the use of the language varieties in linguistically, socially and functionally appropriate ways. To investigate the appropriate use of language at the macro-level, scholars used a functional approach looking to understand the functions of speech as it occurs in context, at the level of speech act, speech event, or speech situation (Hymes, 1974). Fishman proposed a higher level of abstraction, with the notion of 'domain', defined in terms of 'institutional contexts and their congruent behavioral co-occurrences' (1972). Two language-use phenomena: diglossia and code-switching, are examples of language use for appropriateness in multilingual contexts.

Diglossia. Diglossia is a typical example of language use in strict separation of domains. Introduced by Ferguson (1959), the term refers to two varieties of the same language that are functionally specialized and used in mutually exclusive domains by the same speech community. There are superposed variety (H) and regional dialects (L). Fishman (1967) extended the concept of diglossia to include 'serveral separate codes', and recognized two types of compartmentalization: functional and social/political. While Ferguson and Fishman have argued that compartmentalization in language use in diglossic situations contributes to stable societal bilingualism and language maintenance, recent empirical studies on Greek (e.g. Mackridge, 1985), in the Arab world (e.g. Mahmoud, 1984), and in Haiti (e.g. Dejean, 1993), all of which are notable cases of diglossia identified by Ferguson, and elsewhere have suggested that the compartmentalization of H and L may not truly exist because either intermediate varieties may be used or one variety may be displaced by the other. Similarly, Schiffman (1993) claims that diglossia tends to be unstable because the imbalance of power between the two languages or varieties leads to language shift. Whether diglossia can contribute to stable societal bilingualism and language maintenance remains an open question.

Most scholars (e.g. Britto, 1986) have been concerned with developing diglossia typologies rather than applying the notion of diglossia to
language education, however, exceptions include Ferguson (1963) and
Wexler (1971). Given the inherent inequality of language in a diglossic
community, if language maintenance is desirable, protection needs to be
taken. Education can have a direct impact on the power balance in diglossic
languages. Luxembourg is a case of successful triglossia by legal protection and by education (Davis, 1994).

Code-Switching. Code-switching (henceforth CS), a form of language con-
tact, is a phenomenon which frequently occurs in a bilingual community.
Earlier studies of language in contact (e.g. Weinreich, 1953) considered
CS as an interference phenomenon, i.e. the performance of imperfect
bilinguals. Nevertheless, CS had not attracted scholars' attention until
Blom and Gumperz's work (1972) on the dichotomy between situational
and metaphorical CS, which showed CS as motivated by social function.
This work has laid the foundation for continuing investigation of the social
motivations for CS in many different places of the world since the 1970s.

In the early 1980s, using a conversational-/discourse-oriented approach,
Gumperz expanded his view of CS and offered a catalogue of the discourse
functions of CS to account for shifts from one language to another. He
introduced the idea that CS is one of a number of 'contextualization cues'
which addressees use to interpret a conversation. He also characterizes CS
as a stylistic phenomenon, based on the premise that the symbolic distinction between 'we' and 'they' code is embodied in the choice of codes.
This approach contributes to a functional taxonomy of social motivations
for CS. Many scholars (e.g. Heller, 1988) undertook empirical studies and
have advanced CS research along this line in which the concern is with
how linguistic resources acquire social or discourse meaning rather than
with the structural constraints on these linguistic resources.

While Gumperz provides an 'interactional/interpretative' model, which
considers language use as a dynamic event and linguistic choices as a
social strategy, he does not link his interactional-level analyses of data
with macro social aspects, e.g. social organization. This micro – macro
link was developed by other scholars, including Milroy & Wei (1995), who
use a social network approach; and Gal (1988), who uses a macro-approach
to analyze social motivations of CS above the level of conversation. While
Gal sees CS as changing ethnic boundaries and personal relationships and
constructing 'self' and 'other' within a broader political, economic and
historical context, Myers-Scotton (1993) explains CS in terms of a theory
of rights and obligations, based on socio-psychological motivations. She
develops a markedness model of CS and interprets communicative competence in terms of linguistic choice which matches the speech situations in
which speakers find themselves (i.e. rights and obligations).

Research on CS in a variety of bilingual classrooms (e.g. Hornberger, 1988; Zentella, 1981), mostly by using an ethnographic approach with audio-recordings of classroom interactions, has suggested that CS is a sign of bilingual competence, because it is used to fulfill specifiable functions. Studies such as these have provided insights into various bilingual learning environments, teachers' attitudes, classroom interaction, functions of teacher-talk, and pragmatic functions of CS in conversations in a variety of bilingual classes. This provides us an account of what enables or constrains teachers and learners in bilingual classroom communication (see the review by Martin-Jones in this volume).

Research on CS in society in general, and in the classroom specifically, illuminates mechanisms of social and linguistic change in a community. It can be a useful reference for language education policies, particularly for language pedagogy, for example, in the distribution of the two languages of instruction in bilingual education.

Language Maintenance and Shift

A bilingual community without diglossia is categorized as transitional or unstable, which will contribute to a 'minority' language shift. Examples of an unstable bilingual community are immigrant communities such as those in the U.S. or Australia. Concerns for language maintenance (henceforth LM) or language shift (henceforth LS) of immigrant languages drew scholars to collect data on factors and degrees of maintenance. Fishman (1966) was one of the early scholars of LM and LS, who, by using a language survey case study of six groups in the U.S., concluded that all proceed along the same lines in terms of LM and LS but only differ in the rate of change toward Anglicisation. This is also observed by Veltman (1983), who did a careful statistical analysis of LS from minority languages to English, based on the Survey of Income and Education, which was conducted by the U.S. Census Bureau in 1976, and on supplementary data obtained from the High School and Beyond survey conducted in 1980.

It is the different rates of change that interest scholars, a number of whom, using different approaches, have studied LM and LS and correlated factors among different groups around the world. Some favor using a statistical approach, based on self report, as was just mentioned. For example, Pauwels' study (1986) used this approach to look at LM of German and Dutch ethnic groups in terms of two variables: regional dialect and the standard spoken as an immigrant's first language in Australia. Others, however, regard this type of large-scale study as unable to capture the actual language behavior and language attitudes of the members of the community, and thus introduce participant observation into the study. A typical example is Gal's study of LS in Oberwart, Austria (1979). She uses domain theory to detect the degree of mother-tongue shift and claims that 'shifting' is a gradual progress. In a related gesture, some (e.g. Mackey, 1980) use an ecological framework to explain LS in order to avoid drawing the same conclusions about the cause of LS in different groups with different ecological conditions. This framework comes from 'ecology of language', introduced and defined by Haugen as 'the study of the interactions between any given language and its environment' (1972). Integrating three approaches to LS: domain theory, interactional/variationist theory and adaptation theory, McConvell sees LS resulting from 'the loss of the functions of bilingualism' (1991, p. 151).

Another group of researchers study LM and LS from a social psychological perspective. Among them are Giles et al. (1977), who have constructed a model, 'ethnolinguistic vitality' to systematize factors that affect LM and LS, grouped into three categories: status, demographic and institutional support factors. Empirical studies (e.g. Landry & Allard, 1992) show that language shift occurs as ethnolinguistic vitality decreases.

Based on the variables postulated by the previous researchers, those factors that are used to examine how different rates of language change occur are as follows: immigration patterns of a minority group, demographic factors, religious factors, socioeconomic factors, political factors – language policy/institutional support and generational factors. It is the combination of the factors, not any single factor, that accounts for LM and LS. Most importantly, it has to be noted that a single factor may have one effect in one community but the opposite in another. Although these factors provide excellent insights into reasons for LM and LS, they cannot organize any listings or insights into a coherent and comprehensive theoretical framework. Nevertheless, the study of LM and LS is particularly important to those concerned with making language policy in a country. It can help in designing specific programming to meet the needs of specific target populations.

Language Policy and Planning

Given the linguistic complexity of multilingual nations, government policy has to be made for the function of different languages within the nation; such policy is commonly referred to as language planning (henceforth LP), defined as intervention in the process of language change, including three types: status planning, corpus planning and acquisition planning (Cooper, 1989) (see the review by Doğançay-Aktuna in this volume). A dominant language was traditionally chosen for official functions leading to others being shifted or eradicated.

However, due to global social, economic and political changes since the 1960s, LP has taken many forms, even in similar sociopolitical contexts.

For example, among 'developing' nations, Kenya and Tanzania share a similar linguistic background. While Kenya adopted capitalism and English was chosen as the language of instruction in the primary-school level and beyond for developing high-level manpower, Tanzania opted for socialism and Kiswahili was chosen as the language of instruction in the primary-school level for developing rural labor. Similarly, Singapore and Malaysia share similar historical and linguistic backgrounds, but while Singapore adopted a policy of cultural integration of different ethnic groups with English as the supra-ethnic Singaporean identity, Malaysia adopted nationalism and imposed Bahasa Malaysia (Malay) as the sole official language of Malaysia.

Among the 'developed' nations, two different forms of LP are identified. One form (e.g. Belgium) adopted a language policy that separates the different language populations by fixed boundaries. Another form (e.g. the U.S.) adopted a policy that enforces the dominant language as well as allowing minority groups to be educated in their mother tongue through Bilingual Education (henceforth BE).

No matter what language policy is adopted, BE is often carried out in minority children's early school years as a primary tool for acquisition planning and shift policy. The usual practice is to use L1 to acquire L2 proficiency. Hornberger (1991) suggests a heuristic in the form of a typology of BE models and programs, which includes transitional model, maintenance model, and enrichment model. She suggests each of these models can be implemented by a variety of program structures, depending on contextual and structural characteristics. Fishman (1991a) suggests LP to reverse LS of minority languages by allocating societal resources to foster the use of language in more societal functions, by the linguistic 'standardization' of an endangered language and by fostering minority languages in schools.

PROBLEMS AND DIFFICULTIES

Problems and difficulties with the sociology of language include concerns with the reliability and validity of research methods, lack of clarity in defining key concepts, and questions of applying theoretical paradigms. As was mentioned previously, much research in the sociology of language is based on data from census, language surveys or fieldwork (see the review by Baker in this volume). These techniques, although helpful in collecting data, may have serious limitations in terms of presenting a true picture of the sociolinguistic situation at a societal level. National censuses are unreliable particularly in developing nations, and may or may not include a language question, usually limited to asking the informant's mother tongue. Large-scale sociolinguistic surveys are biased in favor of urban, developed and accessible areas. 'Variability' inherent in people's language use is also ignored in census and survey approaches. In fieldwork, the 'Observer's Paradox' (Labov, 1972, p. 209), and specifically the 'response bias' and 'interviewer bias' in an interview are problems that make the reliability and validity of the data questionable. Response bias suggests that data may be influenced by the respondents' social desirability, whereas interviewer bias suggests that data may be influenced by the degree of accommodation between interviewer and interviewee. These forms of bias are particularly pronounced in sociolinguistic interviews because the setting and apparatus of the interview greatly influence the respondent's language use.

The problems of reliability and validity surrounding research techniques are intertwined with conceptual problems of sociolinguistics. Questions about the knowledge or the use of a certain language in certain situations are generally asked no matter what techniques have been employed. However, concepts such as 'language knowledge' and 'language use', 'LM' and 'LS' are hardly defined, because they have not been prescribed or standardized. This inconsistency in the definition of concepts makes self report about language use often unreliable.

The application of theoretical paradigms is also problematic in that a paradigm developed from a certain point of view may be different from that of other points of view. For example, factors and models to account for language spread have been developed mainly from the point of view of the English-speaking countries, but may not be applicable from the point of view of other language-speaking countries. Similarly, models for solutions to questions about the education of minority children may be different, depending on a monolingualism or multilingualism goal, and on different sociolinguistic situations. The various interpretations and compatibility between different positions are not always tested by investigators before application. This is due to the absence of a satisfactory model which can explain and monitor all language behavior. This makes it difficult to know what variables have to be included for investigation or for cross-cultural comparison. Thus, it is hard to move toward a more unified theoretical framework in the sociology of language.

FUTURE DIRECTIONS

After three decades' research in the sociology of language, substantial progress has been made. On the one hand, the rise of domain theory and the functional approach have thrown light on the nature of communicative competence and sociolinguistic change. On the other hand, we have also seen great progress in the quantitative and qualitative study of both stable and unstable bilingualism, in both the 'developing' and 'developed' countries. Those previous studies have laid foundations for delineating future directions which include the incorporation of methods and theories from other disciplines within the enterprise, the establishment of a more unified theoretical framework through comparative studies, and the conduct of longitudinal study on sociolinguistic behaviors.

As an interdisciplinary field of study, the sociology of language draws on theories and methods from other disciplines, particularly from sociology and linguistics. However, as Fishman (1991b) has pointed out, the (macro) sociolinguistic enterprise is undergoing a mid-life crisis because study of language topics (e.g. LP, LM and LS) have been done without (or with few) theoretical and methodological applications from sociology. In fact, sociology can contribute significantly to the sociolinguistic enterprise by applying its theories (e.g. labeling theory and social constructionism) to the study of language topics, e.g. language conflict, and applying its methodology (e.g. multidimensional scaling) for data analysis to increase reliability and validity of the study. In addition, theories and methods from other disciplines could also contribute to the progress of the enterprise. For example, many of the constructs (e.g. attitudes and identity) in social behavior could profit from a sharper theoretical focus in the field of social psychology, and the well established techniques (e.g. matched-guise technique) are useful to measure these complex constructs. Similarly, the study of word use in different sociocultural groups over time, central to the study of the sociology of language, could profit from the theory and research in discursive psychology, which gives real priority to the place of words in thought and in dealing with the world, and to concerns that formal education as a key institution contributes to sociocultural stratification through words (Corson, 1995).

A more unified theoretical framework is yet to be proposed to explain and monitor all language behavior in society. Without such a framework scholars tend to isolate sets of variables and invariables on an ad-hoc basis and thus explore an array of sociolinguistic issues in fragmentary fashion across sociolinguistic contexts. These studies have been insufficient to compare with each other and fall short of explaining similar or different outcomes with the same set of variables. A more consistent framework has to be formulated to enable understanding of parallel issues across numerous cross-cultural comparative studies.

The conduct of longitudinal study on sociolinguistic behavior is also an area for future research. Traditionally studies of the sociology of language are descriptive of sociolinguistic phenomena in different contexts at a particular point in time. We have now to go beyond this description of horizontal multilingualism to conduct study on longitudinal multilingualism, i.e. to investigate how overt behavior toward language in society affects the life of members of the community in social, cultural, economic and cognitive aspects over time. For example, the study of language spread should go further than describing a form-function construct, to investigate how the spread has changed the life of community members in the aspects just mentioned. Similarly, the study of LP should look at how the adoption of an indigenous language has changed the various aspects of people's lives. Studies such as these will be not only descriptive but also suggestive for the progress of human life.

National Hualien Teachers College
Taiwan

REFERENCES

Bailey, R.W. & Gorlach, M. (eds.): 1982, *English as a World Language*, University of Michigan Press, Ann Arbor.

Blom, J.P. & Gumperz, J.J.: 1972, 'Social meaning in linguistic structures: Code-switching in Norway', in J.J. Gumperz & D. Hymes (eds.), *Directions in Sociolinguistics: The Ethnography of Communication*, Holt, Rinehart & Winston, New York, 407–434.

Britto, F.: 1986, *Diglossia: A Study of the Theory with Application to Tamil*, Georgetown University Press, Washington, D.C.

Brosnahan, L.F.: 1963, 'Some historical cases of language imposition', in J. Spencer (ed.), *Language in Africa*, Cambridge University Press, Cambridge, 7–24.

Cooper, R.L.: 1982, 'A framework for the study of language spread', in R.L. Cooper (ed.), *Language Spread: Studies in Diffusion and Social Change*, Indiana University Press, Bloomington, 5–36.

Cooper, R.L.: 1989, *Language Planning and Social Change*, Cambridge University Press, Cambridge.

Corson, D.: 1995, *Using English Words*, Kluwer Academic Publishers, Dordrecht.

Davis, K.A.: 1994, *Language Planning in Multilingual Contexts*, John Benjamins, Amsterdam/Philadelphia.

Dejean, Y.: 1993, 'An overview of the language situation in Haiti', *International Journal of the Sociology of Language* 102, 73–83.

Ferguson, C.A.: 1959, 'Diglossia', *Word* 15, 325–340.

Ferguson, C.A.: 1963, 'Problems of teaching languages with diglossia', in E. Woodworth & R. Di Pietro (eds.), *Report of the Thirteenth Annual Round Table Meeting on Linguistics and Language Studies* (Monograph Series on Language and Linguistics, 15), Georgetown University Press, Washington, D.C., 165–177.

Ferguson, C.A.: 1966, 'National sociolinguistic profile formulas', in W. Bright (ed.), *Sociolinguistics*, Mouton, The Hauge, 309–314.

Fishman, J.A.: 1966, 'Language maintenance and language shift as a field of inquiry', in J.A. Fishman, V.C. Nahirny, J.E. Hofman & R.G. Hayden (eds.), *Language Loyalty in the United States*, Mouton, The Hague, 424–458.

Fishman, J.A.: 1967, 'Bilingualism with and without diglossia, diglossia with and without bilingualism', *Journal of Social Issues* 23(2), 29–38.

Fishman, J.A.: 1971, 'The sociology of language: An interdisciplinary social science approach to language in society', in J.A. Fishman (ed.), *Advances in the Sociology of Language Vol. I*, Mouton, The Hague, 217–404.

Fishman, J.A.: 1972, 'Domains and the relationship between micro- and macro-sociolinguistics', in J.J. Gumperz & D. Hymes (eds.), *Directions in Sociolinguistics: The Ethnography of Communication*, Holt, Rinehart & Winston, New York, 435–453.

Fishman, J.A.: 1991a, *Reversing Language Shift: Theoretical and Empirical Foundations of Assistance to Threatened Languages*, Multilingual Matters, Clevedon (England) & Philadelphia.

Fishman, J.A.: 1991b, 'Putting the 'socio' back into the sociolinguistic enterprise', *International Journal of the Sociology of Language* 92, 127–138.

Fishman, J.A., Cooper, R.L. & Rosenbaum, Y.: 1977, 'English around the world', in J.A. Fishman, R.L. Cooper & A.W. Conrad (eds.), *The Spread of English*, Newbury House, Rowley, Massachusetts, 77–107.

Gal, S.: 1979, *Language Shift*, Academic Press, New York.

Gal, S.: 1988, 'The political economy of code choice', in M. Heller (ed.), *Codeswitching: Anthropological and Sociolinguistic Perspectives*, Mouton, Berlin, 245–263.

Giles, H., Bourhis, R.Y. & Taylor, D.M.: 1977, 'Towards a theory of language in ethnic group relations', in H. Giles (ed.), *Language, Ethnicity and Intergroup Relations*, Academic Press, New York, 307–49.

Gumperz, J.J.: 1968, 'Types of lingusitic communities', in J.A. Fishman (ed.), *Readings in the Sociology of Language*, Mouton, The Hague, 460–472.

Haugen, E.: 1966, 'Dialect, language, nation', *American Anthropologist* 68, 922–935.

Haugen, E.: 1972, *The Ecology of Language*, Stanford Univesity Press, Stanford, California.

Heller, M.: 1988, 'Strategic ambiguity: Codeswitching in the management of conflict', in M. Heller (ed.), *Codeswitching: Anthropological and Sociolinguistic Perspectives*, Mouton, Berlin, 77–96.

Hertzler, J.: 1953, 'Toward a sociology of language', *Social Forces* 32, 109–119.

Hertzler, J.: 1965, *The Sociology of Language*, Random House, New York.

Hornberger, N.H.: 1988, *Bilingual Education and Language Maintenance: A Southern Peruvian Quechua Case*, Mouton, Berlin.

Hornberger, N.H.: 1991, 'Extending enrichment bilingual education: Revisiting typologies and redirecting policy', in O. Garcia (ed.), *Bilingual Education: Focusschrift in Honor of Joshua A. Fishman on the Occasion of His 65th Birthday Vol. 1*, John Benjamins, Philadelphia, 215–234.

Hymes, D.: 1974, *Foundations in Sociolingusitics: An Ethnographic Approach*, University of Pennsylvania Press, Philadelphia.

Hymes, D.: 1984, 'Sociolinguistics: Stability and consolidation', *International Journal of the Sociology of Language* 45, 39–45.

Kloss, H.: 1968, 'Notes concerning a language-nation typology', in J.A. Fishman, C.A. Ferguson & J. Das Gupta (eds.), *Language Problems of Developing Nations*, J. Wiley & Sons, New York, 69–85.

Labov, W.: 1969, 'The logic of nonstandard English', in *Georgetown Monographs on Language and Linguistics* 22, Georgetown University, Washington, D.C. Reprinted in *Language in the Inner City: Studies in the Black English Vernacular* (1972), University of Pennsylvania Press, Philadelphia.

Labov, W.: 1972, *Sociolinguistic Patterns*, University of Pennsylvania Press, Philadelphia.

Landry, R. & Allard, R.: 1992, 'Ethnolinguistic vitality and the bilingual development of minority and majority group students' in W. Fase, K. Jaespaert & S. Kroon (eds.), *Maintenance and Loss of Minority Languages*, Benjamins, Amsterdam, 223–251.

McConnell, G.D.: 1990, 'Three theoretical constructs for the measurement of language spread', in L. Laforge and G.D. McConnell (eds.), *Language Spread and Social Change: Dynamics and Measurement*, Les Presses de L-Universite Laval, Sainte-Foy, 267–282.

McConvell, P.: 1991, 'Understanding language shift: A step towards language maintenance', in S. Romaine (ed.), *Language in Australia*, Cambridge University Press, Cambridge, 143–155.

McKay, S.L. & Hornberger, N.H.: 1996, 'Preface', in S.L. McKay & N.H. Hornberger (eds.), *Sociolingusitics and Language Teaching*, Cambridge Unviersity Press, Cambridge, ix–xi.

Mackey, W.F.: 1980, 'The ecology of language shift', in P. Nelde (ed.), *Language in Contact and in Conflict*, Steiner, Wiesbaden, 35–41.

Mackridge, P.: 1985, *The Modern Greek Language*, Oxford University Press, Oxford.

Mahmoud, Y.: 1984, 'A variable, functional medium', in L. Haynes (ed.), *Studies in Language Ecology*, Steiner, Wiesbaden, 159–169.

Milroy, L. & Wei, L.: 1995, 'A social network approach to code-switching: The example of a bilingual community in Britain', in L. Milroy & P. Muysken (eds.), *One Speaker, Two Languages*, Cambridge Unviersity Press, Cambridge, 136–157.

Myers-Scotton, C.: 1993, *Social Motivations for Codeswitching*. Clarendon Press, Oxford.

Pauwels, A.: 1986, *Immigrant Dialects and Language Maintenance in Australia: The Case of the Limburg and Swabian Dialect*, Foris, Dordrecht.

Schiffman, H.F.: 1993, 'The balance of power in multiglossic languages: Implications for language shift', *International Journal of the Sociology of Language* 103, 115–148.

Stewart, W.A.: 1968, 'A sociolinguistic typology for describing national multilingualism', in J.A. Fishman (ed.), *Readings in the Sociology of Language*, Mouton, The Hague, 532–545.

Veltman, C.J.: 1983, *Language Shift in the U. S.*, Mouton, Berlin.

Wardhaugh, R.: 1987, *Languages in Competition: Dominance, Diversity, and Decline*, Blackwell, Oxford.

Weinreich, U.: 1953, *Languages in Contact: Findings and Problems*, Mouton, The Hague.

Weinstein, B.: 1983, *The Civil Tongue: Political Consequences of Language Choices*, Longman, New York.

Wexler, P.: 1971, 'Diglossia, Language Standardization and Purism', *Lingua* 27, 330–354.

Zentella, A.C.: 1981, '*Ta Bien*, you could answer me *en Cualquier Idioma*: Puerto Rican codeswitching in bilingual classrooms', in R. Duran (ed.), *Latino Language and Communicative Behavior*, Ablex Publishing Co., Norwood, N.J., 109–132.

SERAN DOĞANÇAY-AKTUNA

LANGUAGE PLANNING

Language planning (hereafter LP) refers to activities that attempt to bring about changes in the structure (corpus) and functions (thus, status) of languages and/or language varieties, using sociolinguistic concepts and information to make policy decisions and to implement them, in order to deal with linguistic and/or extra-linguistic problems at the national, international or community level (cf. Cooper, 1989, pp. 30–31). LP is carried out by a variety of agents ranging from governments, to language academies, to individuals. LP is generally located within the domain of the sociology of language that is concerned with 'language varieties as targets, as obstacles and as facilitators, and with the users and uses of language varieties as aspects of more encompassing social patterns or processes' (Fishman, 1972, p. 9). As such, LP is a multifaceted discipline whose aims and goals are interrelated with the political, economic and social aims of the community in question, which are in turn influenced by global events. This review concentrates on the processes, aims, goals and research methods used by language planners. For fuller treatment of language planning theory and its educational links, see the reviews by Schroeder, and by Fettes in Volume 1.

EARLY DEVELOPMENTS

Although governments and grammarians, especially language academies have been making plans and policies about the functions and corpora of languages for centuries, it was not until the 1960s that LP was formalized as a discipline. This was possibly due to the recognition of the fact that language problems are reflections of deeper sociopolitical and cultural issues. There is much to be gained in the sociopolitical, economic and educational arenas through planning seemingly linguistic matters.

Einar Haugen was the first scholar to describe the processes of LP as norm selection, codification, implementation, and elaboration (1966). Following Haugen's model, Rubin (1971) and Fishman (1979) also formulated the processes/stages of LP, adding evaluation as a fifth process while emphasizing the cyclic nature of the undertaking. Rubin lists the stages of LP as fact-finding, selection, development, implementation, and feedback and evaluation, while Fishman talks about decision-making, codification, elaboration, implementation, evaluation and iteration, both in a similar vein to Haugen.

N.H. Hornberger and D. Corson (eds), Encyclopedia of Language and Education,
Volume 8: Research Methods in Language and Education, 15–24.
© *1997 Kluwer Academic Publishers. Printed in the Netherlands.*

In his later work Haugen integrated Kloss' (1969) distinction between status and corpus planning as the two foci of LP (see the review by Fettes in Volume 1), Ferguson's (1968) notions of graphization, grammatication and lexication as procedures for developing a standard language out of a vernacular, and Neustupny's (1974) differentiation between policy and cultivation approaches for the treatment of language problems, to elaborate his model (see Haugen, 1983, p. 275). Status planning is a societal undertaking that focuses on the allocation of functions to varieties of language (i.e., selection) via authoritative policy making. It concerns itself with decisions regarding which language will be assigned for which purposes in a society and procedures for implementing these language policies through education and the mass media. Selection and use of official languages or languages of education are examples of status planning. Corpus planning, on the other hand, refers to efforts by linguists over the code itself, prompting changes in the linguistic structure, the script, the lexicon, styles, and the like, thus seeking to achieve standardization and elaboration of the terminologies and styles, while establishing 'a model of the good language' which is also affected by social, historical, cultural and political factors (Fishman, 1979). The success of status and corpus planning are interdependent and they are both necessary for effective LP because, in most cases, languages that attain new functions via status planning decisions are unprepared in terms of their corpora to fulfill those functions in the most efficient manner, therefore need to be modified and elaborated via corpus planning.

Some examples of Neustupny's (1974) macroscopic, sociological policy approach are the selection of national/official languages and their stratification, standardization, literacy, orthographies, and the like, thus focusing on linguistic varieties and their distribution, and hence, paralleling Kloss's status planning to some degree. Neustupny's cultivation approach, on the other hand, focuses on the functional differentiation of language varieties from one another, putting emphasis on questions of correctness, efficiency, style, and the general modernization of languages, as in corpus planning, thus working more on a micro level than policy planning.

To the status-corpus planning distinction, Cooper adds 'acquisition planning' as a third focus of LP. He defines this as 'increasing the number of users' – speakers, writers, listeners, or readers – of a language, through promoting its learning by giving people the opportunity and the incentive to learn it (Cooper, 1989, p. 33). Thus, LP is defined by Cooper as 'deliberate efforts to influence the behavior of others with respect to the acquisition, structure, or functional allocation of their language codes' (ibid., p. 45), covering not only change in current linguistic behavior, but also including maintenance of the current state of affairs.

The methodological approaches common in the early LP studies were the creation of conceptual frameworks, exemplifying attempts to bring certain guiding principles to the emerging field; the use of extensive survey research comprised of questionnaires and interviews common in sociolinguistics; and analysis and critique of LP policies in light of the conceptual frameworks that tended to reflect an idealized picture of LP and policy making. Examples of these can be found in the early LP literature cited below.

MAJOR CONTRIBUTIONS

After Haugen's initial work, major contributions to LP appeared in volumes such as *Language Problems of Developing Nations* (eds., Fishman, Ferguson, and Das Gupta, 1968), *Can Language be Planned?* (eds., Rubin & Jernudd, 1971), *Language Planning: Current Issues and Research* (eds., Rubin & Shuy, 1973), *Advances in Language Planning* (ed., Fishman, 1974), *Language Planning Processes* (eds., Rubin, Jernudd, Das Gupta, Fishman & Ferguson, 1977), and *Progress in Language Planning* (eds., Cobarrubias & Fishman, 1983). The establishment of the international journal *Language Problems and Language Planning* and the *Language Planning Newsletter* further provided LP scholars forums for their works.

Rabin's (1971) categorization of LP aims as linguistic, semi-linguistic and extra-linguistic and Nahir's (1984) classification of LP goals as endeavors language planners could attempt (and have attempted) added further dimensions to the discipline while helping to separate its processes/stages, as discussed in the LP models (cf. Haugen, 1983; Rubin, 1971), from the rationale and goals of LP. The *Linguistic aims* of LP deal with the cultivation of the corpus by linguists towards achieving greater precision, clarity, and efficiency in the language. The creation or adoption of lexical items to enlarge technical jargon, the development of styles, and the refinement of the syntactic, morphological, and phonological structure of the language are examples of linguistic aims. *Semi-linguistic aims* are the most frequent types of LP and they involve making changes in the writing systems, spelling, orthography, etc. that would not only bring communicative advantages but also serve social and political aims that could be covert or overt. For instance, the shifting of the script of Turkish from Arabic to Latin in the 1920s was done in order to adapt the alphabet to the phonology of the language but it also served to move the newly secular Turkey away from the impact of the Islamic world and towards its goal of westernization (Doğançay-Aktuna, 1995). *Extra-linguistic aims* are primarily political in nature and involve horizontal and vertical language spread, creation of a new language, revival of an unused one, or suppression of existing languages for sociopolitical reasons.

Rabin's typology brought to the foreground the essentially sociopolitical nature of LP that can sometimes be overlooked amid linguistically-oriented definitions. Indeed, as attested by Jernudd and Das Gupta (1971), Rabin

(1971), Karam (1974), Fishman (1979), and Cooper (1989), among others, 'regardless of the type of language planning, in nearly all cases the language problem to be solved is not a problem in isolation within the region or nation but is directly associated with the political, economic, scientific, social, cultural, and/or religious situation' (Karam, 1974, p. 108). The failure of early research to address these aspects of LP is now widely acknowledged. Phillipson (1992, as cited in Corson, 1997), for example, describes early studies in Jordan and Namibia where researchers' (i.e., language planners) failure to consider such factors as cited above accentuated the societal divisions instead of bridging the gaps.

Nahir's (1984) classification of LP goals and functions complements and expands Rabin's work, at the same time establishing clearly the difference between the processes of LP and its functions/goals as reported in various case studies. Nahir lists the goals and functions of LP as internal and external purification of languages, language revival, language reform, standardization, language spread, lexical modernization, terminology unification, stylistic simplification, (facilitating) interlingual communication, language maintenance, and auxiliary-code standardization (i.e., the standardization of sign languages, rules of transliteration, etc.). Hornberger (1994) adds officialization, nationalization, status standardization, proscription, and graphization to this list, while also utilizing some of Stewart's (1968) typology of the societal functions of languages such as the group, religious, literature, etc., as goals of language policy planning, to formulate an integrative framework of LP approaches, types and goals (p. 78).

Language planners may pursue one or more of the above mentioned goals simultaneously. For instance, as decision makers make policies to spread a lingua franca via education due to its perceived instrumental benefits, they can at the same time take measures to protect the purity and the authenticity of the vernaculars from the effects of external borrowings. The particular goal(s) language planners seek reflect their orientations to languages and their users, among which three frequently recurring orientations are language-as-right, language-as-resource and language-as-problem (Ruiz, 1984). The orientations of language planners and their goals are subject to change in line with sociopolitical and economic changes in the nation and outside.

Writing in 1974, Tauli laments that 'LP is ignored by the institutions, journals and congresses which contain the term "applied linguistics"' (p. 56). Yet, owing to the contributions of the above cited scholars, which have paved the way towards the compilation of case studies from around the world, LP is now a recognized and expanding field whose close relationship with applied linguistics and the sociology of language is acknowledged by the regular publication of articles on various aspects of LP in journals like *Applied Linguistics, Journal of Multilingual and Multicultural*

Development, International Journal of the Sociology of Language, and even in the *TESOL Quarterly*, besides the field's own voice, *Language Problems and Language Planning*, while international applied linguistics conferences include papers and symposia on LP. Thus, linguists, educators and social scientists are now cognizant of the fact that the linguistic and sociolinguistic status or development of languages can in fact be planned through organized efforts.

The actual research methods used in LP are taken from various areas of the social sciences. Early LP studies consisted mostly of descriptions of national case studies, using sociolinguistic surveys of various kinds and trying to offer cost-benefit analysis of sample cases in their historical and comparative contexts. Analysis and critique of LP policies were also widespread. These early studies suffered from certain limitations by focusing mainly on overt linguistic issues at the expense of underlying sociopolitical factors as aforementioned, or on one language only without considering the potential effects of LP on the status and corpus of all languages present in that context. Thus, they failed to analyze LP processes, goals and outcomes from the perspectives of all influenced by the event, usually at the expense of the already underprivileged minority groups. Yet, such early descriptions of case studies paved the way to creating conceptual frameworks that brought some systematicity and principles into the emerging field and triggered similar research in different contexts that would, in turn, test the descriptive adequacy of the frameworks offered. Recent LP studies, such as those cited below, recognize more the complexity of LP processes and goals and their interplay with sociopolitical, economic, and cultural issues, besides acknowledging the inherently political nature of LP. They have also moved beyond descriptions to seeking for explanations for phenomena such as language maintenance, shift, spread, and the like (see Grabe, 1993/94).

WORK IN PROGRESS

It is difficult to summarize here the specific LP projects currently undertaken in the world as LP is a multidimensional discipline that uses a variety of means to achieve various ends. This fact notwithstanding, a mention of the changing directions of the field can give a clear indication of its current foci.

In the 1970s and 80s LP discussions centered around descriptions of national case studies of language and policy planning in developing nations. In the 1990s the issues have changed to include the non-national levels of LP in multilingual contexts of both the developing and the developed nations where great attention is given to minority language rights and the role of language-in-education planning, and with stronger emphasis on the social and political contexts of LP activities (see Grabe,

1993/94 for details). Starting in the late 1980s, changes in the sociopolitical and sociolinguistic needs of Eastern and Western Europe and Central Asian Republics, the rise to power of nations in the Pacific Rim Region, the development of greater demands for minority and immigrant rights, the expansion of global information networks, and the worldwide spread of English as an international language have brought prominence to and increased the need for LP both in developed and developing nations.

Consequently, current work in LP deals with issues such as formulating language and language-in-education policies for the European Community (e.g. Coulmas, 1991) and the United States, as well as for other multilingual states (e.g., Corson, 1990 on Australia and New Zealand; Corson & Lemay, 1996 on Canada); coping effectively with linguistic diversity and inequality in areas such as the South Pacific (e.g., Baldauf & Luke, 1990) and the influences of social, economic, ideological, and political factors on LP in national and international contexts (e.g., Lowenberg, 1988; Phillipson, 1992; Jones & Ozog, 1993) (see the review [on school language policies] by May in Volume 1).

Projects such as Erasmus, Lingua, and Mercator within the body of the 1992 Treaty of Maastricht are examples of current European LP which reflect the changing sociopolitical realities of Europe and the pressing need for cultural, educational and linguistic integration in response to the development of regional powers elsewhere. Erasmus aims to provide scholarly mobility for teachers and students in higher education while Lingua is developed to aid in the teaching of two foreign languages across the Community, via financing exchanges of staff, materials, and students in secondary education and to ensure the success of Erasmus. Mercator, on the other hand, aims to support the lesser used languages of Europe, such as Welsh and Irish, in their struggle against larger languages. *Annual Review of Applied Linguistics* special issue on 'Language Policy and Planning' (Vol. 14, ed., Grabe, 1993/94) provides an excellent overview of current concerns of LP research across the world and the ways in which these differ from the earlier concerns of developing nations.

PROBLEMS AND DIFFICULTIES

A problem encountered in LP is the fact that there is as yet no theory of LP with explanatory adequacy. As argued by many, LP has not reached beyond descriptions of case studies and processes (cf. Tauli, 1974; Haugen, 1983; Cobarrubias, 1983; Cooper, 1989). LP case studies might offer valid analysis and rationales for LP processes and outcomes for their particular contexts, yet these cannot usually be generalized to other situations, regardless of the commonalties, due to the complex interplay of sociocultural, economic, political, ideological and linguistic factors, that can lead LP processes and outcomes into rather different directions across contexts.

Moreover, processes of LP as defined in models by Haugen (1983), Rubin (1971), and Fishman (1979) offer idealizations of LP that are not always followed in a planned fashion in real life.

A theory of LP would enable us to explain the motivations, the variety of means, and the outcomes of the LP processes across contexts. As Cooper rightly argues, however, at present an adequate LP theory is not really within our grasp, not only because LP 'is such a complex activity influenced by numerous factors – economic, ideological, political, etc. – and not only because it is directed to many different status, corpus, and acquisition goals, but more fundamentally because it is a tool in the service of so many different latent goals such as economic modernization, national integration, national liberation, imperial hegemony, racial, sexual, and economic inequality, the maintenance of elites, and their replacement by new elites' (Cooper, 1989, p. 182). A satisfactory theory of LP will need to account for all of the above, and thus, Cooper says, it awaits a satisfactory theory of social change (ibid.).

A major problem surrounding LP is the lack of research on evaluations of the undertaking, as attested by many scholars in the field. Some possible reasons relating to this are the political and often covert nature of LP goals, the myriad variables and agents that are involved in the process, and the complexity of doing sociolinguistic surveys and longitudinal studies of such wide coverage. Moreover, as Fishman (1979) explains, evaluations of LP can hardly be purely objective and value-free because even models of the good language have ideological ramifications. Target populations' acceptance and/or rejection of products of LP are greatly influenced by both sociopolitical and psychological factors such that people adopt linguistic innovations and policy decisions more readily when these conform to their ideological orientations. In any event, LP as a discipline would benefit greatly by evaluation attempts that could aid not only in the iterative process of LP but provide LP agencies elsewhere with valid examples in addition to constituting a step toward future theory formulation.

FUTURE DIRECTIONS

Based on current global events and examples of current work, some likely future directions in research and practice of LP include a concern with the formation of new sociopolitical and economic links through linguistic and educational means, as in the European Community and in the Pacific Rim. The linguistic problems of newly forming states will need to be addressed in response to the rise of ethnonationalism. Another main issue would be related to the further global spread of English which triggers LP to both teach the international language in order to participate in information networks and to protect local languages from its influence (for the latter issue, see the special issue of the *TESOL Quarterly*, Vol. 30(3), eds. Hornberger

& Ricento, 1996). Needless to say, as the sociopolitical and economic makeup of nations and regions of the world change, LP aims and goals will also change to satisfy a variety of sociopolitical, economic, cultural, and linguistic needs. This being the case, it appears that the future directions of LP research in particular contexts will relate directly to national and international events.

After reviewing current work on LP, Tucker identifies the following five themes that seem likely to guide future work in LP: The role(s) of LP in foreshadowing or marking major political events; the growing concern for ethnic revitalization and LP directed to indigenous languages in various parts of the world; the correlates and consequences of continuing migration and mobility across national boundaries and the resulting need for foreign languages; the differential perceptions of the role of the mother tongue in primary education and allowances made by LP for educating children of immigrants (i.e., bilingual education); and potential contributions of LP to education and national development (Tucker, 1993/94, pp. 277–283). Currently neglected, Tucker says, are studies on testing language policy efforts and the LP needs of special populations such as the deaf (see reviews by Branson and Miller in this volume and in Volume 1), which are themes also likely to surface among the future concerns of LP research.

So far as the field itself is concerned, it seems that attempts to formulate an adequate theory of LP will need to be a methodological goal of future research. This will be possible only when serious attention is given to objective and comprehensive evaluations of LP attempts, which will not only aid in the formulation of a theory of LP but also provide valid data for justifying or modifying LP efforts. Moreover, research methods used in LP need to address more carefully the actual reasons and accounts of all stakeholders in LP, whose views have too seldom been solicited in early LP research. Triangulation of methods such as ethnographies of communication, critical discourse analysis, conversation analysis, ideology critiquing, among others, can provide emic perspectives that can not only aid in offering insights for theory formulation but also enable us make LP emancipatory for those involved (see Corson, 1997 for details).

Boğaziçi University,
Turkey

REFERENCES

Baldauf, R.B., Jr. & Luke, A. (eds.): 1990, *Language Planning and Education in Australasia and the South Pacific*, Multilingual Matters, Clevedon, Avon.
Cobarrubias, J.: 1983, 'Language planning: The state of the art', in J. Cobarrubias & J.A. Fishman (eds.), *Progress in Language Planning: International Perspectives*, Mouton, New York, 3–26.

Cobarrubias, J. & Fishman, J.A. (eds.): 1983, *Progress in Language Planning: International Perspectives*, Mouton, New York.

Cooper, R.L.: 1989, *Language Planning and Social Change*, Cambridge University Press, New York.

Corson, D.: 1990, *Language Policy Across the Curriculum*, Multilingual Matters, Clevedon, England.

Corson, D.: 1997, 'Critical realism: An emancipatory philosophy for applied linguistics', *Applied Linguistics* 18, 166–188.

Corson, D. & Lemay, S.: 1996, *Social Justice and Language Policy in Education, the Canadian Research*, Ontario Institute for Studies in Education, Toronto, Canada.

Coulmas, F. (ed.): 1991, *A Language Policy for the European Community*, Mouton de Gruyter, Berlin.

Doğançay-Aktuna, S.: 1995, 'An evaluation of the Turkish language reform after 60 years', *Language Problems and Language Planning* 19(3), 221–249.

Ferguson, C.: 1968, 'Language development', in J.A. Fishman, C.A. Ferguson & J. Das Gupta (eds.), *Language Problems of Developing Nations*, Wiley & Sons, New York, 27–35.

Fishman, J.A.: 1972, *The Sociology of Language: An Interdisciplinary Social Science Approach to Language in Society*, Mouton, The Hague.

Fishman, J.A.(ed.): 1974, *Advances in Language Planning*, Mouton, The Hague.

Fishman, J.A.: 1979, 'Bilingual education, language planning and English', *English World-Wide* 1(1), 11–24.

Fishman, J.A., Ferguson, C.A. & Das Gupta, J. (eds.): 1968, *Language Problems of Developing Nations*, Wiley & Sons, New York.

Grabe, W.: 1993/94, 'Foreword', *Annual Review of Applied Linguistics 14*, [Special issue on Language Policy and Planning].

Haugen, E.: 1966, 'Linguistics and language planning', in W. Bright (ed.), *Sociolinguistics*, Mouton, The Hague, 50–71.

Haugen, E.: 1983, 'The implementation of corpus planning: Theory and practice', in J. Cobarrubias & J.A. Fishman (eds.), *Progress in Language Planning: International Perspectives*, Mouton, New York, 269–290.

Hornberger, N.H.: 1994, 'Literacy and language planning', *Language and Education* 8, 75–86.

Hornberger, N.H. & Ricento, T.K. (eds.): 1996, 'Language planning and policy', special issue of *TESOL Quarterly* 30(3).

Jernudd, B.B. & Das Gupta, J.: 1971, 'Towards a theory of language planning', in J. Rubin & B.B. Jernudd (eds.), *Can Language be Planned?: Sociolinguistic Theory and Practice for Developing Nations*, University Press of Hawaii, Honolulu, 195–215.

Jones, G.M. & Ozog, A.C.K. (eds.): 1993, *Bilingualism and National Development* [Special issues of *Journal of Multilingual and Multicultural Development* 14(1/2)].

Lowenberg, H.P. (ed.): 1988, *Language Spread and Language Policy: Issues, Implications and Case Studies, Georgetown University Roundtable on Language and Linguistics*, Georgetown University Press, Washington.

Karam, F.X.: 1974, 'Toward a definition of language planning', in J.A. Fishman (ed.), *Advances in Language Planning*, Mouton, The Hague, 103–124.

Kloss, H.: 1969, *Research Possibilities on Group Bilingualism: A Report*, International Center for Research on Bilingualism, Quebec.

Nahir, M.: 1984, 'Language planning goals: A classification', *Language Problems and Language Planning* 8(3), 294–327.

Neustupny, J.V.: 1974, 'Basic types of treatment of language problems', in J.A. Fishman (ed.), *Advances in Language Planning*, Mouton, The Hague, 103–124.

Phillipson, R.: 1992, *Linguistic Imperialism*, Oxford University Press, Oxford, UK.

Rabin, C.: 1971, 'A tentative classification of language planning aims', in J. Rubin & B.B. Jernudd (eds.), *Can Language be Planned?: Sociolinguistic Theory and Practice for Developing Nations*, University Press of Hawaii, Honolulu, 277–280.

Rubin, J.: 1971, 'Evaluation and language planning', in J. Rubin & B.B. Jernudd (eds.), *Can Language be Planned?: Sociolinguistic Theory and Practice for Developing Nations*, University Press of Hawaii, Honolulu, 217–252.

Rubin, J. & Jernudd, B.H. (eds.): 1971, *Can Language be Planned?: Sociolinguistic Theory and Practice for Developing Nations*, University Press of Hawaii, Honolulu.

Rubin, J. & Shuy, R. (eds.): 1973, *Language Planning: Current Issues and Research*, Georgetown University Press, Washington.

Rubin, J., Jernudd, B.H., Das Gupta, J., Fishman, J.A. & Ferguson, C. (eds.): 1977, *Language Planning Processes*, Mouton, The Hague.

Ruiz, R.: 1984, 'Orientations in language planning', *NABE Journal* 8(2), 15–34.

Stewart, W.: 1968, 'A Sociolinguistic typology for describing national multilingualism', in J. Fishman (ed.), *Readings in the Sociology of Language*, Mouton, The Hague, 531–545.

Tauli, V.: 1974, 'The theory of language planning', in H.A. Fishman (ed.), *Advances in Language Planning*, Mouton, The Hague, 49–67.

Tucker, G.R.: 1993/94, 'Concluding thoughts: Language planning issues for the coming decade', *Annual Review of Applied Linguistics* 14 [Special issue on Language Policy and Planning], 277–286.

ROBERT YOUNG

SOCIAL SCIENCE THEORY IN RESEARCHING LANGUAGE AND EDUCATION

Researching language and education is researching meaning and learning. The theory of meaning and learning employed affects both the method and the outcome of studies of language and education.

Theories of meaning and interpretation may broadly be called 'hermeneutic' theories. Theories of learning may be called theories of 'inquiry.' Some social theories possess only limited and implicit hermeneutic theories, and others, in a majority in the last decade or so, a well-developed hermeneutic theory which lies at the heart of the social theory in question. Theories of learning also vary. Some theories of learning say little about its connection with human inquiry at large, as if the way we learned as individuals had no relevance for an understanding of communities of inquiry such as science. Others such as pragmatism place both meaning and learning at the heart of theory of social life. Such theories are theories of social life as potentially a form of constant more or less methodic adaptation or learning. Inquiry is just a more methodic reflective form of everyday learning in such views.

Hermeneutic theories, whether well developed or not, implicit or explicit, can be classified in terms of the way they deal with the fundamental questions of meaning and its interpretation (Gallagher, 1992). First, how is meaning reproduced, transmitted, or communicated? This may be called the 'communicative question'. Second, what role do power, authority and status play in communication? This may be called the 'authority question'. Third, how does dialogue or communicative interaction influence the communicative process? This may be called the 'discourse question'. Fourth, in the light of answers to these three questions, how is meaning created by communicators, as speakers or writers, and hearers or readers. Just what is interpretation or meaning-taking or making? This may be called the 'ontogenetic question', since it concerns the bringing into being of new meanings and novel interpretations when meanings are uttered and understood. But the bringing of new meanings into existence is also a characteristic of inquiry. The theory of interpretation is inseparable from the theory of inquiry as long as we feel it is useful to ask whether one meaning is in a sense more useful or valid than another. This brings us to a final question, a 'critical' question: How valid are meanings? How should we respond to their 'claim' on us?

There exist many possible sets of answers to these questions, but for

N.H. Hornberger and D. Corson (eds), Encyclopedia of Language and Education,
Volume 8: Research Methods in Language and Education, 25–34.
© *1997 Kluwer Academic Publishers. Printed in the Netherlands.*

the sake of simplicity, it is useful to identify a small number of relatively systematic positions on them – conservative and empiricist hermeneutics, Marxist hermeneutics, moderate hermeneutics, critical-pragmatist hermeneutics, and postmodern or radical hermeneutics. Each of these hermeneutics may be poorly or well-developed in a social theory, and each has different implications for theorising language, for theorising education, and for theorising their conjunction. They also relate to different methodologies for language and education research. These are discussed below.

THE GROWTH OF THEORY AND VIEWS OF THEORY

Much early work on language and education was relatively atheoretical. The once dominant behavioural scientific metatheory in education restricted 'theory' to a shifting array of 'variables', expressing theoretical constructs of a largely psychological kind, and where social structure or culture entered the analysis, it did so as a static, 'black box' variable, such as, socio-economic status (SES). In the 1950s this began to change, as foundational studies departments in Faculties of Education began increasingly to hire sociologists and other non-psychologists, and social science itself began to be influenced by humanistic, phenomenological, structuralist and Marxist meta-theories. These newer social sciences soon took a 'linguistic' and even 'interpretive' turn, influenced by European theoretical ideas and traditions. The notion of 'theory' was itself expanded, from a somewhat restricted conceptual framework, operationalised in a set of measured variables, to a many-layered construction, which ranged widely. Acceptable standards for theorising moved from the view that all concepts should be empirically defined through operationalisation of a method of measuring them, to the postmodern view that 'anything goes' in methodological and theoretical discourse. Arguably, in the process something valuable has been lost. Metaphysical or political-cultural speculation may have its place, but it does not exhaust the range of useful forms of theorising. In turn, behavioural science has moved on, from relatively narrow empiricist meta theory and restrictive doctrines of scientific semantics, through broader cognitive approaches, to a wide range of empirically realised, linguistically – informed analyses – to a 'discursive psychology' (Edwards & Potter, 1992).

One of the assumptions of those who make an exclusive case for forms of theory closely related to empirical evidence is that the chief function of theory is to explain 'surface' phenomena by reference to underlying law-like regularities. In social life, this approach gives rise to the added implication that surface phenomena include the values or preferences of participants in social life while reference to underlying phenomena somehow provides an 'ideology free' basis of explanation. Much the same claim to epistemic privilege-via-theory is made by the older school of Marxists, who tend to view participant's perspectives as being 'in' ideology, while dialectical-material 'science' is able to transcend this. Both views rest on a characteristically 19th century identification of social thought with a self-perception of objectivity among natural scientists. But they also rest on an identification of the purposes of natural and social science as being to explain and even predict phenomena and then to open up the possibility of controlling them or at least, influencing them, by establishing generalisations about relationships between or among phenomena.

But there are other uses to which theory might be put. The linguistic turn in social theory was characterised by a shift from the study of regularities in gross behaviour to the understanding of systems of meaning and the communicative processes through which social life is constructed and reconstructed. From explanation, (prediction) and control, the purpose moved to understanding meaning and how it changed through communicative processes. This was a shift from a theory of elements of structure and their function (in society and the self) to a theory of meaningful action and interpretation (culture theory and hermeneutics). Some early linguistic work remained at a hybrid stage – it recognized social life was constructed communicatively, primarily through language, but its purpose was to provide the means whereby social outcomes, (e.g. in education, learning outcomes), might be controlled by manipulating language (particularly teacher language). Later, the influence of structuralist, hermeneutic and post-structuralist thought, in addition to linguistics, shifted attention away from the view that the linguistically-turned study of educational communication should provide simply another way to manage effective learning of the official curriculum, to a wider range of purposes. Meanings were increasingly seen as matters of choice, rather than blind outcomes of causes, and the focus shifted from explaining existing identities, roles and institutions to making learners aware of the range of creative possibilities available to them in pluralistic moral and cultural milieux. Rather than an uncovering of the hidden 'hard wiring' of social life, the task of social thought was seen as an exposure of the logic of the existing software in the game of life and the fostering of a capacity among students to create an indefinite range of new games.

Today, the question of the degree to which human possibilities are 'hard wired' or 'programmable' is very much an open question, as is the question of whether or not some possible identities, values and ways of life are viable, valid or worthwhile. Today, metaphysical speculation about the nature of human nature – its plasticity, its formation, its universality or lack of it, or its necessity – or lack of it – joins more 'middle range' theory of particular institutional complexes – such as schooling, prisons, language policy, or the family – and connects, too, with more traditional micro-theory about language learning, classroom communication, and literacy. At various levels, different conceptions of theory, connected with different views of human theorising, play different roles. For some, theorising is simply a form of human discourse about choices we face as a species in which academic writing blends into a wider public debate about possible futures and modes of life, for others, it is necessary to maintain some connection with the explanatory agenda of the natural sciences. In some ways, it could be said there is now a surfeit of theory, much of it poorly defined, unanchored in concrete human experience, and uncertain of its own assumptions, for every kind of theory has its own standards, and every discourse has internal criteria of rigour, and too often these are not attended to.

CONSERVATIVE AND EMPIRICIST HERMENEUTICS

Conservative hermeneutic theories are often implicit in conservative social theories. Conservative theories tell a story in which life is depicted as a struggle to maintain a threatened order or to recover an underlying order, now lost. A part of this struggle is a struggle for meanings (beliefs, values, feelings), and for their preservation or recovery. In this view, meanings can be 'preserved' and/or 'recovered'. Texts, or at least well-formed texts, can have a single, best interpretation, and what is uttered in them may be judged according to standards of truth, beauty and goodness. Critique is a matter of the correct application of such standards, or of identification of the formal inadequacies of texts. Authority is a matter of functional necessity, often based on expertise, sensibility or social formation and it is cultural as well as simply 'organizational'. Dialogue is a process of fine-tuning interpretation, by exploring the application of methodological criteria to the truth claims of texts, by the discrimination of correct from excessive or dysfunctional use of authority and by resolving moral disputes by reference to moral principles. In its explicit form, conservative hermeneutic theory may be represented by the work of E. D. Hirsch (1987).

But conservative hermeneutic theory is most commonly an implicit rather than explicit part of social theory. Structural-functional social theory is generally recognized to be conservative (in effect if not intention) because it deals poorly with social change and emphasizes system preservation. In this theory, language and interpretation is treated as something of a 'black box'. That is to say, it is treated the way someone who doesn't understand anything about Compact Disks or their replay treats a CD player. Structural functional (SF) theorists rely on their own, taken-for-granted understanding of meaning and the role of language. It forms an ever present background to their theory and their theory simply assumes that meanings can be preserved i.e. communicated unchanged and that interpretation is straightforward, but SF theorists do theorize culture as a set of meanings – norms, roles etc.

Empiricist approaches to social thought tend to be more fragmented than SF Theory in their approach to meaning, language and culture, in keeping with their more ad hoc and eclectic, occasioned use of clusters of concepts or fragments of theoretical ideas. Empiricism is often found in behavioural approaches to social and educational research. Empiricists frequently adopt an inductive strategy for theory-building. Sometimes they build theory up from relationships among small sets of variables, while at the level of verification of postulated relationships they typically adopt a deductivist approach – deducing consequences of postulated relationships and testing them. In this approach, language, culture, and the business of creating ('uttering') and understanding (reading) meaning is seldom more than an assumed and unexamined background, except where linguistic behaviour is the object of study. When it is the explicit focus of attention, there is a tendency to treat it in terms of an implicit conservative hermeneutics. Commonly, the focus in behavioural studies of communication is on the cognitive and affective obstacles to communication (e.g. Green & Hasker, 1988). It is usually assumed that the removal of obstacles, such as differences in concepts between one speaker and another, will then result in the reproduction of meanings. However recent developments in psychology of discourse promise to change this picture by moving to include accounts of context and the social and cultural 'scripts' that speakers follow and strategically depart from (Edwards & Potter, 1992).

MARXIST HERMENEUTICS

Labels are always a problem, partly because social theorists often choose their own labels and partly because there is a politics of labelling. In addition, labels indicate types and types are usually abstractions, constructed for their semantic neatness or logical purity, while actual theorists have complex views which may change more or less from work to work. The Marxist hermeneutics described in this section may better be called Functional Marxist or 'Class Hermeneutics', as we will see when we come to Pragmatist approaches. In this view of social life and culture we often see an inversion of Structural Functionalist Theory called 'Conflict Theory'. The tacit theory of meaning is focused on the 'ideological' character of meaning and on its change or rather replacement by other meanings rather than its recovery or preservation, but otherwise, meaning, culture, and interpretation is treated pretty much as a black box in this theory, too. Otherwise perceptive theorists; whose major focus is on structured formation of social inequality, the causes of poverty, or the role of the state in capitalist society, may fall short of an adequate view of meaning when they use it as an unexamined background resource in their theorising. Capitalist social relations are credited with a capacity to preserve and reproduce meaning. Analyses in this view tend to focus on the social relationships in which meaning is produced to show how political-economic constraints limit conceptual innovation and shape ideological forms of consciousness.

Typically, the older school of Marxist Theorists, such as Dittmar (1976) or Bowles & Gintis (1977), theorized forms of language and consciousness as products of the differences in experience of classes of people whose role in the economy and workforce was different (subordinate, superordinate; information work, manual work; wage-dependent, capital owning), but little was said about the kind of interpretive processes necessary to the mediation of a relationship between economically determined experience and forms of language and consciousness.

Arguably, Basil Bernstein's structuralist account of hermeneutics, influenced by the French sociologist, Emile Durkheim, could provide a better starting point for a Marxism of meaning that was oriented to the political-economic arguments of the later Marx, than the simple cultural reproduction theories of Bowles and Gintis. Bernstein postulates that differences in family experience, mediated by structural location, (class, form of work, family roles), distribute symbolic capacities differentially. He identifies access to 'codes' as important capacities which are distinguished by the way the resources of language are drawn upon and the way in which utterances are contextually dependent or independent. In his later work he describes the way the school system can constitute a 'pedagogic device' which constructs ideology through a process of recontextualisation (Bernstein, 1990). Working class educational disadvantage is at least partly linguistically mediated, but not by any simple 'deficit' of working class students. Disadvantage is produced by the way school communication codes work upon class differences in coding 'style'.

MODERATE HERMENEUTICS

It is when we come to what I have called moderate hermeneutics that a decisive break with conservative hermeneutics is made. The key figure in this theory of hermeneutics is Gadamer (1989), and in its application to educational thought and development in a critical and social direction (Gallagher, 1992). Moderate hermeneutics both opens up an account of the continuous change of meaning (rather than its reproduction) and the beginnings of a critical hermeneutics, in which connections between understanding meaning-making and understanding learning are able to be explored. Where moderate hermeneutics is limited is in its tendency to adopt a descriptive rather than a normative approach to both interpretation and inquiry.

In this hermeneutics it is recognized that all interpretation is local and that there can be no universal rules which could form the basis for an observer to rule certain interpretations out or in. Interpretation is a product of a process of change for the interpreter and, in interactional contexts, the person being interpreted. However, while there are no universal interpretive rules, there are widespread approaches to interpretation in which it is possible for many to share an abhorrence of violence, or injustice. Conversation or dialogue is a process in which meanings can converge through a kind of negotiation, but this is in tension with social relationships of dependency or authority, which limit dialogue. Interpretation lies somewhere between reproduction and incomprehension, and we accomplish it through a kind of "practical wisdom" or "phronesis" – practical wisdom based on judgement. So much liberally-minded empirical work in language and education appears to draw on an implicit moderate hermeneutics that it would be invidious to list examples.

Where moderate theories appear weak is in their liberal assumption of an unproblematic individual subject who seeks to speak for herself, and in their tendency to a cognitive or "thin" view of dialogue. In critical-pragmatist views, the capacity to speak for oneself is precisely that which is the object of critical striving, and a certain materiality or concreteness is also crucial to speaking positions.

CRITICAL – PRAGMATIST HERMENEUTICS

It is probably easiest to describe critical-pragmatist hermeneutics if we begin with an examination of the hermeneutic theory of systemic-functional linguistics (e.g. Hodge, 1981). The details of systemic linguistics need not detain us. It is an approach to language in which language events (conversations, interactions) are seen as accomplishing social tasks by coordinating actors' roles as transformers of the physical environment, as exchangers of information, and doers of cultural acts of promising, avowing, denying, praising, warning etc. Social situations have, in some sense, a task or expected outcome, which is a practical accomplishment, even if this is simply to have a pleasant talk over coffee. In turn, social situations are distributed in clumps which comprise social institutions and their cultural background, and categories of speakers/actors are distributed across situations. Typically, talk is managed with the help of expectations about the course talk will or should take and the speech roles of categories of participants. Within these roles, categories of actor fulfil their task role by drawing on the resources of language (e.g. by employing a particular vocabulary and style), and using utterances at appropriate times to refer to the way things are and in appropriate ways given their culturally defined relationship with others.

This is essentially a pragmatist view of language. In it, interpretation is something actors do in the light of their cultural knowledge, experience of past patterns of talk accomplishing tasks (e.g. expectations, knowledge of talk genres), and awareness of the resources and conventions of the semiotic field of contrasts which can be realised lexico-grammatically. Interpretation goes beyond actual utterances. It is ampliative relative to the conventional semantic information in speech; that is, it builds on but adds to that information. It is inferential, fallible, and multiple, although not infinitely variable or situationally or linguistically unconstrained. This view is also the starting point for a critical-pragmatic view of meaning, but where systemics has (in the past) been content to describe meaning-making in socially conventional terms at both the lexico-grammatical and interpretive levels, critical-pragmatic theory of meaning goes further (as in the last decade systemics has also begun to do).

In critical-pragmatic theory, individuals are culturally formed within historical relations of dependency and can only emancipate themselves relative to the margin of their historical/biographical formation. They do this when circumstances permit problems to become the subject of more open exploration than is usual, due to the maladaption of past discursive resources in new contexts, sometimes created by the political action of social movements. This probing of assumptions and dialogic reconstruction of disturbed areas of taken-for-granted values, beliefs etc is called 'discourse' (by Habermas, 1982–4). The centrepiece of the theory of interpretation in this view is the notion that all interpretation of meaning, all understanding, involves taking a position on the validity claims inherent in the experiential and interpersonal functions of language. Without validity judgements there is no understanding of the meaning of utterances (note: This is not the same as the 'dictionary meaning' of the sentences uttered). A corollary of this view is the idea that all talk involves ideologising (accepting claims that run counter to one's existential interests) and resistance or critique (resisting or challenging ideological meanings, or re-asserting democratic ones) (Cherryholmes, 1988; Young, 1996).

In this view, emancipation is the outcome of a struggle for ontogenetic agency – a capacity to work at the margin of our culturally formed identity for an equal voice in making our identity and those of others. This view is shared with some versions of postmodern or radical hermeneutics, but the latter differ in offering only a radically non-normative theory of meaning. It is reasonable to see critical-pragmatic and postmodern hermeneutics as informing each other.

POSTMODERN HERMENEUTICS

However, postmodern hermeneutic theories in their most radical form tend to undercut either the possibility of communication of meaning or the possibility of critique – unless by critique you mean undercutting the possibility of all judgements of value or the reduction of them to arbitrary and equal preferences. But most postmodern-influenced views retreat from the more radical positions that some readings of writers such as Foucault (1977) have at times tended to display (e.g. Rorty, 1989). At its best, or most useful, postmodern writing about meaning is a reminder of the constant escape of meaning from the interpretive intention, the ambiguity and ambivalence of interpreters, and the limits of methodologies of adaptation. At its most humane, postmodern-influenced hermeneutics expresses sympathy and insight for all who are denied a speaking position, whose stories are not valorised, and whose meanings are denied. However this 'humanism' is an avowedly 'unprincipled' one, adopted fideistically in the manner of the arbitrary commitments of academic scepticism, and then it is not methodic, nor would it claim to be adaptive in any sense but that in which tolerance and pluralism and the subversion of established hierarchies and systems of power might be said to be adaptive.

Central problems for such a hermeneutics are its inability to discriminate formally between local democracy and dictatorship, or between justifications for injustice or democracy, apart from the personal political commitments of individuals or groups. Its theory of inquiry, insofar as it has one, tends to undercut the very possibility of education, and school systems are seen as based upon a necessary lie – that it is possible for them to foster the moral and intellectual development of individuals (Hunter, 1994). Again, fortunately, it appears possible for many writers to draw on sceptical insights without absolutising them, and so, at the very least, provide a counterpoint to simpler optimisms. At its best, theory of this kind luminously reveals the discursive politics of difference and power (Luke et al., 1995).

METHODOLOGICAL CORRELATES

The research problems that it is possible to tackle are conditioned by the theoretical perspective adopted by the researcher. Conservative theories are generally concerned with problems of the preservation of meaning and the avoidance of misunderstandings, liberal theories with the growth of new understanding through dialogue, radical theories with the subversion of dominant understandings and the ideology of the liberal, self-directing subject, and critical-pragmatic theories with the solution of historical and biographical problems through democratic adaptation.

Research strategies are selected in accordance with research purposes and range very widely, however it is possible to make a broad distinction between descriptive/explanatory methods and normative/critical methods. Problems of the preservation of meaning, and many problems of dialogue (seen as the potentially rational exchange of viewpoints) can be tackled with descriptive methods, whereas problems of ideology critique additionally require normative methods such as 'critical pragmatics.' Postmodern influenced methods may involve less 'methodic', and more aesthetic approaches, including 'deconstruction', forms of 'discourse' analysis, and 'genealogical critique', practised as a subversive 'art'.

The University of Sydney
Australia

REFERENCES

Bernstein, B.: 1975–90, *Class, Codes and Control. Vols 1–5*, Routledge and Kegan Paul, London.

Bowles, S. & Gintis, H.: 1977, *Schooling in Capitalist America*, Basic Books, New York.

Cherryholmes, C.: 1988, 'An exploration of meaning and the dialogue between textbooks and teaching', *Journal of Curriculum Studies* 20(1), 1–21.

Dittmar, N.: 1976, *Sociolinguistics: A Critical Survey of Theory and Application*, Edward Arnold, London.

Edwards, D. & Potter, J.: 1992 *Discursive Psychology*, Sage, London.

Foucault, M.: 1977, *Discipline and Punish: The Birth of the Prison*, Pantheon, New York.

Gadamer, H.G.: 1989, *Truth and Method* (2nd edition), Crossroads Press, New York.

Gallagher, S.: 1992, *Hermeneutics and Education*, SUNY Press, Albany.

Green, J. & Harker, J. (eds.): 1988, *Multiple Perspective Analyses of Classroom Discourse* (Vol XXVIII in Advances in Discourse Processes), Ablex, New Jersey.

Habermas, J.: 1984, *The Theory of Communicative Action Vols 1–2*, Hernemeum Educational Books, London, 1982 and Polity Press, Cambridge.

Hirsch, E.: 1987, *Cultural Literacy: What Every American Needs to Know*, Houghton Mifflin, Boston.

Hodge, B.: 1981, *Communication and the Teacher*, Longman Cheshire, Sydney.

Hunter, I.: 1994, *Rethinking the School: Subjectivity, Bureaucracy, Criticism*, Allen and Unwin, Sydney.

Luke, A., Kale, J., Singh, G., Hill, T. & Daliri, F.: 1995, 'Talking difference: Discourses on aboriginal identity in grade 1 classrooms', in D. Corson (ed.) *Discourse and Power in Educational Organisation*, Hampton Press, Cresskill, 211–232.

Rorty, R.: 1989, 'Education without dogma: Truth, freedom and our universities', *Dissent* (Spring), 198–204.

Young, R.: 1996, *Intercultural Communication: Pragmatics, Genealogy, Deconstruction*, Multilingual Matters, Philadelphia.

COLIN BAKER

SURVEY METHODS IN RESEARCHING LANGUAGE AND EDUCATION

It is important initially to define survey methods. The survey method is not the use of a questionnaire and a large sample with the resulting set of relatively simple statistical analyses. A survey is not synonymous with a particular technique of collecting information. A survey can occur via questionnaires, structured and in-depth interviews, structured or systematic observation, and content analysis of documents (Marsh, 1982; de Vaus, 1986; Babbie, 1990). A survey can occur with one classroom of children, on large and representative samples of teachers and students, and a country's population (e.g. as in a National Census).

Surveys are characterised by a structured and systematic collection of data in the form of variables. By nature, a survey is preordinate in design, quantitative in analysis but not always embedded in positivism. This chapter will outline what, in practice, have been the main forms of surveys in language and education, highlighting methods of approach, but particularly surveys that have been influential in education policy making, education provision and pedagogic practice.

EARLY DEVELOPMENTS

The first section will attempt to show that survey methods in language and education develop from particular traditions and historical developments. Surveys are sometimes wrongly thought of as a product of the twentieth century and emanating from social science. To the contrary, ancient Egyptians, the Romans, the Chinese from the Ming dynasty onwards and the Norman conquerors of Britain all conducted surveys. A bureaucratic society may require data-gathering exercises so as to administer efficiently, assess the characteristics of the population, and particularly to levy taxes. Hence surveys in education firstly derive from information gathering requirements of a bureaucracy. Examples of modern language and education surveys, considered later, fit into this tradition.

Surveys in education also derive from the investigation of social problems. The liberal and utilitarian ideology of the nineteenth century encouraged an investigation of social problems that a capitalist market and industrialism had exacerbated. Early surveys of poverty, health and the unemployed heralded in an era where surveys become part of conscience-

N.H. Hornberger and D. Corson (eds), Encyclopedia of Language and Education,
Volume 8: Research Methods in Language and Education, 35–46.
© *1997 Kluwer Academic Publishers. Printed in the Netherlands.*

building and profile-raising, particularly of forgotten minorities. Surveys of language minorities, including such minorities in education systems, are in this second tradition. This will be exemplified later.

Surveys in language and education have a third root, in national censuses. While censuses have been carried out since Biblical times, regular decennial censuses began in particular countries (e.g. US, UK) from the middle of the nineteenth century. One of the first censuses to include a language question was the 1891 censuses of Britain which allowed Southall (1895) to show the distribution of the Welsh language in Wales. The considerable importance of censuses as surveys providing data on language and education is represented later. However, at this juncture, it is important to state that language censuses around the world provide information about language and education, both in terms of a description of language groups that require education and, in recent times, as one performance indicator of the longer term success or failure of submersion, transitional or maintenance bilingual education programs.

Fourthly, surveys in language and education have been influenced, indeed promoted, by advances in survey methodology. One early development in the use of surveys in language and education derived from the use of attitude scaling techniques. The unidimensional techniques produced by Thurstone & Chave and then by Likert were followed by Guttman's Scalogram analysis, the Semantic Differential Technique and the Matched Guise Technique. Once methodological tools for measuring attitudes were publicized and in vogue, their application to language was quickly recognized. In this sense, one influence on the style of language surveys relating to education has been the availability of a recognized and prestigious methodology. Early work in this tradition concerned attitudes to language groups, attitudes to a language itself, attitudes to the features and uses of a language, attitudes to learning a language, attitudes to bilingual education, and attitudes to language preference and policy (Giles, Hewstone & Ball, 1983). For example, the early work of W.R. Jones (1949, 1950) used a twenty-two item Thurstone scale with schoolchildren to show that there was a decline in a favourable attitude to the Welsh language with age. Such early work can be characterised as measuring attitude to language with implicit rather than explicit theorization, unidimensional measurement, simple bivariate relationships, with more concern for internal reliability than validity (Baker, 1992). Small-scale, unrepresentative sampling and a lack of understanding of the complex relationship between attitudes and behaviour was also a feature of this work.

MAJOR CONTRIBUTIONS

One major contribution in survey methods in researching language and education has been in the internationally widespread use of language questions within national censuses, and recent refinement of such questions. Language censuses analyses provide essential information in the politics, policy making and provision of education. In recent Venezuelan and Gaelic (Scotland) censuses, for example, knowledge of the location and size of language groups aids forward planning, particularly when there are local or regional analyses. Such analyses show the size and distribution of language minority groups in different school-age groups. Both language activists and education administrators may determine needs for educational provision based on such 'age by language' tabulations.

Language information from a census has also recently been conceptualized by central bureaucracy as a measure of outcome. A census provides a performance indicator of success as to whether policies with regard to language in schools have been effective across decades. For example, in governments where there has been high immigration (e.g. the United States), the degree of fluency in the majority language (e.g. English) across decades provides a performance indicator of educational policies which may have aimed at assimilation, integration, maintenance of language minorities or language reversal. In Wales, the decennial census is regarded as a key indicator of the success of bilingual education, even though the equation of language shift or revival is highly complex and debated.

Some countries have a long history of language questions in the census (e.g. Wales), while other countries appear to have avoided inclusion of language questions in their census (e.g. France). A recent development is the addition of a language census question in an increasing number of countries in the world (e.g. Australia, Hungary, Bolivia and Venezuela). Also, the analysis of language census data impinging on education has become relatively sophisticated (e.g. in Canada, United States, Wales, Scotland, Ireland, and Australia). The linguistic detail and attempted precision from recent censuses in Venezuela (Oficina Central de Estadística e Informática, 1993) and Bolivia (Albó, 1995; Díez Astete et al., 1995) are particularly noteworthy.

For example, one of the most impressive current language maps with clear educational importance derives from the 1992 census in Bolivia. This detailed and well conceptualized map not only clearly represents Aymara, Quechua, Guaraní and Spanish, but also many indigenous minority languages. Rather than just using simple colouring or shading, the map shows where there is language contact and bilingualism. The presence of minority languages is represented by coloured dots or letters placed among more widespread languages. The census language map also uses arrows to show the direction of language shift. For example, Portuguese is shown to be advancing in the extreme north west of Bolivia. Spanish is generally advancing on Aymara, Quechua and Guaraní and the many smaller populated indigenous languages, and the map shows specifically where this is occurring in a major way (Albó, 1995; Díez Astete et al.,

1995). Discussion of the role of education in effecting such language shift (and as a means of reversing shift) is stimulated from such a mapping of language.

Another major development has been the movement away from simple census language questions such as 'Do you speak English? Yes/No'. Questions recently tend to include not only oracy but also literacy, separating reading and writing. In the United States 1990 census, question 15a asked: 'Does this person speak a language other than English at home?' If the respondent answered 'yes', they were then asked to write down the name of that language. This U.S. census question also asked: 'How well does this person speak English?' The response scale comprised 'very well/well/not well/not at all'. As an officially stated aim, U.S. census data is made available to help States and Counties benchmark and measure progress in meeting their objectives and legislatively mandated targets (e.g. in English language spread among immigrants). Given the role of education in fostering English among U.S. immigrants, such census data is directly relevant to educational policy making.

How far language census questions have moved forward is revealed in the comparison of the 1990 and the 1910 United States language questions. In the 1910 census, the mother tongue of members of each household was requested. However, the definition of 'mother tongue' excluded those born in the United States. Also, the language of under 10 year olds was ignored, and a person's ability to speak a language other than English was ignored if they were able to speak English. Ability in a heritage language was counted only if a person was unable to speak English.

Alongside the inherently negative profiling of the 1910 United States census, there has been a tendency to ignore surveying the language of immigrants in schooling. A major breakthrough in describing the variety of languages and dialects in schools, revealing the strengths of community languages and cultures, was the Linguistic Minorities Project (1984, 1985) in London and various urban areas of England. Via an attractive cartoon-like questionnaire, this project documented the hitherto unknown extent of bilingualism in schools in key urban areas of England. This project also surveyed the provision of minority language teaching in both mainstream and community-run schools and classes. This was the first large-scale linguistic survey work to be undertaken in Britain.

While the project has received a number of criticisms (e.g. Martin-Jones, 1991) that will be returned to later, this detailed survey had an important impact in putting bilingualism on the agenda in the British educational context. Since no language questions are included in England in the decennial national census, such surveys provide important information and intelligence gathering that impacts on education provision and policy. At the least, such surveys raise the profile of low status, forgotten language minorities and their educational needs.

In the United States, a similar pioneering study of public opinion was by Huddy & Sears (1990) who used a telephone interview survey of a United States national sample of 1170 people. They found that the majority of the public in the mid 1980s tended to be favourable towards bilingual education, although a substantial minority opposed bilingual education when the focus was assimilation, integration or cultural pluralism.

The discussion in this section so far has concerned one major aspect of survey work, that of measuring public opinion, fact finding and information provision. However, there is opposition to this approach. The culling of opinions and the description of the characteristics of the population has been anathema to many sociologists, psychologists, linguists and educationalists who, for example, are critical of a lack of theoretical foundation to such surveys.

The counter-argument is that there is a place within a democracy, not for mob rule by opinion poll, but for the views of the majority being counted and represented. Such public opinions, it is argued, can be balanced against the views of those elected and all forms of persuasionists (e.g. crusading academics, interest groups, language activists and educational campaigners). Factual and opinion surveys have moved from a nineteenth century idea of an informant, to the psychological idea of a respondent, and recently to framing the person answering the questions as a citizen.

In this sense, the survey becomes a polling situation, a collection of votes, a raising of the profile of those who may become neglected by the elected. Such surveys may aid the recognition of language minorities and their needs in education. However, within language and education, surveys can become an intelligence gathering for a centralised ruling class who use the information for manipulation and control. But that is a criticism of government and not of surveys.

If census-type surveys are one part of the language surveys, the other half is surveys that start from a more theoretical perspective. One major criticism of language surveys in education has been the implicit rather than explicit theoretical formulation (De Vries, 1987). Those who use attitude scales to measure language have, in contrast, sometimes commenced from an explicit theoretical basis. For example, utilizing theoretical work on the relationship between attitudes and behaviour, or employing theories of attitude change, attitudes to language can be put in a multivariate, interactive and developmental theoretical framework. One example is research that seeks to establish a probabilistic and interactive, but not deterministic, set of relationships between individual characteristics, schooling, language background, forms of cultural activity, language ability and attitude to language (Baker, 1992). While reductionist in approach, a statistical modelling of language attitude data attempts to uncover weaker and stronger relationships and, at its basis, a finer insight into what support systems are required within formal and informal education to maintain a minority language.

This more theoretically-derived approach in language surveys derives from the pioneering work of Sharp et al. (1973) in developing reliable and valid language scales, but also from the pioneering work of Robert Gardner and colleagues in Canada. Gardner's (1982, 1985) research culminating in his socio-educational model interrelates social and cultural background, intelligence, language aptitude, motivation and attitude, situational anxiety, formal and informal language learning and bilingual proficiency. Recent research from this group has included surveys of students finding patterns in the retention and attrition of a learnt language (Gardner, Lalonde & MacPherson, 1986; Gardner, Lalonde & Moorcroft, 1987 – see also Halsall, 1994).

Another theoretical input into recent survey research is from language maintenance, language shift, social networks and language reproduction. A particularly fine example is O'Riagain's (1992) study entitled Language Maintenance and Language Shift as Strategies of Social Reproduction'. O'Riagain's (1992) survey was based on in-depth interviews with 150 adults in West Kerry, Ireland. His study relates bilingualism in Ireland to extensive socio-economic transformations that have occurred in Ireland this century, with the theoretical input of Pierre Bourdieu particularly influential in analysis and interpretation.

Another trend in recent decades has been in sampling. One of the early patterns of research was rather small-scale survey work. Not only were samples often small, but use of random selection and stratification in sampling was often missing or inadequate. For example, W.R. Jones (1949, 1950) used small and unrepresentative samples (respectively 129 students and 211 students) allowing little generalisation of findings. In comparison, the five year monumental study, the Committee on Irish Language Attitudes and Research (CILAR, 1975) drew-up a stratified random sample for interview in a ratio of 13 respondents per 10,000 members of the Irish population. Another comparison is the sampling technique used in language surveys by von Gleich & Wölck (1994) in Peru. Entitled a 'community profile', von Gleich & Wölck (1994) use local 'guides' to gain information on, for example, the occupational, political, educational, religious, communication and residential organization of a community. Such information enables the social structure of a community to be fully represented in the sample to be interviewed.

Small scale sample survey work is especially justified when there is an intensity of investigation. This is where the margins of survey work merge with techniques such as systematic observation. In this category, the pioneering observational survey work of Gliksman (1976, 1981) deserves mention. In the first study, observation of children's language behaviour in the classroom was carried out for one semester. In the second study,

14 to 16 year olds were observed once every two weeks for four months. The survey comprised systematic observations of students in second language learning classes. The survey collected the number of times a student volunteered information by raising a hand, was asked by teachers without volunteering, answered correctly or incorrectly, asked questions, and received positive, negative or no feed back from the teacher. The survey showed that integratively motivated students volunteered more frequently, gave more correct answers, and received more positive reinforcement from the teacher than non-integratively motivated students. This behaviour was consistent through the semester.

A similar borderline area, this time between surveys and experiments, is the use of the Matched Guise Technique (Giles & Coupland, 1991) to infer attitudes to language varieties (e.g. evaluation of different accents among schoolchildren). Other areas which involve surveys, but also use a psychometric and experimental style, include research on language learning preferences in school, reasons for learning a language, styles of language teaching, and parent's language attitudes. These are well reviewed by Gardner (1985).

A further development in survey work in language and education has been the use of surveys to measure language performance and achievement in school. For example, in the United Kingdom in the early 1980s, the Assessment of Performance Unit carried out surveys of children's abilities in listening, understanding and speaking. In Wales, large representative samples of children throughout Wales were measured on their listening, understanding speaking and writing skills in Welsh (Price & Powell, 1983; Price et al., 1984).

Language surveys in schools have recently been about bench-marking and baselines (e.g. in the National Curriculum in the UK). With a focus on quality assurance and quality enhancement, bench-marks and baselines enable comparisons and accent the need for an upward spiral in centralist-defined educational standards. Language performance surveys enable comparisons across time, across countries, states and counties, across types of school and language groups with the spotlight on performance enhancement, reaching standards of international comparability, raising the performance of individual schools and regions, and locating the 'value-added' contribution that particularly effective schools display in first and second language achievement.

MAJOR WORK IN PROGRESS

There are currently various unconnected initiatives in survey work in language and education. At the European level, as part of a movement of Europeanization and European unity, there are initiatives in the European Union to investigate detailed language use among over forty language minorities. For example, the Euromosaic Project commenced in 1993 to investigate in considerable detail the language vitality or otherwise of lesser used languages in the European Union. Language in education was a prominent part of this survey. Directed by M. Strubell (Politica Linguistica, Generalitat de Catalunya, Barcelona), Peter Nelde (Research Centre for Multilingualism, Catholic University, Brussels) and Glyn Williams (Research Centre Wales, University of Wales at Bangor), relatively intensive data has been collected on the indigenous lesser used language groups of the European Union. This excludes immigrant minorities in countries such as exist in Germany and the United Kingdom. The survey included official policies and legislation in language education, the situation of the language in teaching from preschool level to university, and included adult and continuing education, the provision of curricular material in the lesser used languages, local movements that promote language in education, teacher training, the inspection and monitoring of language teaching, government acts, laws and decrees governing language in education, plus pressure groups in education and language. Apart from education, many other aspects of language vitality within a language minority were explored.

Coleman (1996) surveyed 25,000 British and mainland European students who were learning a foreign language. The survey examined their proficiency in learnt languages, pace of development and progress towards communicative competency, styles of language teaching, attitudes and motivations in learning a language, foreign language testing and assessment, and other variables that relate to more or less successful routes to language learning. This large-scale survey also provides a comparative European examination of national standards in language training, the value of residence abroad, and a currently important issue of whether graduates are being adequately or inadequately prepared for European employment. Such employment increasingly demands foreign language skills, and generally, the United Kingdom lags behind its European partners in this area.

Internationally, there is an expansion in the use of national census, particularly as newer democracies have arisen and require information that will help policy formulation and planning with regard to languages in education. While inevitably language census questions are limited (as so many questions are required in a census), there has been an increasing awareness of the importance of language questions. For example, in Northern Ireland, the 1991 census was the first time that a question was asked about the Irish language. The very detailed language censuses in Bolivia and Venezuela have provided examples of comprehensive and skilful analysis of language census data questions that relate to language and education which other countries are likely to emulate, and from which northern hemisphere countries could learn.

The concept of attitude to bilingualism has been explored (Baker, 1992). Further research is being carried out on this construct, attitude to bilingualism, in the United States (Pittsburgh), Wales (Swansea and Bangor) and Namibia. Surveys of language and education have hitherto tended to focus on single languages. Given that a majority of the world is bilingual rather than monolingual, perceptions of an individual's languages in contact (and sometimes in conflict) has been found worthy of further exploration. This construct fits a cultural pluralist view of languages and bilingual education.

PROBLEMS AND DIFFICULTIES

Surveys are generally surrounded by a series of criticisms and limitations. At one level, there are philosophically based criticisms such as: surveys cannot establish causal connections between variables; they are incapable of uncovering meaningful aspects of social action; people's opinions are not contextualised and therefore are capable of being misunderstood; surveys assume that human action is determined by external forces and neglect the role of human consciousness, intentions and understandings as important sources of action; surveys follow ritualistic methodological rules and lack imagination or depth of penetration in understanding; theoretical input is implicit rather than explicit; only the trivial and superficial is measured, and the construction of surveys fails to penetrate the meanings and understandings of a people who are surveyed but rather arranges answers to fit a conceptualisation that is essentially that of the researcher.

An insightful, critical assessment of survey work is given by Martin-Jones (1991). In discussing the work of the Linguistic Minorities Project, Martin-Jones (1991) indicates many of the practical difficulties in running a survey among immigrant populations and community language groups, and provides an argument for small scale local surveys that pursue the more analytical and interpretive 'how' and 'why' questions in depth.

There are also many technique-based criticisms of surveys within language and education that overlap with the ideological critique. Among the criticisms are the following: surveys are inadequately designed and piloted; the questions are ambiguous, sometimes leading, have in-built social desirability or prestige biases in answers; the questions themselves can create artificial opinions; little evidence is given for reliability or validity; surveys are often unpiloted; there is an over-reliance on single item measurement; the data provides a quick snapshot but no film of interaction and language life; samples are often small and unrepresentative; surveys often lack clear aims with key concepts not being clarified; answer categories insufficiently discriminate between different sensitivities; the interviewer or researcher has an effect on responses; the physical setting of the research and the 'season' in which research is carried out affects responses; evidence is attenuated to simple categorisation and a number system; and ahistorical accounts of issues are presented.

There are furthermore criticisms of the way language is conceived in surveys. These are now listed. A full investigation of language use across a wide variety of domains is rarely presented, including the different domains in schooling. Thus contextual use of language tends to be aggregated to a small number of categories, or in the case of a census, often to merely speaking that language or not. Language census questions sometimes fail to distinguish between use of language and ability in language, and fail to distinguish the various sub-skills of language ability (e.g. listening, speaking, reading, writing, thinking). In such local and national surveys, questions about home language, mother tongue, first language, second language and official language are often ambiguous and distant from the respondent.

The danger is also that a simple census language question may be interpreted as an attitude question. For example, people from a particular ethnic group may feel that they ought to say that they speak the indigenous or heritage language even if they do not. It may be regarded as socially desirable to say one speaks the language, and speaks it well. The opposite may also occur. If a minority language is disparaged and of low status, a speaker of that language may claim not to speak the language. Answers to questions about language on a census form may thus reflect a socially desirable answer and not everyday behaviour. Thus in Ireland, for example, those who never or rarely speak Irish are known occasionally to answer the Irish language census question positively.

FUTURE DIRECTIONS

Within language and education, the dominant methodology is currently not experimental, survey, or similar quantitative approaches. The methodological pendulum has partly swung towards a preference for qualitative, ethnographic and phenomenological types of approach. While quantitative approaches have declined within the study of language and education, it is unlikely they will disappear. As this chapter has shown, survey work in language education lends itself to two movements. The first movement, is the requirement of central government, local government, local education authorities and interest groups to acquire basic factual information about populations, as well as opinions. Thus, the use of national, local and small-scale census-type language surveys is likely to continue.

Such surveys provide language group profiles, collect votes, as well as reveal facts about who speaks what language where and to whom. Thus, as one part of the information collection procedure of a democracy, and as part of the current consumerism ideology, being responsive to public opinion is expected and respected. In this climate, surveys of language will continue.

The second movement, particularly concerned with surveying attitudes, has tended to become more theoretical, using more complex multivariate statistical techniques. On the other hand, the prominence of this approach as a major topic in language and education has decreased since the heyday of the 1970s and 1980s. With major theoretical and research studies having been accepted, replicated, and mostly validated, no major discernible movements in the future are immediately apparent.

One continuously important area appears to be language surveys that measure the performance of children in schools to allow comparisons between institutions and over time. One perspective derives from those assimilationists who are concerned with performance in the majority language (e.g. in the United States and Britain, there is political concern about high standards of oracy and literacy in English). Another perspective comes from those concerned with the preservation, partly by bilingual education, of a minority language. Both assimilationist and maintenance policies seek information about language performance and language achievement to ensure politics and policies are effective. In an increasingly competitive economic world, there is also a need for 'foreign' language competence surveys to ensure strength in trading languages (e.g. attainment in German, Japanese, Cantonese and Mandarin). Such 'foreign language competence surveys' could become the research focus of many future surveys in language and education.

University of Wales Bangor
Wales

REFERENCES

Albó, X.: 1995, *Bolivia Plurilingüe: Guia para Planiticadores y Educadores* (3 volumes), UNICEF-CIPCA, La Paz, Bolivia.
Babbie, E.: 1990, *Survey Research Methods* (second edition), Wadsworth, Belmont, CA.
Baker, C.R.: 1992, *Attitudes and Language*, Multilingual Matters Ltd., Clevedon, Avon.
CILAR (Committee on Irish Language Attitudes Research): 1975, *Report of the Committee on Irish Language Attitudes Research*, Government Stationery Office, Dublin.
Coleman, J.A.: 1996, *Studying Languages: a Survey of British and European Students*, Centre for Information on Language Teaching and Research, London.
De Vaus, D.A.: 1986, *Surveys in Social Research*, George Allen & Unwin, London.
De Vries, J.: 1987, 'Problems of measurement in the study of linguistic minorities', *Journal of Multilingual and Multicultural Development* 8, 23–31.
Díez Astete, A., Riester, J., Mihotek, K. et al.: 1995, *Mapa étnico, territorial y argueologico de Bolivia*, CIMAR, Universidad Gabriel René Moreno, Santa Gruz, Bolivia.
Gardner, R.C.: 1982, 'Language attitudes and language learning', in E.B. Ryan & H. Giles (eds.), *Attitudes Towards Language Variation*, Edward Arnold, London, 132–147.
Gardner, R.C.: 1985, *Social Psychology and Second Language Learning*, Edward Arnold, London.

Gardner, R.C., Lalonde, R.N. & MacPherson, J.: 1986, 'Social factors in second language attrition', *Language Learning* 35, 519–540.

Gardner, R.C., Lalonde, R.N. & Moorcroft, R.: 1987, 'Second language attrition: The role of motivation and use', *Journal of Language and Social Psychology* 6(1), 29–47.

Giles, H. & Coupland, N.: 1991, *Language: Contexts and Consequences*, Open University Press, Milton Keynes.

Giles, H., Hewstone, M. & Ball, P.: 1983, 'Language attitudes in multilingual settings: Prologue with priorities', *Journal of Multilingual and Multicultural Development* 4, 81–100.

Gliksman, L.: 1976. Second language acquisition: The effects of student attitudes on classroom behaviour. Unpublished M.A. thesis, University of Western Ontario.

Gliksman, L.: 1981, Improving the prediction of behaviours associated with second language acquisition. Unpublished Ph.D. thesis, University of Western Ontario.

Halsall, Nancy D.: 1994, 'Attrition/retention of students in French immersion with particular emphasis on secondary school', *The Canadian Modern Language Review* 50, 313–333.

Huddy, L. & Sears, D.O.: 1990, 'Qualified public support for bilingual education: Some policy implications', in C.B. Cazden & C.E. Snow (eds.), *The Annals of the American Academy of Political and Social Science*, Volume 508, 119–134.

Jones, W.R.: 1949, 'Attitude towards Welsh as a second language. A preliminary investigation', *British Journal of Educational Psychology* 19, 44–52.

Jones, W.R.: 1950, 'Attitude towards Welsh as a second language. A further investigation', *British Journal of Educational Psychology* 20, 117–132.

Linguistic Minorities Project: 1984, 'Linguistic minorities in England: A short report on the linguistic minorities project', *Journal of Multilingual and Multicultural Development* 5, 351–366.

Linguistic Minorities Project: 1985, *The Other Languages of England*, Routledge and Kegan Paul, London.

Marsh, C.: 1982, *The Survey Method*, George Allen, London.

Martin-Jones, M.: 1991, 'Sociolinguistic surveys as a source of evidence in the study of bilingualism: A critical assessment of survey work conducted among linguistic minorities in three British cities', *International Journal of the Sociology of Language* 90, 37–55.

Oficina Central de Estadística e Informática: 1993, *Censo Indígena de Venezuela 1992*, Oficina Central de Estadística e Informática, Caracas, Venezuela.

O'Riagain, Padraig: 1992, *Language Maintenance and Language Shift as Strategies of Social Reproduction: Irish in the Corca Dhuibhne Gaeltacht: 1926–1986*, The Linguistics Institute of Ireland (Instituid Teangeolaiochta Eireann), Dublin.

Price, E. & Powell, R.: 1983, *Listening, Understanding and Speaking*, Welsh Office, Cardiff.

Price, E. et al.: 1984, *Survey of Writing Among 10–11 Year Old First Language Welsh Pupils*, Welsh Office, Cardiff.

Sharp, D., Thomas, B., Price, E., Francis, G. & Davies, I.: 1973, *Attitudes to Welsh and English in the Schools of Wales*, MacMillan/University of Wales Press, Basingstoke/Cardiff.

Southall, J.E.: 1895, *The Welsh Language Census of 1891*, Southall Publications, Newport.

von Gleich, U. & Wölck, W.: 1994, 'Changes in language use and attitudes of Quechua-Spanish bilinguals in Peru', in P. Cole, G. Hermon & M.D. Martin (eds.), *Language in the Andes*, University of Delaware, Newark, Delaware.

REBECCA D. FREEMAN

RESEARCHING GENDER IN LANGUAGE USE

Language and gender research has evolved considerably over the last
two decades. In the 1970s and 1980s, through a variety of methodological approaches, researchers demonstrated that language use was gender
differentiated. Sociolinguists offered competing theoretical explanations
based on power and cross-cultural differences for the variation they found
in interaction, and feminists concerned with sexist representations documented considerable bias in the lexicon. From the late 1980s to the
present, ethnographic and discourse analytic research in a wide range of
contexts has begun to reveal complex relations between language, gender,
and power, and to illustrate that gender identity, as one aspect of social
identity, is largely discursively constituted. This work demonstrates how
our language use can reflect and reproduce dominant relations; it can resist
dominant practices in favor of alternatives; or it can create new forms of
representation and interaction that challenge and potentially transform the
social order.

EARLY DEVELOPMENTS

One of the earliest and most influential linguists to write about language
and gender was Robin Lakoff (1975). Her controversial work introduced
feminist analysis into linguistic research. Based on introspection and
native-speaker intuition, Lakoff made a series of claims about women's
language which can be divided into three categories: (1) it lacks resources
for women to express themselves strongly (e.g. women use 'empty' adjec-
tives), (2) it encourages women to talk about trivial subjects (e.g. women
discriminate among colors more than men) and (3) it requires women to
speak tentatively (e.g. women use tag questions and hedges more than
men). Lakoff attributed women's linguistic inadequacies to their political
and cultural domination by men.

Feminist researchers in the 1970s were also concerned with sexist lexical
choice. For example, the so-called 'generic' masculine, that is, the use of
male terms (e.g. *he, him, mankind, chairman*) to refer both to males in
particular and to human beings in general, was targeted for research. Experimental studies suggested that it was unlikely that the 'generic' masculine
was in fact interpreted generically by its readers or hearers (e.g. Bem
& Bem, 1973; Martyna, 1983). Surveys of the lexicon also revealed
this gender bias. For instance, in pairs of words that are distinguished

N.H. Hornberger and D. Corson (eds), Encyclopedia of Language and Education,
Volume 8: Research Methods in Language and Education, 47–56.
© *1997 Kluwer Academic Publishers. Printed in the Netherlands.*

by gender (*dog/bitch; lion/lioness*), the masculine terms are considered 'neutral' whereas the feminine counterparts are semantically marked (Graddol & Swann, 1989). And considerable asymmetry in the lexicon has been identified. For example, Kramarae & Treichler (1990) describe an absence in traditional dictionaries of words representing women's experiences and a bias in dictionary entries that reflects and preserves stereotypes about women. This and other early work on lexical choice has provided a basis for later investigation of the more subtle workings of sexist ideologies.

MAJOR CONTRIBUTIONS

Partially stimulated by Lakoff's claims and partially to examine stereotypes about women's language, feminist sociolinguists in the 1970s and 1980s began to ask questions about how men and women actually used language in face-to-face interaction. Critical of Lakoff's reliance on introspection and native-speaker intuition, these sociolinguists tape recorded, transcribed and analysed naturally occurring conversations (primarily between white middle class heterosexual couples) to understand how linguistic features functioned in interaction. Two major theoretical explanations, the 'dominance' and 'difference' positions, have been forwarded for the gender-based variation that was found. While each has provided insight into language and gender relations, neither is without criticism.

The dominance approach negatively evaluated women's speech, and argued that the linguistic features that men and women respectively used reflected and helped perpetuate the hierarchical nature of gender relations in society. So, for example, findings that men frequently interrupted women in conversation (West & Zimmerman, 1983) and controlled topics in conversation (Fishman, 1983) were interpreted to reflect men's domination of women in conversation. Similarly, findings that women used tag questions and minimal responses more frequently than men (Fishman, 1983) were interpreted to reflect the interactional work that women did to support the conversation. The difference or 'dual-culture' approach criticized the dominance approach for overemphasizing the power that men have over women. This second approach acknowledged that women use language differently than men do, but interpreted women's speech more positively, that is, as a reflection of women's culture. For example, Tannen (1989) demonstrates that not all conversational overlap should be interpreted as interruption/dominating. Rather, some overlap shows conversational involvement and/or solidarity with the speaker. A theme that emerges from this line of research is that men tend to organize their interaction more competitively while women tend to be more cooperative. Because men and women have been socialized to use language differently in their respective subcultures, (unintended) cross-cultural miscommunication can and does arise (Maltz & Borker, 1982; Tannen, 1990). While the dual-culture approach challenges negative stereotypes about women's speech by celebrating women's interactional styles, it has been criticized for its lack of attention to power structures.

Early sociolinguistic work has yielded several major methodological contributions. First, there is no one-to-one mapping of linguistic form and interactional function. Understanding the meaning of a given linguistic form often requires careful attention to the range of possible meanings it can have as well as to its social context of use and to the relationships among speakers (Tannen, 1993). Second, it is not isolated linguistic forms, but communicative styles made up of clusters of linguistic features, that distinguish men's and women's speech in society (Maltz & Borker, 1982; Tannen, 1990). Third, with few exceptions (e.g. pronoun use, some titles, etc.), the relationship between women and the use of any particular linguistic form(s) is not direct (Ochs, 1992). For example, O'Barr & Atkins (1980) looked for the features that Lakoff called 'women's language' in the speech of male and female expert and non-expert witnesses in their study of courtroom testimony. They found that the professional witnesses, whether male or female, used few features of 'women's language' while the nonexpert witnesses used many more of these features, and argued that 'women's language' could more accurately be described as 'powerless language'.

Linguistic anthropological research provides further insight into the nature of relations among language, gender, and power. Beginning with a particular speech community, ethnographers of communication look closely at patterns and functions of language used in situated speech events to elucidate the cultural organization of that community (see the review by Farah in this volume). For example, Sherzer's (1987) ethnography of speaking research among the Cuna Indians of Panama demonstrates how certain cultural rituals are linguistically realized, and shows that the genres and tasks associated with these rituals are differentiated by gender. Thus, the more powerful, public rituals (e.g. chanting of chiefs, speech making of political leaders) are performed by men while the less powerful, private rituals (e.g lullabies, tuneful weeping) are performed by women; the linguistic features and strategies that constitute these genres are associated with the genres themselves and not with men or women directly. Keenan's (1974) work in Malagasy also illustrates a mediated relationship between language and gender. Formal speech activities (e.g. village-to-village negotiation, dispute resolution) are assigned to men because these situations require speaking with care and delicacy and men are seen as more polite in the way they use language. Women are selected for other speech activities where direct confrontation is appropriate (e.g. accusations, bargaining in the marketplace), because they are seen as less polite. In these and other cases, gender is related to language use through men's and women's participation in specific activities; how women and men are assigned to activities and which communicative styles are appropriate for performing those activities reflect local gendered ideologies.

Multidisciplinary research on gendered representations done throughout the 1980s has contributed to our understanding of how ideologies are reflected in texts that we read, write, hear, and speak. Feminist/critical linguists look beyond lexical choice to analyze text representations of who says and/or does what, to whom, under what circumstances, and with what effects (e.g. Cameron, 1990; Poynton, 1989). Intertextual discourse analysis allows the researcher to identify coherence relations across texts, and make abstract, underlying ideologies explicit (Fairclough, 1989; Lemke, 1990). Researchers in cultural or symbolic studies investigate how social groups define cultural categories, how these categories change over time, and how they are systematically related to other areas of cultural discourse. For example, Martin (1987) compares the way that medical textbooks represent menstruation, childbirth, and menopause with the way that women from diverse backgrounds talk about these experiences to demonstrate that women have choices in the ways that they represent and evaluate their bodies. Her intertextual analyses demonstrate how medical texts' use of metaphors reflects dominant cultural ideologies about women and their bodies, which she argues contributes to the alienation of women from their bodies. The working-class women's talk, however, offered more positive, integrated images about their reproductive processes. This research provides one example of the general feminist critique that women's contributions, experiences, and perspectives (i.e. 'voices') have been omitted, marginalized, and stereotyped (i.e. 'silenced') throughout the disciplines.

Research on language, gender, and education conducted primarily in the United States, the United Kingdom, Australia, and New Zealand reflects many of the findings discussed above and has contributed to our understanding of how boys and girls experience schooling in mainstream schools in different cultural contexts in these countries. Close analysis of text representations of curricular materials reveals that women and members of minority groups tend to be excluded, marginalized, or stereotyped within the mainstream curriculum. And interaction analyses of taped and transcribed classroom discourse illustrate a range of ways in which gender differentiation is maintained in mainstream English-speaking classrooms (e.g. boys tend to occupy more space than girls, both in class and at play; boys and girls tend to discuss or write about different topics when they have the choice; girls tend to do the 'fetch and carry' work for boys in practical subjects; teachers often give more attention to boys than girls; see Swann 1993, pp. 51–52, for review of these studies. See also Corson, 1993 for discussion of language, minority education, and gender in other cultural contexts). Implications of these findings for future research on gender socialization through language are suggested below.

WORK IN PROGRESS

Language and gender research today aims to integrate cultural studies of the discursive construction of gendered ideologies with sociolinguistic studies of how gendered identities are socially constituted through face-to-face interaction. Gal's (1995) notion of power as symbolic domination helps link these lines of research. She writes,

the notions of domination and resistance alert us to the idea that the strongest form of power may well be the ability to define social reality, to impose visions of the world. And such visions are inscribed in language, and most important, enacted in interaction (p. 178).

Ethnographic and discourse analytic approaches allow researchers to relate how people describe gender relations in specific communities to how those people actually use language in their everyday interactions. This work is yielding an understanding of how social identity is discursively constituted in situated practice.

Because social groups organize and conceptualize gender alongside of other aspects of social identities in culturally specific and meaningful ways, Eckert & McConnell-Ginet (1992, 1995) argue that research must be grounded in detailed investigation of the social and linguistic activities of specific 'communities of practice'. A community of practice 'is an aggregate of people who come together around mutual engagement in an endeavour. Ways of doing things, ways of talking, beliefs, values, power relations – in short, practices – emerge in the course of this mutual endeavour' (1992, p. 464). Based on Eckert's ethnographic research in a public high school in suburban Detroit, Eckert & McConnell-Ginet (1995) illustrate how gender, class, and power relations are mutually constructed in this setting. Because language is a primary tool that people use to constitute themselves and others as certain 'kinds' of people, i.e. people with certain attributes who participate in certain activities, Eckert & McConnell-Ginet analyzed the language that students used to describe and evaluate each other and the activities in which they participated. They found that there were two communities of practice within the school which were relevant to students (*jocks* and *burnouts*) through which students actively negotiated their social identities. These communities of practice were in opposition to each other and reflected students' class-based responses to school, with *jocks* buying into the dominant school practices and *burnouts* resisting them in favor of alternative practices. Within these communities of practice, gender differentiation was evident in the activities that boys and girls pursued to continually define themselves as community members.

This discussion brings us to an important methodological point that is evident in much of the recent work on language and gender. That is, researchers need to consider the activity, as opposed to the individual or the cultural group, as the basic unit of analysis. Eckert did not begin her study by looking at how girls and boys used language at school. Rather, gender differentiation emerged when she looked closely at the activities and attri-abutes toward which *jocks* and *burnouts* oriented themselves. Goodwin (1990) also examined a wide range of speech activities (directives, argu-ment, gossip-dispute, instigating, and stories) and of play activities (playing house – girls, making slingshots – boys, making glass rings – girls, arguments – girls and boys) in her ethnographic and conversation analytic study of the different social structures created by African-American boys and girls. Her analysis illustrates that in some activities, girls and boys build systematically different organizations through their use of talk. How-ever, in others, they build similar structures (e.g. when playing house girls build hierarchical structures similar to those that boys build). She writes,

stereotypes about women's speech thus fall apart when talk in a range of activities is examined; in order to construct social personae appropriate to the events of the moment, the same individuals articulate talk and gender differently as they move from one activity to another (p. 9).

To this point, the discussion has concentrated on research in gender and language use. Ochs (1992) offers a framework for understanding how gender is socially constructed, which derives from studies of language socialization across cultures (e.g. Schieffelin & Ochs, 1986). She proposes that linguists study how gender is constituted through acts (e.g. question-ing, requesting), stances (e.g. accommodation, hesitancy), and activities (e.g. caregiving, storytelling), by investigating how the acts, stances, and activities associated with culturally preferred gender roles are linguistically realized in specific cultural contexts. Her comparative discussion of the social construction of 'mothering' in white middle class (WMC) United States society and traditional Samoan society illustrates how children are socialized through their participation in caregiving situations to understand a culturally shaped image of mother, and by extension of women.

For example, in the US, the WMC caregiving activity is associated with an accommodating stance by mothers; this stance is constituted by certain clusters of discourse features and strategies that mothers use when giving care (e.g. shorter sentences, phonological and morphosyntactic simplification, repetition, etc.). Through their participation in caregiving situations with mothers, WMC children are socialized to see mothers as accommodating. Unless these novices see other images of women in other roles with other stances (e.g in the workplace as assertive), the ideological notion of woman as accommodating is likely to become part of the cultural expectation for woman. In traditional Samoa, in contrast, children are the ones who are expected to be accommodating. Thus, the caregiving activity is linguistically constituted differently, for example with little simplification of the mother's speech, and children develop a different cultural expectation for mothering and for women. Och's work provides considerable insight into how children and other novices in society are socialized through language to acquire an understanding of what activities, acts, and stances are performed by whom, and how they are linguistically realized. Their communicative competence in these activities depends on their abilities to perform the associated acts and stances in ways that are culturally appropriate.

The theoretical orientation and methodological approach described here is exemplified in Hall & Bucholtz (1995). This collection of essays illustrates how in some communities, hegemonic constructions of gender are imposed on girls and women through language use; in other communities, women demonstrate their agency and use language to resist dominant ideological structures for alternatives that constitute women more favorably; and yet in other communities, women create new social identities for themselves that aren't determined in advance by existing gender ideologies. In each case,we see the central role of community values, meanings, and practices in the social construction of identity, which is demonstrated to be a dynamic, situated, negotiated, and negotiable process.

PROBLEMS AND DIFFICULTIES

The theoretical orientation that underlies the work in progress described above helps researchers address several problems and difficulties in much research on language and gender. For example, two common but mistaken assumptions underlie much sociolinguistic research:

The first assumption is that gender is always relevant. The second is that gender is best studied when it is maximally contrastive. Together, these two assumptions have led to a number of "get-your-data-and-run-studies," in which a researcher tapes an interaction or two, assumes that the differences evident in the interaction are due to gender, and too quickly overgeneralizes findings to all men and boys and all women and girls (Freeman & McElhinny, 1995, p. 243).

In addition, several problems have arisen from failure to critically examine the fundamental categories, 'man' and 'woman'. First, many researchers have looked at gender in isolation. However, as Eckert & McConnell-Ginet's (1995) discussion of class and gender relationships illustrates, researchers need to question how gender interacts with other aspects of social identity. Second, researchers' focus on differences in the ways that men and women use language has tended to essentialize gender, that is, to reify these differences and understand them as categorical (McElhinny, 1995). McElhinny proposes that researchers focus not just on differences between women and men, but on the 'existence and competition of different feminine or masculine identities in any given context' (p. 219). Her ethnographic and conversation analytic study of the gender performances of women police officers in the traditionally masculine, all male, working-class job of policing demonstrates how a female officer may, at any given moment, be perceived as a woman, as a man, or simply as a police officer. McElhinny shows how these female officers strategically display stances associated with middle class masculinity (e.g. rationality and emotional control) as a means of challenging the dominant definition of policing that centers on physical force and emotional aggression. Her work provides an excellent example of how a focus on situated activities within specific communities of practice can further our understanding of complex relations among language, social identity, and power.

FUTURE DIRECTIONS

In response to the strong criticism of the prevalence of language and gender research done by white English speaking middle class heterosexual women within white middle class English speaking heterosexual contexts, we can expect to see much more work done in a wider range of communities. The multidisciplinary ethnographic and discourse analytic studies that emerge will provide more insight into how social identity (i.e. gender, race, class, profession, religion, ethnicity, etc.) is negotiated and displayed through language in situated activities in specific contexts. Ongoing, open-ended conversational interviews, analysis of site documents, and extended participant-observation in context (e.g. family, school, workplace, church, society), enables the researcher to explore a wide range of questions about ideological representations. For example, within specific communities of practice, what are the relevant social categories? What is the historical and current relationship among community members? How do members represent and evaluate their own activities and attributes in relation to those of other communities of practice? The answers to these kinds of questions are rich data for intertextual discourse analysis that will reveal abstract, underlying ideologies that structure local community relations.

Perhaps more important than *what* people say about each other is *how* they interact with each other. Transcriptions of audiotaped and/or video-taped recordings of the range of activities in which community members participate provides data for detailed, systematic, discourse analysis of the negotiation and display of social identity. Questions such as the following guide this level of inquiry: Which types of conversational acts, speech activities, affective and epistemological stances, participant roles in situations, etc. enter into the social construction of identity within the community of practice? In what ways? When is gender relevant, and in what relationships with which other aspects of social identity? Which of the acts, stances, activities, and roles are marked for whom? And which are unmarked? What does the micro-level interaction reveal about ideological patterns of domination and resistance? Longitudinal research is especially needed in families, peer groups, and schools to further our understanding of how novices are socialized through language to develop their social identities relative to each other in the communities of practice in which they participate. When discriminatory practices are identified, alternatives that position all more favorably can be proposed.

University of Pennsylvania
USA

REFERENCES

Bem, S. & Bem, D.: 1973, 'Does sex-biased job advertising "aid and abet" sex discrimination?', *Journal of Applied Social Psychology* 3(1), 6–18.

Cameron, D.: 1990, *The Feminist Critique of Language: A Reader*, Routledge, New York.

Corson, David: 1993, *Language, Minority Education and Gender: Linking Social Justice and Power*, Multilingual Matters, Clevedon, Avon/Bristol PA.

Eckert, P. & McConnell-Ginet, S.: 1992, 'Think practically and look locally: Language and gender as community-based practice', *Annual Review of Anthropology* 21, 461–490.

Eckert, P. & McConnell-Ginet, S.: 1995, 'Constructing meaning, constructing selves: Snapshots of language, gender, and class from Belten High', in K. Hall & M. Bucholtz (eds.), *Gender Articulated: Language and the Socially Constructed Self*, Routledge, New York, 469–507.

Fairclough, N.: 1989, *Language and Power*, Longman, New York.

Fishman, P.: 1983, 'Interaction: The work women do', in B. Thorne, C. Kramarae & N. Henley (eds.), *Language, Gender and Society*, Newbury House, Cambridge, MA, 89–102.

Freeman, R. & McElhinny, B.: 1995, 'Language and gender', in S. McKay & N. Hornberger (eds.), *Sociolinguistics and Language Teaching*, Cambridge University Press, Cambridge, MA, 218–280.

Gal, S.: 1995, 'Language, gender, and power: An anthropological review', in K. Hall & M. Bucholtz (eds.), *Gender Articulated: Language and the Socially Constructed Self*, Routledge, New York, 169–182.

Goodwin, M.H.: 1990, *He-Said-She-Said: Talk as Social Organization among Black Children*, Indiana University Press, Bloomington.

Graddol, D. & Swann, J.: 1989, *Gender Voices*, Basil Blackwell, Oxford.

Hall, K. & Bucholtz, M.: 1995. *Gender Articulated: Language and the Socially Constructed Self*, Routledge, New York.

Keenan, E.O.: 1974, 'Norm-makers, norm-breakers: Uses of speech by men and women in a Malagasy community', in R. Bauman & J. Sherzer (eds.), *Explorations in the Ethnography of Speaking*, Cambridge University Press, Cambridge, 125–143.

Kramarae, C. & Treichler, P.: 1990, 'Words on a feminist dictionary', in D. Cameron (ed.), *The Feminist Critique of Language: A Reader*, Routledge, London, 148–159.

Lakoff, R.: 1975, *Language and Woman's Place*, Harper and Row, New York.

Lemke, J.: 1990, *Talking Science: Language, Learning, and Values*, Ablex, Norwood, NJ.

Maltz, D. & Borker, R.: 1982, 'A cultural approach to male-female miscommunication', in J. Gumperz (ed.), *Language and Social Identity*, Cambridge University Press, Cambridge, 195–216.

Martin, E.: 1987, *The Woman in the Body: A Cultural Analysis of Reproduction* Beacon Press, Boston, Beacon Press.

Martyna, W.: 1983, 'Beyond the he/man approach: The case for nonsexist language', in B. Thorne, C. Kramarae & N. Henley (eds.), *Language, Gender and Society*, Newbury House, Cambridge, MA, 25–37.

McElhinny, B.: 1995, 'Challenging hegemonic masculinities: Female and male police offi-cers handling domestic violence', in K. Hall & M. Bucholtz (eds.), *Gender Articulated: Language and the Socially Constructed Self*, Routledge, New York, 217–243.

O'Barr, W. & Atkins, B.: 1980, ' "Women's Language" or "Powerless Language"?', in S. McConnell-Ginet, R. Borker & N. Furman (eds.), *Women and Language in Literature and Society*, Praeger, NY, 93–110.

Ochs, E.: 1992, 'Indexing Gender', in A. Duranti & C. Goodwin (eds.), *Rethinking Context*, Cambridge University Press, Cambridge, 335–358..

Poynton, C.: 1989, *Language and Gender: Making the Difference*, Oxford University Press, Oxford.

Schieffelin, B. & Ochs, E. (eds.): 1986, *Language Socialization across Cultures*, Cambridge University Press, Cambridge, MA.

Sherzer, J.: 1987, 'A diversity of voices: Men's and women's speech in ethnographic perspective', in S. Philips, S. Steele & C. Tanz (eds.), *Language, Gender and Sex in Comparative Perspective*, Cambridge University Press, Cambridge, 95–120.

Swann, J.: 1993, *Girls, Boys and Language*, Basil Blackwell, Oxford.

Tannen, D.: 1989, 'Interpreting interruption in conversation', in B. Music, R. Graczyk & C. Wiltshire (eds.), *CLS 25: Papers from the 25th Annual Regional Meeting of the Chicago Linguistic Society (Part 2: Parasession on Language in Context)*, Chicago Linguistic Society, Chicago, 266–287.

Tannen, D.: 1990, *You Just Don't Understand: Women and Men in Conversation*, William Morrow, New York.

Tannen, D.: 1993, 'The relativity of linguistic strategies: Rethinking power and solidarity in gender and dominance', in D. Tannen (ed.), *Gender and Conversational Interaction*, Oxford University Press, NY, 165–185.

West, C. & Zimmerman, D.: 1983, 'Small insults: A study of interruptions in cross-sex conversations between unacquainted persons', in B. Thorne, C. Kramarae & N. Henley (eds.), *Language, Gender and Society*, Newbury House, Rowley, MA, 102–117.

Section 2

Language, Variation, and Education:
Recent Advances in Approaches, Methods, and Topics

STELLA MARIS BORTONI-RICARDO

VARIATIONIST SOCIOLINGUISTICS

The evolution of two basic premises in 20th-Century structural linguistics created the conditions for the emergence of variationist sociolinguistics as an interdisciplinary field. These premises are cultural relativism and orderly linguistic heterogeneity. Cultural relativism is an anthropological tradition inherited by linguistics, according to which no culture or language of a speech community is classified as inferior or underdeveloped irrespective of the level of Western technology that the speech community has achieved. Under the influence of the principle of cultural relativism, linguists posited the 'functional equivalence and essential equality of all languages, and rejected mistaken evolutionary stereotypes' (Hymes, 1974, p. 70). At a first stage the relativistic premise applied to comparisons across languages but when the orderly heterogeneity premise was postulated by variationist sociolinguists in the late 60's, it evolved to comparisons across different varieties or styles of a same language. No variety within a language would be considered inherently superior to the others as concerns its structure even though functional distinctions among them would be acknowledged.

These new assumptions have motivated a group of linguists to describe the orderly differentiation in many languages. They developed empirical studies of language samples recorded in natural settings and started to correlate linguistic variation with social factors such as ethnicity, regional background, socioeconomic status, age brackets, gender, formality of the interaction and so on as well as with structural linguistic factors. The data so gathered received a quantitative treatment.This treatment was made possible with the introduction of the concept of variable rules, that are designed to meet a general principle of accountability, as Labov (1972, p. 94) explains: 'Any variable form (a member of a set of alternative ways of "saying the same thing" should be reported with the proportion of cases in which the form did occur in the relevant environment, compared to the total number of cases in which it might have occurred.' The quantitative treatment was mathematically refined by David Sankoff and associates (see Sankoff, 1988). For each area of variation in a given language it is necessary to identify the constraints that are determinants, in a statistical sense, of the relative proportions of each variant of the variable rule, i.e. of each possible realization of the variable rule. The constraints (also referred to as factors) can be defined as forces that operate simultaneously

N.H. Hornberger and D. Corson (eds), Encyclopedia of Language and Education,
Volume 8: Research Methods in Language and Education, 59–66.
© *1997 Kluwer Academic Publishers. Printed in the Netherlands.*

to make the application of the rule more or less probable (Naro, 1981). There is presently a computer program with several versions, known as VARBRUL, that operates this quantitative analysis with much refinement (Pintsuk, 1988).

EARLY DEVELOPMENTS

From its outset in the 1960's, variationist sociolinguistics argued in favor of the essential equality of the varieties of any language and had to deal with correlations between a child's dialect with her educational achievement. In fact, the reading achievement of children from nonmainstream families or from ethnic minorities was in the 1960's – and still is – well below the national norms in several countries. An example of this is given by Stubbs (1980, p. 141) who reproduces the results of a reading survey carried out by Kellmer-Pringle et al., in 1966, in the United Kingdom. They grouped 11,000 seven-year-olds into three categories: good, medium and poor readers, using as a parameter their performance on the Southgate word-recognition test. The percentage of poor readers in the upper classes was 7.1 per cent; in the middle class it was 18.9 per cent; in the lower classes, the percentage went up to 26.9 per cent.

Stubbs points out that the study may have a bias toward the overestimation of the reading abilities of upper class youths but nonetheless results like these were consistent with nationwide school achievement of minority children and many scholars tended to explain them with the hypothesis derived from Basil Bernstein's theory of social codes. Children from the lower classes were speakers of what Bernstein (1971) called restricted code and were deprived at home of the linguistic skills necessary to successful learning. This fact, some influential educators argued, had a negative effect on their cognitive abilities. This explanation came to be known as the deficit model. The sociolinguists found this hypothesis not convincing at all and offered an alternative explanation that was known as the difference hypothesis. They argued firstly that all languages and dialects were systematic and showed an equivalent structural complexity, and secondly that the dialect speakers possessed the same capacity for conceptual learning as speakers of more prestigious varieties. As they discussed the differences between nonstandard varieties and the school language, they started to search for other explanations for the reading failure of economically deprived children. Nothing was intrinsically wrong with the children's linguistic forms, they argued, but with society as a whole, and that included the teachers, who regarded these forms as a sign of stupidity. As Wolfson (1989) observes, the notion behind this attitude was that nonstandard speakers were attempting to speak English (the standard variety) but were too lazy or sloppy and ignorant to succeed. A seminal article written with the purpose of demonstrating the verbal and cognitive capacity of ghetto children was Labov's (1969) *The Logic of Nonstandard English* (see the review on non-standard varieties by Corson in volume 1).

The variationist sociolinguists'efforts in regard to the African American Vernacular (AAV) at this point followed two related trends: 1) to reject vehemently the deficit model and the remediation educational policy that it gave rise to; and 2) to explore the relationship of language to reading and new approaches to teaching reading. This is well documented in a collection of papers edited by Joan Baratz and Roger Shuy in 1969 in the Center for Applied Linguistics of Washington, D.C. (Baratz & Shuy, 1969). The general assumption shared by the authors in the volume was that reading problems originated from differences in the linguistic systems of AAV and Standard English as well as in the mismatch between the African-American children's cultural orientation and the school's expectations. Labov (1969) made a clear distinction between structural conflicts stemming from differences between linguistic structures, and functional conflicts, which are a cross cultural phenomenon. For him, ghetto children's reading problems were rooted in a situation of reciprocal ignorance where teachers and students were ignorant of each other's system. He strongly recommended that teachers learn to make a distinction between differences in pronunciation and grammar and mistakes in reading.

Several authors of the volume proposed the use of dialect readers whereby children would be taught to read first in their dialect and then transfer the reading skills to the standard variety. They believed that if the primers were written in the dialect, the child would be spared the double load of learning to read and also learning a new variety of English. As Shuy (1969, p. 117) put it ' the child would read adequately if the material and method were consistent with his linguistic behavior patterns.' This dialect reading method was identified by Stewart (1969) as a native-to-foreign approach to literacy. There was a strong and a weak version of it. The former advocated the use of a special orthography which would reflect more closely the dialect pronunciation. The weak version accepted Fasold's contention that alphabetic symbols represent phonological segments on a more abstract level and 'therefore the main, conventional English orthography is as adequate for Black English speakers as it is for Standard English speakers' (Fasold, 1969, p. 85). This is presently a well established point (see Stubbs, 1980).

Despite the initial academic enthusiasm, the dialect reader proposal did not prove to be a solution to the reading underachievement of socially marginalized children as the pioneer variationists expected it to be (see Toohey, 1986). Fasold (1990) points out that the idea of teaching children in a stigmatized variety was distressing to society at large, which traditionally holds the standard written variety in high regard. Indeed, such proposals raised much controversy in the U.S. and Europe. Cheshire et al. (1989, p. 7) for example refer to the pamphlet *The Language Trap* written by John Honey in 1983, which claimed that the doctrine of equality spoused by linguists and sociolinguists was contributing to the declining moral and educational standards in British schools.

There are however reports of good results of the use of spoken dialect in the classroom. Edwards (1989) argues that such use represents a move to a child-centered philosophy that builds on existing knowledge. Accordingly, Bull (1982) claims that Norwegian dialects have been acknowledged in Norwegian schools for over 100 years and this approach has proved successful. Nonetheless the prevailing position nowadays is stated by Fasold (1990, p. 279): 'At the moment, it seems that language differences are not the greatest problem in teaching reading. Labov would agree, although he is convinced that black and white vernaculars are diverging.' For Labov (1987, p. 10) 'the primary cause of educational failure is not language differences but institutional racism.' But he acknowledges that linguists have yet to make a significant contribution to better school curriculum. According to him (p.c.) the main issue to be investigated is whether or not the nonstandard features in the reading of a dialect speaking child preclude his/her understanding of the reading content. On this issue, Fasold (1990) argues that a teacher can be even more confident that the child understood what s/he is reading when s/he translates a standard form of the text into a dialect one, rather than simply decoding the standard forms.

MAJOR CONTRIBUTIONS AND FUTURE DIRECTIONS

We have seen that over the past 30 years the use of dialect in the classroom has been a very debatable issue. As Edwards (1989, p. 317) notes, 'the co-existence of standard and dialect grammar is now widely recognized as giving rise to problems in educational systems.' Wolfram & Christian (1989) deal specifically with these problems and emphasize that the notion of grammmatical correctness is always a subjective judgment. Every student should be taught the written standard, as well as the regional oral standard. But they recommend that teachers should take as parameter the social acceptability and not the linguistic acceptability of any particular form. In order to do this teachers must be aware of linguistic variation and information concerning dialect diversity must be part of the school curriculum (see the reviews by Corson in Volumes 1 and 6).

Thus, the current trend is not to choose between the standard and the dialect as a medium of instruction, but rather to consider both varieties as functional components of the teachers' and the pupils' repertoire. In a study that combined ethnographic observation and quantitative analysis in a rural school in Brazil, Bortoni-Ricardo (1996) identified four types of teacher-led events according to their interactional configurations, 'marked by ways of speaking, ways of listening, ways of getting the floor and holding it, and ways of leading and following' (Erickson & Schultz, 1977, p. 6).

The first type of event was made up of highly context dependent short utterances. The second one consisted of longer stretches of instructional conversation. They were both typical events of orality. The third type was the three-part exchange structure made up of teacher initiation (I), pupil response (R) and teacher evaluation (E) (see Sinclair & Coulthard, 1975). The fourth type of event can be classified as an event of secondary orality, as it consisted of readings or of expositions based on a written plan. The events were divided into utterances and a VARBRUL analysis was carried out. The dependent variable was the utterance and two variants were postulated: utterances produced in colloquial standard Portuguese and utterances produced in popular/rural Portuguese. The analysis showed that literacy-related events were carried out mostly in the standard whereas orality-related events were performed in a non-standard variety of Brazilian Portuguese.The continuum of events from type 1 to type 4 runs parallel to a continuum of standardness. The results also showed that classrooms are multidimensional sociolinguistic domains where teachers intuitively monitor their speech according to a widespread system of beliefs regarding school literacy.

This evidence hinges on the debatable issue that basic linguistic traits are not transmitted across group boundaries simply by exposure to other dialects in the mass media or in schools (Labov & Harris, 1986). Of course it is not expected that schools will influence the students' vernacular. Rather the purpose of language teaching in schools is the development of monitored styles that are superimposed on the vernacular. And in fact there is much evidence that the school contributes to the enlargement of the pupils' stylistic repertoire.

A variationist study of noun phrase agreement in interview style carried out with 4th graders and their parents in a school in Brasília brings striking evidence of the role of schooling in imparting the linguistic resources that are necessary for the performance of monitored styles (Freitas, 1996). The frequencies of noun phrase agreement in the mothers' speech were 0%; 26%; 32%; and 84%. In their children's speech the frequencies were, respectively, 94.4%; 100%; 85.7%; and 100%. A similar pattern of differences in the speech of literate youths and that of their illiterate parents was described in a low-income community in Brazil (Bortoni-Ricardo, 1985), as well as in bilingual contexts.

The influence of school on language acquisition is well demonstrated in a survey using variationist methodology carried out among students enrolled in Ontario's French-language schools, with the twofold purpose of 1) assisting in the evaluation of the students' proficiency in French and 2) providing data which could be used to develop materials for the teaching of French (Mougeon & Beniak, 1991). Percentage of francophones in the communities where the students came from, use of French at home and grade level were the independent variables in the study. The dependent variable was mastery of the reflexive pronouns in French. The results showed that the students that were predominant users of English at home did not reach the level of mastery of reflexive pronouns in French achieved by grade 2 students from French-speaking homes and led to the argument that it is unrealistic to expect that schooling in a minority/second language setting will on its own ensure full development of skills in that language. On the other hand, however, it is noteworthy that there was an increase from 35% to 75% in French proficiency of the students from non-French speaking homes throughout their schooling years. This is evidence of the success of the French program in the schools.

In a recent volume dedicated to the description of variation in the speech of Rio de Janeiro (Silva & Scherre (eds.), 1996) Silva and Paiva discuss the influence of the factor of education on language variation and give a detailed description of 22 variationist studies in Portuguese, in English, in French and in Spanish, in which the lower frequency of the stigmatized variant correlates with the higher levels of schooling.

Finally, there is a trend toward application of variationist findings to the development of teaching materials. Mollica and associates (1996) have been conducting school experimental research in which the experimental treatment is the training of pupils with exercises based on results of variationist studies. The observed outcomes of their work show that this type of teaching can be very effective. Three basic principles are followed in the designing of the exercises: 1) going from larger units to smaller ones (e.g. from discourse to the sentence; from word to phoneme etc.); 2) going from most frequent to least frequent forms; and 3) going from most probable to least probable occurrences.

Over the thirty years of its existence, variationist sociolinguistics has made many contributions to education and has offered quantitative tools that can be used in combination with other approaches in the effort to better the school performance of nonstandard speaking pupils. It has also been the target of much criticism and has certainly overcome the stage of naive belief that the study of variation by itself could solve all educational problems. The main problem, as Labov (1987) has claimed, is not language difference but institutional racism (see the reviews by Baugh in this volume and in Volume 1). However, information on language heterogeneity is a valuable instrument to help fight social inequalities and ethnic prejudices. In order to treat children equally their cultural and linguistic differences must be considered.

University of Brasília
Brazil

REFERENCES

Baratz, J.C. & Shuy, R.W. (eds.): 1969, *Teaching Black Children to Read*, Center for Applied Linguistics, Washington, DC.

Bernstein. B.B.: 1971, *Class, Codes and Control* (vol. 1), Paladin, London.

Bortoni-Ricardo, S.: 1996, 'Codeswitching in a bidialectal school', in J. Arnold et al. (eds.), *Sociolinguistic Variation, Data, Theory, and Analysis, Selected Papers from NWAVE 23 at Stanford*, CSLI Publication, Stanford, 377–386.

Bortoni-Ricardo, S.: 1985, *The Urbanization of Rural Dialect Speakers: A Sociolinguistic Study in Brazil*, Cambridge University Press, Cambridge.

Bull, T.: 1982, 'Mother tongue teaching and learning: Teaching beginners to read and write in the vernacular', mimeo.

Cheshire, J., Edwards, V., Münstrermann, H. & Weltens B.: 1989, 'Dialect and education in Europe: A general perspective', *Journal of Multilingual and Multicultural Development* 10, 1–10.

Edwards, V.: 1989, 'Dialect and education in Europe: A postscript', *Journal of Multilingual and Multicultural Development* 10, 317–323.

Erickson, F. & Shultz, J.: 1977, 'When is a context? Some issues and methods in the analysis of social competence', *The Quarterly Newsletter of the Institute for Comparative Human Development* 1(2), 5–10.

Fasold, R.W.: 1990, *Sociolinguistics of Language*, Basil Blackwell, Oxford.

Fasold, R.W.: 1969, 'Orthography in reading material', in J.C. Baratz & R.W. Shuy (eds.), 68–91.

Freitas, V.L.: 1996, 'A Variação Estilística de Alunos de 4ª Série em Ambiente de Contato Dialetal', M.A. unpublished thesis, University of Brasília.

Hymes, D.: 1974, *Foundations of Sociolinguistics*, University of Pennsylvania Press, Philadelphia.

Labov, W.: 1987, 'Are black and white vernaculars diverging?', *American Speech* 62(1), 5–12.

Labov, W.: 1972, *Language in the Inner City*, University of Pennsylvania Press, Philadelphia.

Labov, W.: 1969, 'The logic of nonstandard English', *Georgetown Monograph on Language and Linguistics*, Center for Applied Linguistics, Washington, DC (Reprinted in Labov, 1972).

Labov, W. & Harris, W.A.: 1986, 'De facto segregation of black and white vernaculars', in Sankoff, D. (ed.), *Diversity and Diachrony*, John Benjamins B.V., Amsterdam, 1–24.

Mollica, M.C.: 1996, 'Sociolingüística e Ensino de Língua', Paper read at the SBPC Annual Conference.

Mougeon, R. & Beniak, E.: 1991, *Linguistic Consequences of Language Contact and Restriction*, Clarendon Press, Oxford.

Naro, A.J.: 1981, 'The social and structural dimension of a syntactic change', *Language* 57(1), 63–98.

Pintsuk, S.: 1988, VARBRUL programs, unpublished manuscript.

Sankoff, D.: 1988, 'Variable rules', in U. Ammon, N. Dittmar & J. Klauss (eds.) *Sociolinguistics*, Academic Press, New York, 119–126.

Shuy, R.W.: 1969, 'A linguistic background for developing beginning reading materials for black children', in Baratz & Shuy (eds.), 117–137.

Silva, G.M. de O. & Paiva, M.: 1996, 'Visão de Conjunto das Variáveis Sociais', in Silva & Scherre (eds.), 335–378.

Silva, G.M. de O. & Scherre, M.M. (eds.): 1996, *Padrões Lingüísticos*, Tempo Brasileiro, Rio de Janeiro.

Sinclair, J. McH. & Coulthard, M.: 1975, *Towards an Analysis of Discourse*, Oxford University Press, London.

Stewart, W.A.: 1969, 'On the use of negro dialect in the teaching of reading' in Baratz &
    Shuy (eds.), 156-219.
Stubbs, M.: 1980, *Language and literacy*, Routledge & Kegan Paul, London.
Toohey, K.: 1986, 'Minority educational failure: Is dialect a factor?' *Curriculum Inquiry*
    16(2), 128–145.
Wolfram, W. & Christian, D.: 1989, *Dialects and Education: Issues and Answers*, Prentice
    Hall, Englewood Cliffs, NJ.
Wolfson, N.: 1989, *Perspectives – Sociolinguistics and TESOL*, Newbury House
    Publishers, New York.

TARA GOLDSTEIN

LANGUAGE RESEARCH METHODS AND CRITICAL PEDAGOGY

I want to begin this review of language research methods and critical pedagogy by saying that what I know and can say about the topic comes from a particular set of social experiences. These include the conversations I have had with the people who supervised my doctorate work (at the Ontario Institute for Studies in Education in Canada); my engagement with texts published in the academic journals I read regularly (all of which are written in English) and my engagement with the conference presentations I have attended (mostly in North America because it is so expensive to travel "overseas"). The reason I want to say this at the very beginning has to do with questions concerning the authority this review carries. In their book *Language, Authority, and Criticism: Readings on the School Textbook*, Suzanne de Castell, Allan Luke and Carmen Luke (1989) tell us that school textbooks hold a particular and significant social function. They "represent to each generation of students an officially sanctioned, authorized version of human knowledge and culture" (1989, vii). Rarely, maintain de Castell, Luke and Luke, do educators or researchers reflect upon the unique status of the textbook as the primary medium of formal education, or consider the theoretical and practical questions that arise when that status is recognized.

Acknowledging that this text can be read as "an authorized version of human knowledge" on the topic of language research methods and critical pedagogy, I want to say that there are many questions that could and should be asked about the content of this piece. Questions such as "Why present *this* knowledge, *this* literature, *these* ideas, *these* particular approaches?" (de Castell, Luke & Luke, 1989, ix). Like other researchers, what I know, what I share with you in this text, and what you will know about the topic of language research methods and critical pedagogy after reading this piece is embedded in a sampling of the particular knowledge and understandings I have gained as a result of my academic training and my everyday academic life. There are other things that might be said and other ways to write about this topic. It is with this in mind that I begin a discussion of the ways language researchers have studied language learning and language use and how their research is informed by those interested in the ideas, principles and practices of critical pedagogy.

67

N.H. Hornberger and D. Corson (eds), Encyclopedia of Language and Education,
Volume 8: Research Methods in Language and Education, 67–77.
© *1997 Kluwer Academic Publishers. Printed in the Netherlands.*

EARLY DEVELOPMENTS: WORKING IN THE INTERESTS OF JUSTICE AND EQUALITY

Educators, researchers and theorists working within the framework of critical pedagogy are interested in describing how unequal societal power relations are manifested in schools and what educators and students can do to challenge the inequities that result from imbalances of power. For example, in the second edition of his book *Life in Schools* Peter McLaren (1994) talks about critical pedagogy as an approach to schooling that is committed to the imperatives of "empowering" students and transforming the larger social order in the interests of justice and equality (1994, vii). Empowering students means providing students with schooling that enables them to analyze the ways they experience oppression and to take steps to redress the conditions that perpetuate discrimination (1994, 14).

Such an approach involves working with educators so that they can teach for empowerment. Critical pedagogy theorist Roger Simon (1988) talks about what it means to teach for empowerment in his work on "the pedagogy of possibility". For Simon, there is a distinction between teaching and pedagogy. "Teaching" refers to the specific strategies and techniques educators use in order to meet predefined, given objectives. However, such strategies and techniques are insufficient for creating a practice that strives to increase students' access to power, or in Simon's words, "a practice whose aim is the enhancement of human possibility". What is required is "a discourse about practice that references not only what we as educators might actually do, but as well, the social visions such practices would support. 'Pedagogy' is simultaneously about the details of what students and others might do together *and* the cultural politics such practices support" (1988, 2). Critical pedagogy, the details and politics of what we might do together, has been described by educators John Rivera & Mary Poplin (1995) as a process which "draws out student voices and puts these voices into dialogue with others in a never ending cycle of meaning making that is characterized by reflection/action/reflection/new action" (1995, 223). It is the learning which emerges from such dialogue that can be used to work towards social transformation.

Language researchers interested in notions from the field of critical pedagogy focus on the ways that language use and language learning interact with social dimensions such as class, ethnicity gender and race to reproduce inequities both inside and outside school. They also explore the ways that educators might work towards challenging these inequities. In doing so, these researchers choose to look at language learning and language use as something more than a psycholinguistic phenomenon which has been the traditional practice in the field of applied linguistics (cf., e.g., Pennycook, 1994).

In the growing literature on critical approaches to language education, authors usually use the words "critical pedagogy" to align themselves with the thinking of a group of writers who have built up an academic discourse known as "critical pedagogy" (these include Apple & Weiss, 1983; Giroux, 1988; McLaren, 1994, Simon, 1988, 1992; Weiler & Mitchell, 1992). Some language educators, however, do not use the words "critical pedagogy" in reports of their work, but write about language education in ways that seem to reflect the vision of social justice which lies at the heart of critical pedagogical approaches. For example, Jim Cummins (1996) writes about "education for empowerment" in his latest work on education for minority language children and Elsa Auerbach and Nina Wallerstein (1987) write about a "problem-posing" approach to adult ESL education that has grown out of their reading of work done by Brazilian educator Paulo Freire (e.g., 1973) (see the review by Auerbach in Volume 2). Freire's work around education for critical consciousness has also influenced the writings of many critical pedagogy theorists. Recently, in response to criticisms of prescriptivism and the exclusion of feminist voices and perspectives in critical pedagogy (e.g., Ellsworth, 1989; Gore, 1992; Simon, 1992), some writers have begun to use the terms "critical pedagogies" or "critical pedagogical approaches" in addition to "critical pedagogy" to signal that they are not referring to some prescriptive – patriarchal – set of practices but to a set of common pedagogical and political visions for social and educational justice (see reviews by Wallace, Clark and Ivanić, and Wortham in Volume 6).

LANGUAGE RESEARCH METHODS AND CRITICAL PEDAGOGICAL APPROACHES: A SAMPLING OF CURRENT WORK

As mentioned earlier, critical language researchers are interested in the ways that language use and language learning interact with other social processes to reproduce inequities both inside and outside educational settings. They then use their findings to discuss what educators, policy makers, parents and students can do to challenge the inequities that result from imbalances of power. In the work featured below, researchers have combined critical pedagogical perspectives with the research methodologies of ethnography, micro-ethnography, discourse analysis and diary-study to answer questions about language, learning and unequal relations of power.

Critical Ethnography

In a Canadian study that asked questions about the languages Portuguese immigrant workers chose to use at work and the consequences that these language practices had for their lives (Goldstein, 1997), I worked with the methodology of ethnography. Originally developed in anthropology to describe the "ways of living" of a social group (Heath, 1982), the goal of ethnography is to provide a description and an interpretive-explanatory account of what people do in a particular setting (such as work), the outcome of their interactions in that setting, and the way they understand what they are doing (see Erickson, 1988; see also the review by Watson-Gegeo in this volume for more on the method of ethnography). Using the ethnographic data I had collected, I was able to trace a relationship between the workers' language practices, the gendered structure and dynamics of their Portuguese families and the class positions they held in Canadian society. I then examined the relevance of the job-specific English language training program we had designed for the workers in light of this analysis. Arguing that such training could not generally invoke change in the lives of many working-class Portuguese workers because of structural processes and constraints that limit possibilities for workers in Canadian society, I suggested an alternative ESL curriculum for immigrant workers, a curriculum "for economic protection and control over everyday living conditions and relationships" (Goldstein, 1997).

Other language researchers who have used ethnography to examine questions of language use and access to educational and economic resources are Numbuso Dlamini who examined the ways English and a number of African languages were being used by high school students and teachers in South Africa (Dlamini, 1997); Monica Heller (1996) who analysed the social origins and consequences of language practices in a French-language minority high school in Ontario (Canada) and Suresh Canagarajah (1993) who explored the complexities of domination and resistance that were being played out in an ESL class of Tamil students in Sri Lanka (see the review by May in this volume).

Critical Micro-Ethnography

Ethnographers who engage in the study of one-on-one, face-to-face-interactions often refer to their work as micro-ethnography (see the reviews by Garcez and Heap in this volume). Judy Hunter (in press) has conducted a micro-ethnographic study that examines teacher and student interactions in a grade 4 and 5 process writing class in Toronto (Canada). Hunter's analysis of the female students' strong social investments in popular media and the way those investments were silenced in the classroom leads her to argue for a pedagogical approach that recognizes girls' investments and preferred knowledge and problematizes the assumptions of schooling that reject them.

In their study of "bilingual support" provided by bilingual teaching assistants in primary classrooms in Lancashire (England), Marilyn Martin-Jones & Mukul Saxena (1996) also use a fine-grained analysis of classroom interaction to show how bilingual teaching assistants are often positioned as marginal to the "main action" of the classroom which is defined and orchestrated by monolingual English-speaking teachers. They use their findings to argue that while bilingual assistants are able to use code switching to provide students with linkages between the students' knowledge and the knowledge of school, ultimately their code switching practices serves to reinforce the dominance of English in the classroom.

The ethnographic studies by Monica Heller, Marilyn Martin-Jones and Mukul Saxena have been published as part of a special two-volume issue of *Linguistics and Education* entitled *Education in Multilingual Settings: Discourse, Identities and Power.* The special issue contains other sociolinguistic studies that examine the relationship between education and the production/reproduction of relations of power in different parts of the world. Included are articles about practices in Botswana (Arthur 1996); Burundi (Ndayifukamiye, 1996); Malta (Camilleri, 1996); Brazil (Cavalcanti, 1996); and Australia (Moore, 1996). Also included is an examination of race relations and the use of "Stylised Asian English" by Panjabi-speaking students in England (Rampton, 1996).

Critical Discourse Analysis

Discourse analysis is the study of patterns in linguistic organization that occur in continuous stretches of language. In her study of classroom Cantonese and English code switching in Hong Kong, Angel Lin (1996) uses discourse analysis to demonstrate how students of the dominant group, who already have knowledge of English from outside school, are positioned advantageously in comparison to poorer students, who do not have the same access. Lin looks at how different teachers make use of different varieties of discourse formats to organize different types of lesson activities for their students. She shows how" doing-English-lessons" in poorer classrooms seems to have the effect of reproducing the students' sociocultural world and their lack of interest in and access to English linguistic and cultural resources. This is problematic for the students since the ability to use English in Hong Kong can provide much access to important economic and educational resources (see the review by Lin in Volume 5).

Another researcher who has combined discourse analysis with a critical perspective is Sue Starfield (1995) who followed the progress of a group of South African ESL students as they were inducted into the "discourse community" of their Sociology department. As an English instructor at the same university, Starfield's job was to help ESL students acquire the "disciplinary language" needed for success in their content areas (1995, 2). She undertook this research study in order to obtain a finer understanding of the Sociology Department's induction processes and the nature of the pedagogic genres that were used in the department (these included essays, tests and oral presentations). Such information allowed her to trace the relationship of these processes and genres to students' academic success or failure and to re-think the nature of her work as a university English teacher (see the review by Norton in this volume).

Critical Diary-Study

Finally, in her Canadian study of natural language learning outside the classroom, Bonny Peirce (1995) uses a combination of questionnaires, interviews and diary study to investigate how opportunities for immigrant women to practice English are socially structured. The diary study proved to be the most important source of information for Peirce as it provided her with data on what participants thought, felt and did in response to different language learning situations and allowed her to analyse the ways the women acted upon social structures to create, use or resist opportunities to practice English.

FUTURE DIRECTIONS

The Challenge of "Writing Culture"

Much of the research reviewed in this article locates itself within the realm of anthropological, ethnographic inquiry. Thus, one of the challenges facing critical language researchers is the writing and construction of ethnographic texts. In their influential book *Writing Culture: The Poetics and Politics of Ethnography*, James Clifford & George Marcus (1986) subject traditional anthropological writing to a sophisticated textual analysis and demonstrate that the writing of ethnography is both a literary and a political act. Asserting that anthropologists can not presume that their ethnographies are transparent mirrors of culture, Clifford and Marcus propose a new agenda for anthropology, an agenda that encourages more innovative, dialogic, reflexive and experimental writing and that "reflects a more profound self-consciousness of the workings of power and the partialness of all truth, both in the text and in the world" (Behar & Gordon, 1995). The challenge, then, for language researchers who use ethnographic approaches in their work is to find ways of writing and constructing texts that meet this new agenda. Responding to the challenge with an anthology entitled *Women Writing Culture*, anthropologists Ruth Behar & Deborah Gordon (1995) have collected 21 "experiments in writing" – all by women – that illustrate many innovative ways to "write culture" differently. This work serves as an inspiration and model for critical language researchers who need to explore new ways of writing and constructing ethnographic texts.

Engaging with African-American Scholarship

A second challenge facing language researchers who draw ideas from the discourse of critical pedagogies is to respond to those who have criticized the field for its lack of engagement with African-American scholarly writing around issues of race and racism. Educational theorist Beverly Gordon (1995) writes, "While the issue of race, as well as race in conjunction with class and gender, has been part of the history of critical discourse as an object of study [e.g., Apple & Weiss, 1983] only recently have proponents of this discourse seriously engaged the theoretical constructs generated by African Americans [e.g., Giroux, 1992]" (Gordon, 1995, 190).

An example of work that situates itself within an African-American critical pedagogical discourse is Annette Henry's (1992) Canadian study of five Black women teachers. Henry shows how the teachers' "Black womanist practice" has developed out of their life experiences as Black women living, mothering and teaching in a hegemonically Eurocentric society. Her challenge to educators and researchers is to recognize the development of "alternative pedagogical intents and strategies [e.g., "Black womanist practice"] that are context-specific and rooted in particular histories" (1992, 402) (see the reviews by Baugh in this volume and in Volume 1).

Conducting Research Across Linguistic, Cultural and Racial Differences

A third challenge facing critical language researchers is the challenge of conducting research in settings where the linguistic and cultural practices and/or racial identity of the researcher(s) and the research participants differ. As a non-speaker of Portuguese who developed an ethnographic research project that involved members of Toronto's Portuguese community, I responded to this challenge by working with a linguistic and cultural interpreter (Goldstein, 1997). While this meant working with two layers of interpretation, it also meant that I had access to the sociocultural, sociolinguistic background knowledge necessary for understanding talk by the Azorean workers participating in the study. This knowledge, the importance – and complexity – of which has been discussed by sociolinguists interested in intercultural interview situations (e.g., Belfiore & Heller, 1992; Briggs, 1983; Gumperz, 1992), was not accessible to me without a linguistic and cultural interpreter. It is knowledge which I argue strengthens my analysis. The work of linguistic and cultural interpretation in the project was undertaken by a Portuguese colleague of mine who taught ESL and Portuguese literacy classes for immigrant men and women from Portugal and the Azores. Her interest in the research project was sparked by her own questions about language use in her community and classrooms. Recently, we have begun to hear a lot about the benefits of "action research" projects in the field of second language education (e.g., Crookes, 1993). Looking towards the future, there is great potential in facilitating opportunities for ESL teachers from diverse linguistic, cultural, and racial backgrounds to team up with each other and with formally trained researchers to conduct "action research" projects around questions of language teaching and learning.

Bringing the notion of power into this discussion of working across linguistic, cultural and racial differences, feminist educational philosopher Kathryn Pauly Morgan writes about "a multiplicity of axes of privilege and oppression that affect all of us in educational settings" (1996, 105). "Privilege involves the power to dominate in systematic ways, which are simultaneously ideological and material, institutional and personal" while "oppression involves the lived, systematic experience of being dominated by virtue of one's position on various particular axes" (1996, 106). Morgan believes that in North America everyone occupies a particular point of "specific juxtapositon on the axes of privilege and oppression and that this point is simultaneously a locus of our agency, power, disempowerment, oppression and resistance" (1966, 106). Her work is important for language researchers working across cultural, linguistic, and racial differences for several reasons. First, as suggested by Henry's work (1992), the eyes (or perspectives) with which researchers view the world, the eyes with which researchers create research instruments, make observations during fieldwork, analyse data and write up their analyses are a reflection of their position of privilege and oppression in our hegemonically Eurocentric society. The rigorous, complex, sophisticated research analysis is one in which researchers have reflected deeply upon the ways their own location in society might influence their work. Such deep reflection provides researchers with a way of developing the "self-consciousness of the workings of power and the partialness of all truth" that is a major current concern in anthropology. However, it is not only deep reflection upon power, privilege and oppression that will help researchers create a rigorous piece of research. It is the action they take as a result of their reflection on the workings of power within their research projects that is important. As suggested above, such action should involve engagement with scholarship and writing that may lie outside the canon in which they were trained. It should also involve consideration of the cultural, linguistic, and racial diversity represented on the research team and the diversity of perspectives that are being brought to bear on the research design, execution, analysis, and write up. By asking the questions, "Whose views, whose knowledge, whose understandings are represented on this project and whose are not?" and then, by ensuring that a variety of views and people are represented on a project, critical researchers not only set up their projects for rigorous analysis, they may, in certain circumstances, also be able to challenge the hegemony of white Eurocentric thought and privilege in their own research projects.

In this review, I have attempted to outline the ways that language research has been informed by the ideas, principles and practices of critical pedagogy. From an interest in language use to an interest in writing to an interest in bilingual education, what the projects described here all have in common is an interest in the ways educators can work towards equity and social justice. In closing, I'd like to say is that it is important for researchers to find ways of disseminating the findings of our projects into domains where they can be accessed by educators, parents and students in the service of their own work towards equity and social justice. In doing so, we might be able to answer provocative questions posed earlier: "Why present *this* knowledge, *this* literature, *these* ideas, *these* particular approaches?"

Ontario Institute for Studies in Education,
University of Toronto, Canada

REFERENCES

Apple, Michael & Weiss, Lois (eds.): 1983, *Ideology and Practice in Schooling*, Temple University Press, Philadelphia.

Arthur, Jo.: 1996, 'Code switching and collusion: Classroom interaction in Botswana primary schools', *Linguistics and Education* 8(1), 17–34

Auerbach, Elsa Roberts & Wallerstein, Nina: 1987, *ESL for Action: Problem-Posing at Work*, Addison-Wesley, Reading, MA.

Behar, Ruth & Gordon, Deborah: 1995, *Women Writing Culture*, University of California Press, Berkeley and Los Angeles.

Belfiore, Mary Ellen & Heller, Monica: 1992, 'Cross-cultural interviews: Participation and decision-making', in B. Burnaby & A. Cumming (eds.), *Sociopolitical Aspects of ESL*, OISE Press, Toronto, 233–240.

Briggs, Charles: 1986, *Learning How to Ask: A Sociolinguistic Appraisal of the Role of the Interview in Social Science Research*, Cambridge University Press, Cambridge.

Camilleri, Antoinette: 1996, 'Language values and identities: Codeswitching in secondary classrooms in Malta', *Linguistics and Education* 8(1), 85–104.

Cavalcanti, Marilda: 1996, 'Collusion, resistance and reflexivity: Indigenous teacher education in Brazil', *Linguistics and Education* 8(2), 175–188.

Canagarajah, Suresh: 1993, 'Critical ethnography of a Sri Lankan classroom: Ambiguities in student opposition to reproduction through ESOL', *TESOL Quarterly* 27(4), 601–626.

Clifford, James & Marcus, George (eds.): 1986, *Writing Culture: The Poetics and Politics of Ethnography*, University of California Press, Berkeley.

Crookes, Graham: 1993, 'Action research for second language teachers: Going beyond teacher research', *Applied Linguistics* 14(2), 130–144.

Cummins, Jim: 1996, *Negotiating Identities: Education for Empowerment in a Diverse Society*, California Association for Bilingual Education, Ontario, California.

de Castell, Suzanne, Luke, Allan & Luke, Carmen: 1989, 'Editorial introduction: Language, authority and criticism', in Suzanne de Castell, Allan Luke & Carmen

Luke (eds.), *Language, Authority, and Criticism: Readings on the School Textbook*, Falmer Press, New York.

Dlamini, Numbuso: (in press/1997), 'Defining cultural and linguistic borders and the politics of identity', *Critical Arts: A Journal of Cultural Studies*.

Erickson, Frederick: 1988, 'Ethnographic description', in U. Ammon, N. Dittmar & K. Mattheier (eds.), *Sociolinguistics: An International Handbook of the Science of Language and Society*, Walter de Gruyter, Berlin/New York.

Ellsworth, Elizabeth: 1989, 'Why doesn't this feel empowering? Working through the repressive myths of critical pedagogy', *Harvard Educational Review* 59(3), 297–324.

Freire, Paulo: 1973, *Education for Critical Consciousness*, Seabury Press, New York.

Giroux, Henry, A.: 1988, *Schooling and the Struggle for Public Life: Critical Pedagogy in the Modern Age*, University of Minnesota Press, Minneapolis.

Giroux, Henry: 1992, *Border Crossings: Cultural Workers and the Politics of Education*, Routledge, Chapman and Hall, New York.

Goldstein, Tara: 1997, *Two Languages at Work: Bilingual Life on the Production Floor*, Mouton de Gruyter, Berlin/New York.

Gordon, Beverly M.: 1995, 'Knowledge construction, competing critical theories, and education', in James A. Banks & Cherry A. McGee Banks (eds.), *Handbook of Research on Multicultural Education*, Macmillan Publishing, New York.

Gore, Jennifer: 1992, 'What we can do for you! What can "we" do for "you"? Struggle over empowerment in critical and feminist pedagogy', In Carmen Luke & Jennifer Gore (eds.), *Feminisms and Critical Pedagogy*, Routledge, New York.

Gumperz, John J.: 1992, 'Interviewing in Intercultural Situations', in P. Drew & J. Heritage (eds.), *Talk at Work: Interaction in Institutional Settings*, Cambridge University Press, Cambridge, 302–327.

Heath, Shirley Brice: 1982, 'Questioning at home and at school: A comparative study', in G. Spindler (ed.), *Doing the Ethnography of Schooling: Educational Anthropology in Action*, Holt, Rinehart and Winston, New York.

Heller, Monica: 1996, 'Legitimate language in a multilingual school', *Linguistics and Education* 8(2), 139–158.

Henry, Annette: 1992, 'African Canadian women teachers' activism: Recreating communities of caring and resistance', *Journal of Negro Education* 61(3), 370–377.

Hunter, Judy: 1997, 'Power and gendered discourses: Girls learning school writing', in J. Addison & S. McGee (eds.), *Feminism and Empirical Writing Research: Emerging Perspectives*, Heineman, Boyton and Cook, New York.

Lin, Angel: 1996, 'Bilingualism or linguistic segregation? Symbolic domination, resistance and code switching in Hong Kong schools', *Linguistics and Education* 8(1), 49–84.

Martin-Jones, M. & Saxena, M.: 1996, 'Turn-taking, power, asymmetries, and the positioning of bilingual participants in classroom discourse', *Linguistics and Education* 8(1), 105–124.

McLaren, Peter: 1994, *Life in Schools: An Introduction to Critical Pedagogy in the Foundations of Education*, Second edition. Longman, New York.

Moore, Helen: 1996, 'Telling what is real: Competing views in assessing ESL development', *Linguistics and Education* 8(2), 189–213.

Morgan, Kathryn Pauly: 1996, 'Describing the Emperor's New Clothes: Three myths of educational (in-)equity', in Ann Diller, Barbara Houston, Kathryn Pauly Morgan & Maryann Ayim (eds.), *The Gender Question in Education: Theory, Pedagogy, and Politics*, Westview Press, Boulder, Colorado.

Ndayifukamiye, Lin: 1996, 'Bilingualism or linguistic segregation? Symbolic domination, resistance, and codeswitching', *Linguistics and Education* 8(1), 35–48.

Peirce, Bronwyn Norton: 1995, 'Social identity, investment and language learning', *TESOL Quarterly* 29(1), 9–31.

Pennycook, Alastair: 1994, *The Cultural Politics of English as an International Language*, Longman, London.

Rampton, B.: 1996, 'Youth, race and resistance: A sociolinguistic perspective', *Linguistics and Education* 8(2), 159–174.

Rivera, John & Poplin, Mary: 1995, 'Multicultural, critical, feminine and constructive pedagogies seen through the lives of youth: A call for the revisioning of these and beyond: Toward a pedagogy for the next century', in Christine Sleeter & Peter McLaren (eds.), *Multicultural Education, Critical Pedagogy and the Politics of Difference*, State University of New York Press, Albany, NY.

Simon, Roger: 1988, 'For a pedagogy of possibility', in J. Smyth (ed.), *The Critical Pedagogy Networker* 1(1), Deakin University, School of Education, Victoria, Australia, 1–4.

Simon, Roger I.: 1992, *Teaching Against the Grain: Essays Toward a Pedagogy of Possibility*, Bergin and Garvey, Boston.

Starfield, Sue: 1995, 'I'll go with the group: Discourse community, genre, power in academic writing', Paper presented at the TESOL 30th Annual Convention, Chicago, Illinois.

Weiler, Kathleen & Mitchell, Candace (eds.): 1992, *What Schools Can Do: Critical Pedagogy and Practice*, SUNY Press, Albany.

LUDO VERHOEVEN

EXPERIMENTAL METHODS IN RESEARCHING LANGUAGE AND EDUCATION

In experimental research on language and education an attempt is made to build theories which explain the mental processes behind language and literacy learning, the individual differences that go along with these processes and the outcomes of differential treatments meant to stimulate such processes. Implicit in experimental research is the idea that it is possible to make valid claims from the particular to the general and that new knowledge becomes available from processes of inductive inference. In order to obtain answers to research questions a balanced design needs to be created going from the writing of hypotheses to the statistical analysis of data. Usually the researcher starts out with a plan, outlining the variables under consideration, their operationalization and the methods used to gather and analyze the data.

With regard to methods of data analysis a distinction can be made between experimental designs for the analysis of individual differences and correlational techniques (including correlational analysis, factor analysis, and structural equation models), aimed to explore the relationship between research variables. In this section a short review of these methods will be presented, along with some research examples.

EXPERIMENTAL DESIGNS

Experiments are designed to test theories by the use of controlled observation. In an experiment the researcher manipulates and controls one or more independent variables and observes the variation of the dependent variable(s) as a result of the manipulation of the independent variables. An experimental design enables the researcher to manipulate an independent variable while controlling other independent variables. For instance, an investigator may manipulate feedback on children's reading attempts to produce differential outcomes of reading instruction. In a classical experiment the researcher has the power to assign subjects to experimental groups, or to assign experimental treatments to the groups. In classroom-based studies subjects normally cannot be randomly assigned to treatments. Nevertheless, since the structural and design features of these classroom-based studies are similar to those in true experiments this research is called 'quasi-experimental' (cf. Cook & Campbell, 1979).

N.H. Hornberger and D. Corson (eds), Encyclopedia of Language and Education,
Volume 8: Research Methods in Language and Education, 79–87.
© *1997 Kluwer Academic Publishers. Printed in the Netherlands.*

An independent variable in an experiment can be a classification variable, present prior to the experiment, such as sex, age or socio-economic status, or a treatment variable controlled by the experimenter. Any independent variable is labeled as a factor of which the possible values are defined as levels. In case the effects of two independent variables are investigated simultaneously the experiment is called 'two-factor'. Most experiments include a single treatment variable with two or more levels. In many experiments a group of subjects is randomly divided into a number of independent groups. A different treatment is then given to each group, while no treatment is given to a control group. By means of comparisons between treatment groups and the control group the effect of the treatments can be determined. Usually, a pretest – treatment – posttest design is followed in order to estimate the experimental effects. Sometimes a retention measure is also taken some time after the treatment has taken place in order to find out whether the effects remain stable as time goes on. A problem with experimental designs is that contaminating variables may influence the outcomes of experimental treatments. Let us consider, for instance, an experiment in which the outcome of a specific reading program for children with decoding problems is investigated. Given the fact that decoding proficiency is related to children's intelligence and phonological abilities a maximum control of these unwanted variables that may have an effect on the experimental outcomes is required. This can be realized by comparing differential treatments in one and the same group of subjects, by random assignment of subjects to treatments, or by matching the subjects in the different treatment groups on the supposedly contaminating variables.

The effects of experimental treatments can be evaluated by means of analysis of variance (cf. Winer, 1962). This statistical technique divides the variation observed in experimental data into different parts related to the experimental factor. In case the effects of a number of treatments are under consideration, the analysis of variance is used to test the significance of the differences between the mean scores of the various samples. The null hypothesis that the samples are drawn from populations which have the same mean score can then be tested. In case the simultaneous effect of more than one experimental variable is investigated the effects of each factor, as well as the interaction between factors, can be computed. The statistical analysis of time measures in experimental designs is a special case. By means of analysis of variance with repeated measures the effects of time and experimental treatment can be evaluated separately. For an overview of new developments on statistical methods in longitudinal research see Von Eye (1990).

CORRELATIONAL ANALYSIS

Correlational techniques are used in order to test the interrelationship between research variables. Measures of correlation are conventionally defined to take values between −1 and +1. A value of +1 refers to a perfect positive correlation, a value of 0 to the absence of correlation, and a value of −1 to a perfect negative correlation. By computing the square value of a correlation coefficient the percentage of common variance of two variables can be expressed. If, for example, the correlation coefficient between the variables of intelligence and reading ability in a group of children is 0.70, we may conclude that 49 per cent of the variance of one variable is predictable from the other, and that the remaining 51 per cent is due to other factors.

Variables with different measurement scales can be used in research. Nominal variables represent entities, such as numbers referring to the two sexes, without any suggestion that they can be subjected to mathematical analyses. Ordinal variables refer to entities that can be ordered from high to low without any indication of the size of individual differences. Scores on a motivation questionnaire form a case in point. Interval scales involve a rank ordering of entities with information about relative distance between the ranks. If there is also information about a rational zero to which the distances can be related, we speak of ratio scales. The specification of people's length is an example here. With ordinal variables usually *rank-order correlations* are used, whereas *contingency coefficients* are normally computed in order to describe nominal variables. With rank-order correlations the ranking of entities on different dimensions are related. For example, the ranking of the taste and the color of a dozen wines by experienced judges. An example of a contingency coefficient concerns the correlation between sex (male vs female) and examination outcome (pass vs fail).

The measure of correlation most widely used is the Pearson *product-moment correlation coefficient.* Its use is confined to variables of the interval, or ratio type. As an example of Pearson correlation, in many studies the interrelationship between word reading efficiency and phonological awareness has been studied. By means of correlational analysis it was examined to what extent a measure of word decoding in children in the early grades of primary school relates to their phonological awareness. Generally, it was found that there was a positive correlation between phonological awareness and word decoding skill. However, in such correlational studies three problems remain unresolved.

First of all, a correlation only indicates a relationship between two variables without providing information about a causal direction in one way or the other. As such, the problem of causality remains unsolved in the type of study introduced above. On the one hand, Bradley & Bryant

(1983) argued that the degree of phonological awareness in children is a good predictor of word decoding. On the other hand, Perfetti, Beck & Hudges (1981) claimed that children in acquiring word decoding skills become more aware of the nature of written language. As such, phonological awareness is seen as a consequence of becoming literate. Even a third option is found in the literature, saying that the relationship has a reciprocal nature. Training studies have given some evidence for the latter option. Ehri & Wilce (1985) showed that young children can be trained in phonemic awareness prior to formal instruction in conventional reading, provided they have a certain amount of letter knowledge when the instruction begins.

Second, differences in language or literacy outcomes may have multiple causes. The possibilities of more complex multiple-factor theories must therefore be admitted. A possible technique is multiple regression. This technique enables the user to predict language and literacy outcomes from a number of independent measures (e.g. Finn, 1977). However, though in educational prediction studies the multiple regression technique can be justified, an obvious limitation of multiple regression is that equations between dependent and independent variables can only be tested one by one and not as a hierarchical set.

Third, there is the question of how the variables under consideration should be operationalized. In different studies usually the research variables are operationalized in varying ways. For instance, in exploring the relationship between phonological awareness and word decoding the former variable has been measured by such tasks as word rhyming, judgments of number of phonemes in spoken words, in segmentation tasks which require the pronunciation of separate phonemes in a word, and word synthesis tasks which require the child to recognize a word when a string of phonemes is presented (see Wagner, 1988). It is by no means clear to what extent the differences in operationalization of variables has influenced the outcomes of the studies involved. A closer insight into the content validity of variables is offered by factor analysis. This technique enables the researcher to find commonalities among related variables.

FACTOR ANALYSIS

Factor analysis is a method for reducing a large number of variables to a smaller number of underlying hypothetical variables, called factors. These factors can be derived from the correlations between variables. Only if variables are substantially related, one or more factors can emerge. As such, factors reflect the variances shared by variables. Correlations between the original variables and the underlying factors are called factor loadings. A factor of a data matrix can be seen as a linear combination of the variables in the matrix. By means of rotation a given factor structure can be further simplified.

In a study by Verhoeven (1991) the bilingual proficiency of 6-year-old Turkish children, living in the Netherlands, was examined by using factor analysis. An attempt was made to operationalize pragmatic conversational and decontextualized grammatical aspects of the children's first and second language proficiency. The assessment of pragmatic language proficiency started with the recording and transcription of spontaneous speech using three different tasks: giving a spatial description, describing a series of events, both on the basis of pictures, and some free conversation between the child and an interviewer. Native speakers of Turkish and Dutch acted as interviewers in each of both languages. Several parameters of language use were assessed from the transcriptions. As measures of lexical variety in discourse, the numbers of different content and function words occurring in 75 utterances (25 random utterances from each task) were computed. In order to measure the use of morphosyntactic devices in the two languages, the mean number of morphemes in the longest utterances (10% of each individual corpus) was computed. Moreover, the percentage of subordinated clauses over 150 utterances (50 random utterances from each task) was determined.

The assessment of decontextualized grammatical proficiency involved tests measuring phonological, lexical and morphosyntactic subskills in Turkish and Dutch. The phonological test required children to make similar-different distinctions of word pairs that differ in one phoneme, the position of phonemes, or the number of phonemes. To test both productive and receptive lexical skills, children were required to label pictures and to select the correct referent out of four pictures for a spoken word. Morphosyntactic abilities in the two languages were measured by a 24-sentence imitation task. The children's reproductions were scored for the proportion of correct imitation of function words, word final markers and clause linking.

Factor analysis was used to determine to what extent the eight measures for proficiency in the two languages could be reduced to a smaller number of factors. Common factor analysis for the measures of Turkish language proficiency yielded a two-factor solution, explaining 59 percent of the total amount of variance. The language measures with high loadings on the first factor primarily referred to pragmatic language use. The measures of lexical variety, utterance length and proportion of subordinated clauses all concerned the unconscious use of linguistic knowledge in a communicative situation. The language measures with high loadings on the second factor, on the other hand, all referred to grammatical proficiency. Moreover, these measures involved a situation where the focus of the learner is to perform a linguistic task out of context. The phoneme discrimination task, the vocabulary tasks and the sentence imitation tasks all demanded a decontextualized orientation on the part of the child.

Factor analysis on the measures of Dutch proficiency also yielded a two-factor solution. 69 percent of the variance in proficiency scores was explained by the two factors. The pattern of factor loadings highly corresponded to the one found for the Turkish data. Language measures with high loadings on the first factor primarily referred to contextual pragmatic skills, whereas the ones with high loadings on the second factor drew on decontextual grammatical skills.

The conclusion is that the children's proficiency in both Turkish and Dutch can be seen as two-dimensional constructs. In either case the underlying dimensions can be easily interpreted in terms of Cummins' theoretical framework in which contextual pragmatic language skills are distinguished from decontextual language skills (cf. Cummins, 1984, 1989).

STRUCTURAL EQUATION MODELS

A relatively new technique for the study of variation of language and literacy development over time is analysis of structural equations. In this technique, hypotheses concerning the interaction between independent and dependent variables are formulated as a set of structural equations of covariances between variables which can be subsequently tested. Estimations of parameters of these equations as well as a test of goodness of fit can be done by application of Linear Structural Relations Analysis, or LISREL (Jöreskog & Sörbom, 1993). LISREL not only offers the opportunity to evaluate the model's fit, it also enables the user to employ observed as well as latent variables. The latter argument makes it possible to measure the same underlying factor with various tests. LISREL makes use of maximum likelihood procedures to assess the measurement and structural components of a particular causal model. The measurement model describes the relationship between the measures taken and a latent variable. The structural model describes the underlying causal relationship among the latent variables. By testing alternative models, the best fitting model can be sought for.

Verhoeven (1990) gives an example of a study in which LISREL is used to explain individual variation in second language reading of Turkish children in the Netherlands. An attempt was made to account for bottom-up factors in the second language reading process by relating reading comprehension scores to the children's word reading efficiency scores, their ability to discriminate Dutch phonemes and their meta-linguistic abilities. A series of LISREL programs was conducted in order to examine the temporal variation in Dutch reading comprehension during the first two grades. In designing the explanatory models both longitudinal and cross-sectional effects were included. From a longitudinal point of view it was clear that the children's metalinguistic abilities have hardly any predictive power for similar abilities after one year of literacy instruction. The longitudinal relationships for phoneme discrimination and for reading comprehension were moderate, the one for word reading efficiency was strong. From a cross-sectional point of view, phonemic discrimination appeared a substantial predictor of metalinguistic abilities and of reading comprehension. Metalinguistic abilities strongly predicted the children's word reading efficiency, which in turn highly predicted reading comprehension. Given the present model about two thirds of the variance in reading comprehension abilities was explained.

PROBLEMS AND DIFFICULTIES

In experimental research there is the problem of test reliability and test validity. A reliability problem may derive from the lack of consistency in the data collection procedures being followed. For example, language and literacy can be measured on the basis of self-evaluation which facilitates the introduction of an element of subjectivity into replies. Another measurement problem concerns sampling. With respect to sampling, empirical studies on language and education have often failed to control the socio-economic and linguistic background of learners. Most importantly, however, there is a validity problem. The kind of assessment techniques used, and research methodology followed is partly dependent on the aim at which language and literacy data are to be collected. In some studies, the operationalization of variables can be questioned, given the possibility that with tests only 'test-wiseness' is measured, an ability which incorporates a desire to do well on artificial tasks. If this turns out to be the case, the relationship between various language and literacy measures can be no more than a tautology.

The study of language and literacy development may gain benefit from using item response theory methodology (see Messick, 1987). In that case tasks representative for language and literacy skills can be scaled using item response theory, a mathematical model for estimating the probability that a person will respond correctly to a particular task. Both difficulty parameters of the tasks and proficiency levels for individuals and groups can then be estimated. If on a task children from varying backgrounds yield equivalent estimations of item parameters, it could be concluded that the items on the task can be scaled along one and the same dimension. Moreover, the conception of multiple scales instead of the traditional single scale makes it possible to assess a multifaceted construct of language proficiency.

Given the complex nature of language in education, there is an urgent need of longitudinal quasi-experimental studies in which children of different backgrounds under varying instructional approaches are followed over time. So far, the bulk of educational research has been cross-sectional. It can be argued that in cross-sectional studies language proficiency can be conceived of as an intervening effect rather than as a causal factor. In studies with a cross-sectional design it is unclear whether it is language proficiency or cognitive maturity that predicts academic proficiency. Therefore we are in need of studies in which children's language development and academic achievement are followed over time. Willett (1989) discusses the implications of longitudinal measurement of change for the design of studies of individual growth.

Sampling can be seen as a special concern as regards the study of individual differences in language and literacy learning. In many studies certain groups, such as dialect speakers, ethnic minorities, transient groups, or disabled children are, if represented at all, underrepresented. Besides overall assessment it may be important to have insight on groups of children who are at risk of being functionally illiterate. As far as ethnic minorities are concerned, the choice of language of literacy tasks can be questioned. In a multilingual society different ethnic groups may use various oral and written codes at different competence levels, because these codes have at least partially distinct sets of functions.

Finally, experimental research in language education might profit from combining insights from research on characteristics of instructional processes and research on individual differences in learning (see Byrne, 1995). It should be explored how different styles of language teaching have different impacts on different learners. In such aptitude-treatment interaction studies neither educational methods, nor children's abilities are considered to be fixed. Instead an optimal fit of students and instructional alternatives is sought. For an overview of studies on programs that adapt instruction to the learning characteristics of individual children see Dunn, Beaudrey & Klavas (1989).

University of Nijmegen
The Netherlands

REFERENCES

Bradley, L. & Bryant, P.E.: 1983, 'Categorizing sounds and learning to read, a causal connection', *Nature* 301, 419–421.
Byrne, B.: 1995, 'Individual differences, instruction and the way ahead', *Issues in Education* 1(1), 71–75.
Cook, T.D. & Campbell, D.T.: 1979, *Quasi-Experimentation: Design and Analysis Issues for Field Settings*, Rand McNally, Chicago.
Cummins, J.: 1984, 'Wanted: A theoretical frame for relating language proficiency to academic achievement among bilingual students', in: C. Rivera (ed.), *Language Proficiency and Academic Achievement*, Multilingual Matters, Clevedon.

Cummins, J.: 1989, 'Language and literacy acquisition in bilingual contexts', *Journal of Multilingual and Multicultural Development* 10(1), 17–31.

Dunn, R., Beaudrey, J.S. & Klavas, A.: 1989, 'Survey of research on learning styles', *Educational Leadership* 46(6), 50–58.

Ehri, L.C. & Wilce, L.S.: 1985, 'Movement into reading: Is the first stage of printed-word learning visual or phonetic?', *Reading Research Quarterly* 20, 163–179.

Finn, J.D.: 1977, *A General Model for Multivariate Analysis*, Holt, Rinehart & Winston, New York.

Jöreskog, K.G. & Sörbom, D.: 1993, *LISREL-8, User's Reference Guide*, Scientific Software International, Chicago.

Messick, S.: 1987, 'The once and future issues of validity: Assessing the meaning and consequences of measurement', in H. Wainer & H. Braun (eds.), *Test Validity*, Erlbaum, Hillsdale NJ.

Perfetti, C.A., Beck, I., Bell, L.C. & Hughes, C.: 1987, 'Phonemic knowledge and learning to read are reciprocal: A longitudinal study of first grade children', *Merrill-Palmer Quarterly* 33(3), 283–319.

Verhoeven, L.: 1990, 'Acquisition of reading in a second language', *Reading Research Quarterly* 25(2), 90–114.

Verhoeven, L.: 1991, 'Assessment of bilingual proficiency', in L. Verhoeven & J.H.A.L. de Jong (eds.), *The Construct of Language Proficiency*, John Benjamins, Amsterdam/Philadelphia, 125–136.

Verhoeven, L.: 1994, 'Linguistic diversity and literacy development', in: L. Verhoeven (ed.), *Functional Literacy: Theoretical Issues and Educational Implications*, John Benjamins, Amsterdam/Philadelphia, 199–219.

Von Eye, A. (ed.): 1990, *Statistical Methods in Longitudinal Research*, Academic Press, San Diego.

Wagner, R.: 1988, 'Causal relationships between the development of phonological-processing abilities and the acquisition of reading skills: A meta-analysis', *Merrill-Palmer Quarterly* 34, 261–279.

Willett, J.B.: 1989, 'Some results on reliability for the longitudinal measurement of change', *Educational and Psychological Measurement* 49, 587–602.

Winer, B.J.: 1962, *Statistical Principles in Experimental Design*, McGraw-Hill, New York.

TERESA PICA

SECOND LANGUAGE ACQUISITION RESEARCH METHODS

Research methods in second language acquisition (SLA) are used to address questions about SLA processes, developmental sequences, conditions, contexts, and outcomes, and to identify their linguistic, social, cultural, and cognitive characteristics. Methodology is both eclectic and innovative, with application and adaptation of approaches from the social sciences, most notably, linguistics, psychology, anthropology, and education, and with increasing development and refinement of instruments, procedures, and techniques within the field itself. Emphasis has been more consistent with nomothetic than hermeneutic research. However, questions raised by the complexity of SLA phenomena have required approaches from both traditions. Thus, research design can be theory-driven and hypothesis testing, as well as data-driven, through pattern identification, interpretation, and analysis. Data may be collected longitudinally and cross-sectionally, under instructed and untutored conditions, following experimental intervention, during naturally occurring social interaction, and through elicitation, interview, and observation. Analyses employ quantitative procedures, including descriptive and inferential statistics, and qualitative approaches of triangulation, description, reflection, and interpretation (see reviews in Volume 4).

EARLY DEVELOPMENT

Early methodology took the form of parental diaries that described children's simultaneous acquisition of two languages (for example, Leopold, 1939–1949). During the late 1940s through early 1970s, quantitative methods were used to compare the impact of instructional methods on student achievement (reviewed in Levin, 1972). Questions regarding instruction were also addressed through 'contrastive analysis,' as researchers worked within structuralist linguistics and behaviorist psychology to identify differences between forms in the second language (L2) and students' native language (NL,) believed to 'interfere' with L2 learning, and to develop lessons accordingly (Stockwell, Bowen & Martin, 1965).

Research methods expanded throughout the 1970's, stimulated by child language studies and psycholinguistic theories on language acquisition as

N.H. Hornberger and D. Corson (eds), Encyclopedia of Language and Education,
Volume 8: Research Methods in Language and Education, 89–99.
© *1997 Kluwer Academic Publishers. Printed in the Netherlands.*

a predisposed activity of rule formation, simplification and overgeneraliza-
tion. These processes were viewed as errors and developmental features
of the learner's grammar or 'interlanguage,' only some of which were NL
related (Selinker, 1972). 'Error analysis' categorized errors according to
linguistic features and functions of communication and learning (Richards,
1974), while 'performance analysis' described sequences in the emergence
of L2 grammatical morphemes, verb phrase negation, questions, and relative clauses over time (See examples in Hatch, 1978).

Data were collected longitudinally and cross-sectionally, from individuals and groups of children and adults, of diverse language backgrounds
and learning contexts, across developmental stages. Longitudinal case
studies were conducted by Hatch and colleagues, and by Ravem (1968),
Cazden, Cancino, Rosansky & Schumann (1975), and Hakuta (1976),
and others, excerpts from which appear among chapters in Hatch (1978).
Data were collected through interviews, elicitation, and conversation, then
aggregated for error and performance analysis.

Cross-sectional approaches sampled learner groups across developmental levels, using techniques of picture description and interviews that
provided contexts for L2 grammatical morpheme suppliance. Percent-
ages of suppliance were calculated for each morpheme, then rank ordered.
Spearman's rho and Pearson product moment statistics sought correlation among the rank orders shown by different learner groups, usually
with positive results. Despite weaknesses in these correlational measures,
and differences in morpheme suppliance between expressive and receptive modalities (Larsen-Freeman, 1975), the correlations were applied to
theoretical claims for a developmental order in SLA that transcended age,
NL, and learning context (Dulay & Burt, 1973; Krashen, 1977). Publication of Hatch & Farhady (1982), brought SLA its own research methods
text.

MAJOR CONTRIBUTIONS

Research methods have become a major focus of attention in the field
of SLA, reflected by the plethora of books and articles, conference
papers, symposia, and workshops on methodological issues and procedures. Methods texts (Brown, 1988; Johnson, 1992; Nunan, 1992)
and manuals (Hatch & Lazaraton, 1991) have been written for novices
and sophisticated researchers. Numerous journals have published special
issues on SLA research methods. A book series was established by Gass
& Schachter in 1994.

With the advent of university-based, often nationally funded, centers
for the study of SLA throughout the United States, Canada, Europe, and
Australia, have come financial and personnel resources to support work on
developing instruments and procedures for collection of valid and reliable

data, often with the aid of technology. Data bases have been established and maintained through computer storage and organization, from which researchers can access, retrieve, and donate L2 data to be used in future studies. Software has been developed to assist data analysis by facilitating coding, organization, and storage of data (Pienemann, Jansen, Johnston, Patten & Sipkes, 1991).

Early methods have been modified to accommodate new research questions as well as address questions of continued concern. Thus, diary methodology has been extended, to describe and reflect on affective factors in classroom SLA (reviewed in Bailey & Oschner, 1983), to study L2 learning conditions and processes over time (Schmidt & Frota, 1986), and to record observations, interpretations, and analyses of L2 learning contexts (Watson-Gegeo, 1988). This reflects the increased application of qualitative, anthropological approaches in SLA research, including ethnographic methods of participant observation, self-reflection, and triangulation of data from multiple sources, including written documents, interviews, and other forms of oral account (See Johnson, 1992 for review).

Further refinement of these methods is found in the use of participatory action research design to address social inequities as they bear on L2 learning. Here, L2 learner participants, usually from disadvantaged backgrounds, are involved with researchers in all phases of the research process, as they identify research problems, initiate research questions, gather, analyze, and interpret data, and apply their findings toward transformation of educational, occupational, and other dimensions of their social context (See Auerbach, 1995).

As early approaches of contrastive, error, and performance analysis were found to be too narrow in scope for understanding and explaining SLA, researchers turned to principles of linguistic markedness and universal difficulty, and to the possible interaction among the L2, the learner's NL, and a potentially active innate, universal grammar. Drawing on theories from linguistics, researchers have been able to make testable predictions as to learning processes, learner knowledge, and L2 outcomes, and to advance new approaches to data collection and analysis. They sample across learners of different NLs learning the same L2, and follow principles of markedness and universal grammar when selecting linguistic forms and processes by which to compare developmental outcomes. Because such features are realized through complex structures and constituent relationships that are difficult to access through interview and conversational techniques, data collection has been primarily through grammaticality judgments (White, 1987), elicited imitation, and translation.

Analysis has moved beyond cataloguing and describing learner errors and aggregating interlanguage data, as longitudinal approaches have become more focused, to respond to theoretical questions about interlanguage form and function relationships (Huebner, 1983), conversational bases for L2 grammar development (Sato, 1986), linguistic, social, and cognitive processes in SLA (Schmidt & Frota, 1986), and retention of instructional treatments (reviewed in Lightbown & Spada, 1993). Cross-sectional design has continued to dominate, with sampling based on learners' linguistic background, gender, age, and proficiency level. Several studies have combined longitudinal and cross-sectional approaches (Meisel, Clahsen & Pienemann, 1981) to further understand SLA developmental sequences, and to link them with social and cognitive factors.

The field has also sustained an interest in questions about the impact of instructional interventions through approaches that focus attention on learners and their classroom strategies rather than the evaluation of global teaching methods. Long (1983) employed techniques of meta-analysis to develop categories about teaching and learning in instructional contexts, and then apply them to results of previous studies on classroom learning. His analysis revealed that instruction did not alter developmental order, but was correlated with greater accuracy and to an accelerated rate of acquisition. This gave impetus to classroom process research that links instruction to learning outcomes, focuses on independent variables drawn from theories on perceptual processing and linguistic complexity (Pienemann, 1984), markedness (Doughty, 1991), and L1–L2 similarities and differences (White, 1991), and employs instructional treatments motivated by SLA theory, and operationalized and isolated for study over time (reviewed in Lightbown & Spada, 1993).

Emergent theoretical claims about the role of conversation in L2 development called for analytical tools that transcended word and sentence level description. Discourse analysis became a widely used approach for organizing conversational data from everyday social interaction and in classroom and community contexts (See Chaudron, 1988). Van Lier (1992) developed contingent analysis to detect inequities among participants in such contexts, and to link the inequities with broader sociological forces at work in their L2 classrooms.

Observation schemes and inventories for classroom studies have been used to gather and classify linguistic and communicative behavior, and to document particular strategies or methods whose purported effects are under study (Allen, Frolich & Spada, 1984). Introduction of ethnomethodological features of negotiation, including clarification and confirmation questions (Long, 1983), enabled researchers to study how the learner accessed L2 forms and features in conversation and during classroom interaction. Also critical to this line of research has been the use of interactive tasks for data collection and for insight into the role and variation among input, interactional, and instructional resources to learners. Interactive tasks with classroom validity have been developed to elicit targeted structures. See Pica, Kanagy & Falodun (1993) for review. Other examples appear among the chapters in Gass & Crookes (1993).

Quantitative analysis typically tests significance of findings through chi-square, t-tests, and analysis of variance. Factor analysis, regression, and multiple analysis of variance are used in larger studies to determine underlying variables that account for correlations among observed variables. An alpha level of 0.05 has become a standard level of significance. Experimental methods have been refined from pre-experimental to quasi-experimental in design. As few studies have been able to meet experimental conditions of pre-post testing and random assignment of subjects, analysis of covariance has been used to adjust data for initial differences across subject groups (Spada, 1987). Implicational scaling has been used to show consistency and variability in the order of occurrence of interlanguage features (Meisel, Clahsen & Pienemann, 1981).

Qualitative analysis is used to illuminate quantitative findings, through detailed description of representative examples, as well as to organize descriptive findings, and to create analytical categories for them. Attention is often given to providing a 'thick explanation' of findings (Watson-Gegeo, 1988), and to drawing connections between L2 learning theories, classroom practice, and social forces (See Tollefson, 1995).

Of further interest has been the development of work in sociopragmatic competence, due largely to an expansion of the notion of language competence to include rules for social appropriateness. Data have been collected through observation of naturally occurring social interaction. Role plays and discourse completion tasks have also been used because of the difficulty in accessing such data, and to maintain a uniformity across languages studied (reviewed in Wolfson, 1989).

With traditional techniques of data collection found ineffective to address questions regarding learner strategies toward communication and learning, introspective and retrospective techniques gained consideration. Through think aloud protocols, learners report on and analyze their cognitive, linguistic, and communication behaviors, while engaged in a learning or performance task. In retrospection, learners are asked to reflect on these processes, often through diaries and journals (See Faerch & Kasper, 1987).

WORK IN PROGRESS

New approaches to data collection and analysis are being developed, and existing approaches modified, to respond to emerging theoretical concerns and research questions. Of particular interest have been questions as to learners' need to focus attention on both the meaning and the form of the L2 they are learning, and to obtain negative evidence when features of their interlanguage are not grammatical within the L2. The highly focused nature of these questions suggests that data be collected through tightly controlled experimental studies, yet the pertinence of such questions to pedagogical issues also requires instruments and procedures that have validity for classroom communication.

To address these methodological needs, grammar-focused communication tasks are being developed, often with adaptation from classroom activities (See Gass & Crookes, 1993). In addition, instructional treatments, including corrective feedback, metalinguistic instruction, and form focused input, and instructional L2 targets are being derived from theory and research across a number of fields, including linguistics, psychology, and from within the field of SLA itself (See Long, 1996). To address questions concerning the impact of these interventions and the retention of instructional features over time, researchers have also been working closely with classroom teachers to design experimental classrooms and to implement appropriate forms of assessment (reviewed in Lightbown & Spada, 1993).

Researchers are also looking toward ways to shape computer-controlled learning settings so that they might serve as pedagogically valid contexts for these treatment options (Doughty, 1991). As interest continues in the acquisition of L2 sociolinguistic rules, there has been an increasing focus on the extent to which the kinds of instructional interventions described above can also facilitate the social dimensions of SLA. These new developments in tasks and treatments are beginning to provide a principled basis for decisions in research design, instrumentation, and procedures that have implications for both basic research and classroom application (See Long, 1996).

Emerging theoretical questions about the contributions to SLA of cognitive processes such as awareness and attention have challenged researchers to develop reliable procedures through which to identify such processes at work in the learner, and to be able to document their impact on learning outcomes. One approach has been through carefully designed experimental studies, carried out under strict laboratory conditions (Hulstijn & DeKeyser, 1997). Another approach has been to require greater participation of learners, themselves, in the data collection. Here, in addition to the more traditional methods of diary, interview, and observation, the verbal report has emerged as both valid and viable (Cohen, 1996).

PROBLEMS AND DIFFICULTIES

Problems and difficulties in SLA research methodology reflect the scope and ambition of its research questions and the challenge of accessing valid data to address them. Questions posed must be researchable, and entail observable features. Suitable subjects and settings must be located, and appropriate instruments and procedures chosen for data collection and analysis. Decisions in these areas bear considerable impact on the internal and external validity of the research.

Many SLA constructs are difficult to define operationally, particularly those for cognitive processes such as attention and awareness, or for motivation and other affective features. Some constructs, such as acquisition and intake, have both process and outcome definitions. Others, such as communicative competence, L2 proficiency, or comprehensible input, are defined by a multiplicity of features, only some of which might be studied at the same time. Reference to the construct, target like use, has been problematic as a measure of development, because it assumes a standard L2 variety, which may be inaccessible to the learner.

Selection of subjects and settings can be hampered by their accessibility to the researcher. Sample size may be constrained by research requirements for internal validity in experimental design or ethnographic study, or mundane considerations such as subjects' availability and willingness to participate. Ethical standards can prevent investigation of a question which deprives one group of learners of a particular treatment.

Data collection instruments and procedures must provide valid data samples. Despite the assumption that naturally occurring speech provides the most authentic data, it is often difficult to gain sufficient samples of sociolinguistic features or complex structures. Controlled data collection might be preferred for consistency across subjects and instructional interventions. Researchers face decisions about whether to be present for data collection, and possibly intrusive, or to remove themselves, thereby risking failure of recording equipment or subjects' misinterpretation of a data collection task. Instruments effective in gaining data samples might fail to address other questions of concern. Sentence-level, grammaticality judgment tasks are easy to administer and score for accuracy, but it is seldom possible to determine whether judgments are based on the grammar of a sentence or some other dimension such as vocabulary.

A lack of consistency in the field in organizing conversational data as T-units and fragments, turns, or utterances has limited the extent to which comparisons can be made with respect to L2 discourse. Similarly, the field has yet to agree upon an index of development that could be used to establish baseline L2 proficiency or change over time. Many of the features of interest to researchers are in high inference categories of operationalization, which challenge conditions for inter-rater reliability, and require consensus through multiple trials of coding, discussion, and revision.

Research training and research time are often problematic. Researchers come from varied backgrounds of linguistics, psychology, education, modern languages, and literature, and find themselves in academic departments where emphasis is on the methods specific to these related fields. Few possess sufficient training to employ quantitative and qualitative methods. Often, they are pressured to apply basic research findings to solution of actual classroom problems. Few studies have had piloting phases, and there has been little replication of studies. Nearly all phases of methodology take up time for locating subjects and settings, observing in or visiting the research site, setting up experiments, or transcribing and analyzing data. This situation can be further constrained by researchers' lack of funding or other professional obligations.

FUTURE DIRECTIONS

Methodology will continue to develop as the field moves toward construction of a unified theory of SLA. This work will entail a range of different approaches, each guided by the need to test theoretical claims or to gather data on SLA processes, sequences, and outcomes, and the conditions that underlie them. There will be continued refinement of instruments and procedures, so that they can be based on principles of SLA theory and findings of previous research, have classroom validity, and meet reliability requirements. Efforts will continue to design studies whose outcomes will effect educational change.

Thus, work will continue on development of grammar-focused communication tasks that can be used to address questions about the learner's need for form focused input and instruction, as well as on adaptation of current tasks such as the dictogloss, a form of lecture reconstruction, which shows promise in this area. Instructional treatments and L2 targets will continue to be refined, with further derivation from theory and research. Researchers and classroom teachers will continue to work together across a range of options, including collaboration in action research and classroom ethnography, convergence of efforts to design and implement instructional programs and to study their impact over time, with compatibility of interests in learning processes and classroom interventions.

The increasing use of computers across educational settings will impact SLA research methods in a variety of ways, including continued development of controlled instruments and procedures for testing the impact of instructional interventions on L2. Computers will also allow researchers to accumulate data bases, to better store, code, and retrieve data, and to share data across communities.

The field will see increasing inclusion of learners' perspectives and beliefs. As definitions of language competence broaden into social and strategic areas, researchers will seek instruments and procedures that can describe learning processes in these areas, and identify sequences in their development. Emerging theoretical questions about the contributions to SLA of cognitive processes such as awareness and attention challenge researchers to develop reliable procedures through which to identify such processes at work in the learner, and to document their impact on learning outcomes. The challenge will be to coordinate experimentation with observation of naturally occurring social interaction, and to balance the roles of researchers and learners in these processes.

New theoretical claims about the role of neural networks in language learning have led to questions as to neurological correlates specific to SLA, and to research that has been carried out largely by cognitive and computer scientists, whose background and methodologies are often distinct from those of SLA researchers. This context provides one of many methodological challenges that will face current and future SLA researchers, as theories and questions continue to expand.

University of Pennsylvania
USA

REFERENCES

Allen, J.P.B., Frolich, M. & Spada, N.: 1984, 'The communicative orientation of language teaching: An observation scheme', in J.Handscombe, R. Orem & B. Taylor (eds.), *On TESOL '83, The Question of Control*, TESOL, Washington, DC, 231–252.
Auerbach, E.: 1995, 'The politics of the ESL classroom: Issues of Power in pedagogical choices', in J.W. Tollefson (ed.), *Power and Inequality in Language Education*, Cambridge University Press, Cambridge, England, 9–33.
Bailey, K.M. & Ochsner, R.: 1983, 'A methodological review of the diary studies: Windmill tilting or social science?', in K.M. Bailey, M.H. Long & S. Peck (eds.), *Second Language Acquisition Studies*, Newbury House, Rowley, Mass, 188–198.
Brown, J.D.: 1988, *Understanding Research in Second LanguageLearning: A Teacher's Guide to Statistics and Research Design*, Cambridge University Press, Cambridge.
Cazden, C., Cancino, H., Rosansky, E. & Schumann, J,: 1975, *Second Language Acquisition Sequences in Children, Adolescents and Adults*, Final Report, U.S. Department of Health, Education, and Welfare.
Chaudron, C.: 1988, *Second Language Classroom: Research on Teaching and Learning*, Cambridge University Press, Cambridge.
Cohen, A.D.: 1996, 'Verbal reports as a source of insights into second language learner strategies', *Applied Language Learning* 7, 7–26.
Doughty, C.: 1991, 'Second language instruction does make a difference: Evidence from an empirical study of second language relativization', *Studies in Second Language Acquisition* 13, 431–469.
Dulay, H. & Burt, M.: 1973, 'Should we teach children Syntax?', *Language Learning* 23, 245–258.
Faerch, G. & Kasper, G.: 1987, *Introspection in Second Language Research*, Multilingual Matters, Clevedon, England.
Gass, S. & Crookes, G. (eds.): 1993, *Tasks in a Pedagogical Context Integrating Theory and Practice*, Multilingual Matters, Clevedon, England.
Gass, S. & Schachter, J.: 1994, *Second Language Acquisition Research: Theoretical and Methodological Issues*, Lawrence Erlbaum Associates, Inc., Hillsdale, NJ.
Hakuta, K.: 1976, 'A case study of a Japanese child learning English as a second language', *Language Learning* 26, 321–351.
Hatch, E.: 1978, 'Discourse analysis and second language acquisition', in E. Hatch (ed.), *Second Language Acquisition: A Book of Readings*, Newbury House, Rowley, MA, 401–435.

Hatch, E. & Farhady, H.: 1982, *Research Design and Statistics for Applied Linguistics*, Newbury House, Rowley, MA.

Hatch, E. & Lazaraton, A.: 1991, *The Research Manual: Design and Statistics for Applied Linguistics*, Newbury House/Harper Collins, New York.

Huebner, T.: 1983, *A Longitudinal Analysis of the Acquisition of English*, Karoma Publishers, Ann Arbor, MI.

Hulstijn, J.H. & DeKeyser, R.M.: 1997, 'Testing SLA theory in the research lab', *Studies in Second Language Acquisition 19, Special Issue*.

Johnson, D.: 1992, *Approaches to Research in Second Language Learning*, Longman, New York.

Krashen, S.: 1977. 'Some issues relating to the monitor model', in H. Brown, D. Yorio & R. Crymes (eds.), *On TESOL '77: Teaching and Learning English as a Second Language: Trends in Research and Practice*, TESOL, Washington, DC, 144–158.

Larsen-Freeman, D.: 1975, 'The acquisition of grammatical morphemes by adult ESL students', *TESOL Quarterly* 9, 409–420.

Larsen-Freeman, D. & Long, M.: 1991, *Second Language Research*, Longman, New York.

Leopold, W.F.: 1939, 1947, 1949, *Speech Development of a Bilingual Child: A Linguist's Record*. Vol. 1, *Vocabulary Growth in the First Two Years*. Vol. 2, *Sound Learning in the First Two Years*. Vol. 3, *Grammar and General Problems in the First Two Years*. Vol. 4, *Diary from Age 2*, Northwestern University Press, Evanston, Ill.

Levin, L.: 1972, *Comparative Studies in Foreign Language Teaching*, Almqvist and Wiksell, Stockholm.

Lightbown, P. & Spada, N.: 1993, *How Languages Are Learned*, Oxford University Press, Oxford.

Long, M.: 1983, 'Linguistic and conversational adjustments to non-native speakers', *Studies in Second Language Acquisition* 5, 177–194.

Long, M.: 1991, 'The least a theory of second language acquisition needs to explain', *TESOL Quarterly* 24, 649–666.

Long, M.: 1996, 'The role of the linguistic environment in second language acquisition', in W.C. Ritchie & T. Bhatia (eds.), *Handbook of Language Acquisition*. Volume 2, *Second Language Acquisition*, Academic Press, New York, 413–468.

Meisel, J., Clahsen, H. & Pienemann, M.: 1981, 'On determining developmental stages in natural second language acquisition', *Studies in Second Language Acquisition* 3, 109–135.

Nunan, D.: 1992, *Research Methods in Language Learning*, Cambridge University Press, Cambridge.

Pica, T., Kanagy, R. & Falodun, J.: 1993, 'Choosing and using communication tasks for second language research and instruction', in S. Gass & G. Crookes (eds.), *Tasks and Language Learning: Integrating Theory and Practice*, Multilingual Matters, London, 9–34.

Pica, T.: 1994, 'Research on negotiation: What does it reveal about second-language learning conditions, processes, and outcomes?', *Language Learning* 44, 493–527.

Pienemann, M.: 1984, 'Psychological constraints on the teachability of languages', *Studies in Second Language Acquisition* 6, 186–214.

Pienemann, M., Jansen, L., Johnston, J., Patten, R. & Sipkes, F.: 1991, 'COALA: Computer-aided linguistic analysis', ms, *Language Analysis Research Center*, Sydney University, Sydney, Australia.

Ravem, R.: 1968, 'Language acquisition in a second language environment', *IRAL* 6, 175–185.

Richards, J.(ed.): 1974, *Error Analysis*, Longman, London.

Sato, C.: 1986, 'Conversation and second language development: Rethinking the connection', in R.R. Day (ed.), *Talking to Learn: Conversation in Second Language Acquisition*, Newbury House, Rowley, MA, 23–95.

Schmidt, R.W. & Frota, S.: 1986, 'Developing basic conversational ability in a second language: A case study of an adult learner of Portuguese', in R.R. Day (ed.), *Talking to Learn: Conversation in Second Language Acquisition*, Newbury House, Rowley, MA, 237–326.

Selinker, L.: 1972, 'Interlanguage', *IRAL* 10, 219–231.

Spada, N.: 1987, 'Relationship between instructional differences and learning outcomes: A process-product study of communicative language teaching', *Applied Linguistics* 8, 137–161.

Stockwell, R., Bowen, J. & Martin, J. (eds.): 1965, *The Grammatical Structures of English and Spanish*, University of Chicago Press, Chicago.

Tollefson, J.: 1995, *Power and Inequality in Language Education*, Cambridge University Press, Cambridge, England.

Van Lier, L.: 1992, 'Not the nine o'clock linguistics class: Investigating contingency grammar', *Language Awareness* 1(2), 91–108.

Watson-Gegeo, K.: 1988, 'Ethnography in ESL: Defining the essentials', *TESOL Quarterly* 22, 575–592.

White, L.: 1987, 'Markedness and second language acquisition: The question of transfer', *Studies in Second Language Acquisition* 9, 261–286.

White, L.: 1991, 'Adverb placement in second language acquisition: Some effects of positive and negative evidence in the classroom', *Second Language Research* 7, 133–161.

Wolfson, N.: 1989, *Perspectives: Sociolinguistics and TESOL*, Newbury House, Harper and Row, New York.

BIRGIT HARLEY

RESEARCHING AGE IN LANGUAGE ACQUISITION AND USE

Among the many factors that researchers have examined for their relevance to language acquisition and use, age is one of the easiest to measure. Any initial impression that research on age is a cut-and-dried affair is soon dispelled, however. Despite an impressive number of studies, the role of the language learner's age has remained controversial. In part, this is due to the apparent incompatibility of findings emanating from different research approaches, but more fundamentally it is caused by the difficulty of determining what age differences really mean. Chronological age reflects life experience as well as biologically determined maturation, and in interpreting their age-related findings, researchers have continued to debate how much weight should be accorded to each. This article outlines some hypotheses that provided a major stimulus to research, describes various strategies that researchers have used to investigate age-related issues, and concludes with some thoughts on future research directions (also see the review by Singleton in Volume 4).

ORIGINS OF THE RESEARCH

Infants do not master speech all at once; they coo and babble before producing identifiable words and only later start putting words together. The idea that there are approximate age levels at which particular speech milestones normally occur is one that is rooted in the human experience. Early age in this case appears to limit what the young child can do. In contrast, it is increasing age that is commonly perceived as a limitation in second language (L2) acquisition, with children widely believed to have an advantage over older learners. In the 1950s and 60s, these ideas found expression in the neurologically based hypotheses of Penfield (e.g. Penfield & Roberts, 1959) and Lenneberg (1967), who used evidence from clinical studies of aphasia to argue that children have a remarkable capacity for language acquisition that is not shared by older learners. They observed, for example, that after damage to the speech areas of the dominant left hemisphere of the brain, children were much more likely than adults to regain speech, and they reasoned that a turning point between child and adult language capabilities comes with the completion of lateralization of speech function to the left hemisphere.

N.H. Hornberger and D. Corson (eds), Encyclopedia of Language and Education,
Volume 8: Research Methods in Language and Education, 101–109.
© *1997 Kluwer Academic Publishers. Printed in the Netherlands.*

Penfield argued that brain plasticity up to about age 10 to 12 makes it possible for children to learn two or three languages as easily as one. This view was educationally influential, encouraging the introduction of foreign language instruction in elementary schools and the initiation in his home city, Montreal, of early French immersion for English-speaking children. Lenneberg's more closely argued 'critical period hypothesis', emphasizing an innately preprogrammed language acquisition mechanism, had a greater impact on language acquisition theory. A critical period for language acquisition, according to Lenneberg, begins between the second and third year of life with a gradual unfolding of innate capacities on a language-specific maturational schedule, and ends around puberty with a rapid decline in language learning ability as lateralization for language is completed. On L2 learning, he observed, adults *can* learn to communicate in a new language because the cerebral matrix for language skills has been established in childhood, but after puberty there is a rapid increase in language learning blocks and adults are obliged to learn languages 'through a conscious and labored effort' (1967, p. 176). Although the neurological arguments given for a sharp decline in language acquisition ability around puberty did not stand up to subsequent scrutiny, Lenneberg's critical period hypothesis has continued to this day to attract considerable attention from researchers.

RESEARCH APPROACHES

Identifying the Timing of Milestones in First Language (L1) Acquisition

If language acquisition proceeds according to a preprogrammed, language-specific timetable, one would expect to find a similar timing of speech milestones across children, little influenced by variation in environmental conditions. Milestones such as the emergence of single words around age one and two-word utterances around age two across a wide variety of languages and environmental circumstances are indeed regularly cited as support for an innate basis for language learning (e.g. Gleitman, 1988). According to Gleitman, any differences in children's final attainment 'pale into insignificance when compared with the samenesses among children' (p. 161). Over a century of observational studies of early child language provide the major source of relevant data. In a synthesis of findings from longitudinal research, Singleton (1989) concluded that there is 'a stable sequence of stages, with each of which it is apparently possible to associate a normative age-range' (p. 14).

Age 'norms' do not indicate lack of variation, however. In a large-scale longitudinal study of English L1 development, involving 125 preschool children each recorded at 3-monthly intervals over 3 $\frac{1}{2}$ years, Wells (1985) identified the ages at which different interpersonal functions, sentence meaning relations, and grammatical features emerged in spontaneous speech. From this fine-grained analysis, he derived a 10-level scale of language development that showed substantial differences in the ages at which individual children reached specific levels (especially the higher levels), although the route of acquisition was broadly similar for all. In interpreting the variation in rate of development found, Wells pointed to an interaction between maturational and environmental factors, including children's individual attributes and the quality and quantity of their conversational experience with adults. Variation in rate of development is also revealed by research that uses a crosslinguistic approach to the study of L1 acquisition. A pioneer in this field, Slobin (e.g. 1982) demonstrated through test data obtained from matched samples of children in four countries that the age at which specific linguistic subsystems are acquired varies according to the particular L1 to which children are exposed. Exposure to Turkish L1, for example, makes for earlier acquisition of inflections than in English, Italian, or Serbo-Croatian.

Alongside such studies of children's acquisition of various linguistic subsystems, research on speech perception has provided a new perspective on the question of when language acquisition begins. In ingenious experiments that began in the 1970s, researchers have determined that infants are sensitive to phonetic distinctions long before they can speak, and even within a few weeks of birth. Experiments have involved, for example, observing changes in infants' sucking speed or their head turning behaviour as they react to changes in recorded syllables. Although the human infant's initial ability to discriminate speech sounds appears to be shared by other species, 6–8 month old infants have been shown to attend specifically to phonetic category boundaries and not just to acoustic changes in speech stimuli (Werker & Lalonde, 1988). Linguistically relevant behaviour is thus evident at a much earlier age than Lenneberg proposed, and maybe even at birth, raising the possibility that there is no unique timing to the onset of language as the critical period hypothesis would claim. In keeping with Lenneberg's nativist perspective on language acquisition, however, such experiments have demonstrated that infants are sensitive to phonetic distinctions that are not present in the language of their environment, implying that at least this aspect of language ability is innate. By 10–12 months of age, as infants begin establishing an L1 sound system, this sensitivity wanes (Werker & Tees, 1984), suggesting that language experience also plays an important part in age-related changes.

Assessing Outcomes of Language Acquisition at Different Onset Ages

Much research effort has been devoted to investigation of Penfield's and Lenneberg's claim that children have an advantage over older learners in language acquisition. Second language learners have most often been the sample in such studies, both because of the relevance of this age question for educational policy and, of course, because the starting age for L1 acquisition is under normal circumstances in infancy for all children.

Comparing Different Starting Ages for L2 Classroom Instruction. The 1960s and 70s saw a spate of studies in the United States, Britain, and Europe designed to evaluate the effectiveness of an early introduction to foreign language instruction. These large-scale educational evaluations compared the achievement of experimental groups of students with that of comparison groups whose instruction began at an older age. Overall, they lent little support to an early start. A classic example is a longitudinal study conducted in Britain by Burstall, Jamieson, Cohen & Hargreaves (1974). In this study involving thousands of children, the L2 achievement of students beginning French instruction at age eight was compared with that of students in the traditional French program beginning at age 11. After the same amount of instruction (three years), L2 test results mostly favoured the older learners in the traditional program, although the younger students did better in speaking. When all were assessed again at age 16, the earlier start with three additional years of instruction showed a small longterm advantage on only one of four tests, namely listening comprehension.

Burstall et al. interpreted their results as counter-evidence to the critical period hypothesis, arguing that the relative cognitive maturity of older learners makes for more efficient second language learning. This interpretation was soon challenged on the grounds that there were equally valid environmental reasons for the results obtained (Stern, 1976). For example, experimental and comparison students were often mixed in the same classes at the secondary level, an administrative decision that somewhat compromised the experimental research design. However, a rate-of-acquisition advantage for more mature older learners has been a consistent finding across various classroom (and non-classroom) environments, particularly on measures of syntax and morphology (Krashen, Long & Scarcella, 1979) and even when testing conditions in the shape of oral conversations are geared to children (Harley, 1986). This older-age advantage has remained an awkward fact to reconcile with the notion of a critical period for L2 acquisition. Also beyond the ability of the critical period hypothesis to explain is that age-related differences emerge among adults as well. Seright (1985), for example, tested adult French speakers' aural comprehension of English after 300 hours of L2 instruction and found that when she divided them into two age groups, younger adults (aged 17–24) obtained significantly higher scores than older ones (aged 25–41). This study, in keeping with more recent ones comparing the outcomes of different adult arrival ages in a natural L2 environment (e.g. Birdsong, 1992; Scott, 1994), indicates a need for greater research attention on the role of age in adult L2 acquisition (see also Singleton, 1989).

Relating Age of Arrival to L2 Success in a Natural Environment. One possibility proposed by Cummins (1981), is that the cognitive advantage for older school-aged learners observed by Burstall et al. applies more specifically to cognitive-academic aspects of L2 such as morphology, syntax, and literacy-related skills. Using native-speaker grade norms as the criterion, Cummins established that age of arrival in Canada made little difference to the length of time – five years on average – that it took minority language students to reach grade norms on standardized tests of academic skills in English. Since grade norms are naturally higher for older students, they must in fact have learned more than the younger ones in absolute terms. Such norm-oriented research serves to alert educators to the danger of assuming that young minority students who may achieve basic conversational L2 fluency within two years are already performing at full potential in their academic L2 skills.

More in keeping with the notion of a childhood advantage in L2 acquisition have been studies designed to assess ultimate L2 attainment after longterm residence in the L2 environment. In pronunciation, for example, numerous correlational studies have shown a strong linear relationship between arrival age and ultimate success when length of residence is controlled. The earlier the age of arrival, the more likely that an individual will be rated as a native (e.g. Oyama, 1976) or near-native (e.g. Thompson, 1991) speaker of the L2. These high ratings are typical of those arriving before age 7; it is a rare adult learner that achieves a near-native rating. A similar correlational approach has been taken in studies of the acquisition of morphology and syntax. Johnson & Newport (1989), for example, tested longterm US residents who had arrived at different ages on an oral grammaticality judgment task in English; they found a high negative correlation of -0.77 between age of arrival and test scores. Only those who had arrived before age 7 achieved a native level of performance. By dividing the sample into two age-of-arrival groups (ages 3–15 versus 17–39), Johnson & Newport uncovered a clear pattern of declining scores for arrival ages up to 15 but no relationship between arrival age and scores in the 17–39 group. This 'turning point' at age 15 was interpreted as support for the close of a critical period at puberty. A reanalysis by Bialystok & Hakuta (1994), however, showed that dividing the sample at arrival-age 20 instead of 15 produced exactly the same pattern of decline in the younger age-of-arrival group and also revealed a modest pattern of decline with age among the adult arrivals. This reanalysis counters the claim for a turning point at puberty, but reaffirms the more general relationship between declining L2 scores and older arrival ages in adults as well as children.

Linguistic theory has been influential in determining what L2 features have been chosen as the focus of more recent research on ultimate attainment. For example, in another test of the critical period hypothesis, Johnson & Newport (1991) gave a more difficult grammaticality judgment task in English focused on a principle of Universal Grammar that linguists had argued is part of the infant's innate endowment. The question was whether this principle would still be available to later arriving L2 learners when it was not manifested in their L1 (Chinese in this case). None of the adults in this study, not even those who had arrived in the US before age 7, achieved a native level of performance, but the familiar pattern of declining performance by later arrivals emerged. If, as Long (1990) has argued, complete native-like acquisition of the L2 is the mark of success for a critical period learner, then this study, along with Thompson's on L2 pronunciation, casts doubt on the relevance of the critical period concept for L2 acquisition. According to Cook (1992), however, this monolingual standard is inappropriate to deal with the 'multicompetence' of the bilingual, whose knowledge of two languages is not the same as that of a monolingual in either language. If multicompetence is the criterion for success, then high L2 attainment by young immigrants who lose their L1 in the process (e.g. Wong Fillmore, 1991) is no cause for celebration. The relevant question to ask becomes instead: At what age and under what conditions is the highest level of multicompetence achieved? To date, the age-related research has not been designed to tackle this question.

Investigating Late Acquisition of L1. The question of ultimate attainment in L1 by learners of different onset ages for acquisition has been more difficult to investigate than in L2. For many years, the study of this phenomenon was limited to isolated cases of severe child abuse or feral children, where findings of postpubertal inability to acquire full L1 competence could well have been due to a variety of causes beyond the late start itself. More recently, however, the comparative study of groups of congenitally deaf adults who were first exposed to American Sign Language (ASL) at different ages has provided more solid evidence of age-related effects. As in the L2 domain, Newport (1990) and Mayberry & Eichen (1991) found that age of initial exposure to ASL as a first full language of communication was predictive of ultimate attainment in adulthood: longterm adult users first exposed to ASL at ages 4–6 did not perform as well on ASL tests as those whose exposure began in infancy, and increasing age of onset was associated with declining accuracy. Evidence that prior language experience, and not maturation alone, has a role to play comes from Mayberry (1993), whose study included a group of adults who had become deaf between age 9 and 15. The ultimate attainment of this group of L2 learners of ASL was better on some aspects of an elicited imitation task in ASL than that of a group who had begun at the same age to learn ASL as their first full language.

Examining the Acquisitional Capacities of Adults. Rather than comparing older and younger onset ages, some researchers have turned to closer investigation of adult language acquisition capacities. Under facilitative laboratory conditions, when provided with instruction, and not required to simultaneously process meaning, at least some adults are able to discriminate non-native phonetic contrasts (e.g. Logan, Lively & Pisoni, 1991) or produce native-like L2 pronunciation (Neufeld, 1977). Also, when Birdsong (1992) tested 20 highly proficient French L2 speakers who had arrived in France at various adult ages, he found 15 whose judgments of the grammaticality of written French sentences were comparable to those of native speakers. These studies suggest that postpubertal language acquisition capabilities remain intact, although it is not clear that adults are equally capable of nativelike spontaneous L2 use. Such studies can be seen as counterevidence to the critical period hypothesis, but on the other hand if talented adult L2 learners are in some way neurologically exceptional, the hypothesis could still be tenable. Several case studies of individual adult learners have examined this issue and, based on test data and personal histories, have suggested tentative links between language talent and an unusual neuropsychological profile (e.g. Schneiderman & Desmarais, 1988; Ioup, Boustagui, Tigi & Moselle, 1994).

Searching for Age-related Differences in Acquisition Processes

Over the years, researchers have looked, mostly in vain, for evidence that the L2 acquisition process is different in children and older learners as Lenneberg appeared to suggest. Studies of L2 error patterns, developmental sequences, and sentence processing strategies have failed to reveal any substantial age-related differences. Recently, however, Harley & Hart (in press) investigated the relationship between aspects of language aptitude and L2 proficiency among high school students who had entered French immersion programs at different ages (in grade 1 or 7). Regression analysis showed that for the early immersion students, a memory measure predicted scores on several L2 tests, while for the late immersion students it was inductive language learning ability that was predictive of L2 scores. This study suggests in line with Lenneberg's hypothesis that later learners, in a classroom context at least, tend to employ different, more analytical abilities in acquiring L2 than earlier learners do.

PROBLEMS AND PROSPECTS

No overarching theory of the role of age in language acquisition and use currently exists that can account for the full range of findings summarized above. Despite the wide variety of research approaches brought to bear, the critical period hypothesis that Lenneberg proposed with its language-specific onset and terminus timing has received little firm support from subsequent research. In a more flexible form, however, the critical period concept may still have considerable relevance in language acquisition research, particularly if due attention is given to the potential contribution of individual differences and the interaction of maturational and environmental factors in age-related changes. It is no longer enough simply to establish that age-related differences exist; more studies are needed that probe specific reasons for any differences found. As is evident from speech perception research and from Mayberry's (1993) study of the L1 and L2 acquisition of ASL, for example, language experience is one important factor that cannot be ignored. Not just L1 background, but amount and quality of contact with native speakers, may affect age-related results (e.g. Scott, 1994). Ultimate L2 attainment studies will also need to embrace broader samples of adults, beyond those with university educations who may not be equally representative of their different age-of-onset groups. Perhaps most important from an educational perspective is the need for research designed to gain further understanding of age-related differences in the development of 'multicompetent' individuals.

Ontario Institute for Studies in Education,
University of Toronto, Canada

REFERENCES

Bialystok, E. & Hakuta, K.: 1994, *In Other Words: The Science and Psychology of Second-Language Acquisition*, Basic Books, New York.
Birdsong, D.: 1992, 'Ultimate attainment in second language acquisition', *Language* 68, 706–755.
Burstall, C., Jamieson, M., Cohen, S. & Hargreaves, M.: 1974, *Primary French in the Balance*, National Foundation for Educational Research, Slough.
Cook, V.: 1992, 'Evidence for multicompetence', *Language Learning* 42, 557–591.
Cummins, J.: 1981, 'Age on arrival and immigrant second language learning in Canada: A reassessment', *Applied Linguistics* 11, 132–149.
Gleitman, L.R.: 1988, 'Biological dispositions to learn language', in M.B. Franklin & S.S. Barten (eds.), *Child Language: A Reader*, Oxford University Press, New York, 158–175.
Harley, B.: 1986, *Age in Second Language Acquisition*, Multilingual Matters, Clevedon, Avon.
Harley, B. & Hart, D.: In press, 'Language aptitude and second language proficiency in classroom learners of different starting ages', *Studies in Second Language Acquisition*.
Ioup, G., Boustagui, E., Tigi, M.E. & Moselle, M.: 1994, 'Reexamining the critical period hypothesis: A case study of successful adult SLA in a naturalistic environment', *Studies in Second Language Acquisition* 16, 73–98.
Johnson, J.S. & Newport, E.L.: 1989, 'Critical period effects in second language learning: The influence of maturational state on the acquisition of English as a second language', *Cognitive Psychology* 21, 60–99.

Johnson, J.S. & Newport, E.L.: 1991, 'Critical period effects on universal properties of language: The use of subjacency in the acquisition of a second language', *Cognition* 39, 215–258.

Krashen, S., Long, M. & Scarcella, R.: 1979, 'Age, rate, and eventual attainment in second language acquisition', *TESOL Quarterly* 13, 573–582.

Lenneberg, E.H.: 1967, *Biological Foundations of Language*, Wiley, New York.

Logan, J.S., Lively, S.E. & Pisoni, D.B.: 1991, 'Training Japanese listeners to identify /r/ and /l/: A first report', *Journal of the Acoustical Society of America* 89, 874–886.

Long, M.H.: 1990, 'Maturational constraints on language development', *Studies in Second Language Acquisition* 12, 251–285.

Mayberry, R.I.: 1993, 'First-language acquisition after childhood differs from second-language acquisition: The case of American sign language', *Journal of Speech and Hearing Research* 36, 1258–1270.

Mayberry, R.I. & Eichen, E.B.: 1991, 'The long-lasting advantage of learning sign language in childhood: Another look at the critical period for language acquisition', *Journal of Memory and Language* 30, 486–512.

Neufeld, G.: 1977, 'Language learning ability in adults: A study of the acquisition of prosodic and articulatory features', *Working Papers on Bilingualism* 12, 45–60.

Newport, E.L.: 1990, 'Maturational constraints on language learning', *Cognitive Science* 14, 11–28.

Oyama, S.: 1976, 'A sensitive period for the acquisition of a nonnative phonological system', *Journal of Psycholinguistic Research* 5, 261–283.

Penfield, W. & Roberts, L.: 1959, *Speech and Brain Mechanisms*, Princeton University Press, Princeton NJ.

Schneiderman, E.I. & Desmarais, C.: 1988, 'A neuropsychological substrate for Talen in second-language acquisition', in L.K. Obler & D. Fein (eds.), *The Exceptional Brain: Neuropsychology of Talent and Special Abilities*, Guilford Press, New York, 103–126.

Scott, M.L.: 1994, 'Auditory memory and perception in younger and older adult second language learners,' *Studies in Second Language Acquisition* 16, 263–281.

Seright, L.: 1985, 'Age and aural comprehension achievement in francophone adults learning English', *TESOL Quarterly* 19, 455–473.

Singleton, D.: 1989, *Language Acquisition: The Age Factor*, Multilingual Matters, Clevedon, Avon.

Slobin, D.I.: 1982, 'Universal and particular in the acquisition of language', in E. Wanner & L.R. Gleitman (eds.), *Language Acquisition: The State of the Art*, Cambridge University Press, Cambridge, 128–170.

Stern, H.H.: 1976, 'Optimal age: Myth or reality?', *Canadian Modern Language Review* 32, 283–294.

Thompson, I.: 1991, 'Foreign accents revisited: The English pronunciation of Russian immigrants', *Language Learning* 41, 177–204.

Wells, G.: 1985, *Language Development in the Pre-school Years*, Cambridge University Press, Cambridge.

Werker, J.K. & Lalonde, C.E.: 1988, 'Cross-language speech perception: Initial capabilities and developmental change', *Developmental Psychology* 24, 672–683.

Werker, J.K. & Tees, R.C.: 1984, 'Cross-language speech perception: Evidence for perceptual reorganization during the first year of life', *Infant Behavior and Development* 7, 49–63.

Wong Fillmore, L.: 1991, 'When learning a second language means losing the first', *Early Childhood Research Quarterly* 6, 323–346.

JOHN BAUGH

RESEARCHING RACE AND SOCIAL CLASS IN LANGUAGE ACQUISITION AND USE

A combination of interdisciplinary research traditions intersect in the present review. Language scholars who study race and social class have been intellectually cut off from most linguistic studies of language acquisition, but the relationship between these topics is made explicit in this review. The discussion begins with a brief survey of early research in the respective fields, and readers should likewise consult other reviews within this volume regarding related topics (see, for example, reviews by Chen, Doğançsy-Aktuna, Bortoni-Ricardo, Goldstein, May and Norton).

Preliminary discussion lays the foundation to contemplate prospects for contemporary integration of research and analyses, and to consider their intellectual and social utility. Many scholars have produced important research related to this topic, which is surveyed under the heading of 'promising research trends.' A brief summation concludes these remarks immediately after a discussion of future challenges facing integrated research on topics related to language acquisition in socially stratified speech communities that also have a history of racism.

EARLY RESEARCH DEVELOPMENT

Sapir (1921) was among the first to draw specific attention to the relationship between language and race, and the well known Sapir-Whorf hypothesis (Sapir, 1949) that introduced the concepts of "linguistic determinism" and "linguistic relativity" was indirectly related to race; that is, in the sense that different speech communities were often composed of different racial groups. Boas (1940), Kroeber (1948), and Hymes (1964) embody the anthropological linguistic tradition where studies of language occur within the ethnographic context of speakers' lives, and since much of that work focused on language in tribal settings, social stratification within the speech community was rarely paramount.

French dialectologists, including Gauchat (1905), Meilliet (1921), and Martinet (1955), gave rise to early sociolinguistic work in the United States, as reflected in Weinreich's (1953) *Languages in Contact*, and Labov's (1966) study of the social stratification of English in New York City. Since

N.H. Hornberger and D. Corson (eds), Encyclopedia of Language and Education,
Volume 8: Research Methods in Language and Education, 111–121.
© *1997 Kluwer Academic Publishers. Printed in the Netherlands.*

then there have been numerous language studies that relate to social class (and caste) throughout the world, and Gumperz' (1971) studies of linguistic diversity in India are illustrative of interdisciplinary language studies that shed light on complex speech communities. Dialectologists have made us keenly aware of regional differences in speech (Kurath, 1949; McDavid; 1979; Preston, 1993), and sociolinguists have increased understanding of racial divisions within speech communities (Labov et al., 1968; Baugh, 1983; Edwards, 1991), but language acquisition, and education, among disenfranchised racial minorities remains a neglected topic.

Linguistic analyses of child language development and first language acquisition began to mature in the wake of the Chomskian revolution when Skinner's reinforcement theory of child language development was rebuffed. Briefly, Skinner (1969) hypothesized that children learned to speak based on positive reinforcement from older speakers with whom they interacted. We now know that Skinner's theory was inadequate and simplistic, and Chomsky (1964) emphatically argued that all normal children have an innate capacity to learn language without the aid of formal instruction. He also pointed out severe limitations in Skinner's theory, while at the same time laying the foundation for the emergence of generative grammar that he inherited from his mentor (Harris, 1951). Drawing largely from the theoretical foundations and advances embodied in Chomsky's research, Slobin (1967), Gleitman & Gleitman (1971), Clark (1993), and many others have developed research on universal aspects of child language acquisition, but much of that work is devoid of racial or social demarcation; that is, in an effort to confirm general principles of child language development, pioneering studies have not focused on the race or social class of children.

Bickerton's (1981) *Roots of Language* presents an interesting hypothesis that has indirect racial and social implications, because he draws parallels between language development in the child, and new language developments that grow from pidginization and creolization processes. According to Bickerton, the birth of a new language – resulting from contact derived from two or more parent languages – gives rise to parallel processes, particularly with respect to simple-to-complex stages of development. Again, matters of race and class are not explicit in Bickerton's theory, but most pidgins and creoles have been created when people from an established (isolated?) speech community have been contacted (and subordinated?) by members from another (dominant?) speech community. The resulting contact language is a newly formed pidgin, and when children acquire that pidgin as their mother tongue it is transformed into a creole (see the reviews by Corson on 'non-standard varieties' in Volumes 1 & 6). It is this creolization process that demands greater linguistic complexity, leading to innovations that Bickerton claims are similar to the increasing complexity of language development by individual children as they mature and become competent users of their native language(s).

CONTEMPORARY RESEARCH ISSUES

The Ebonics controversy, which emerged in Oakland, California, represents an example of where the legacy of racial bigotry, language acquisition, and educational policies coincide. Oakland Educators were seeking ways to teach standard American English to African American students who were enrolled in their school district. Under the consultation of Afrocentric scholars, who were not linguists, they passed a controversial resolution claiming that Ebonics "is not a black dialect or any other dialect of English." They later revised this statement, claiming that Ebonics is not merely a dialect of English.

School administrators in Oakland believed that black students enrolled in their school district acquired a language other than English, owing to the linguistic legacy of American slavery which began during the colonial era long before the United States declared its independence from England. The extreme interpretation of Ebonics; that is, as a language other than English, is based on the belief that African Americans have lived in racial isolation from English and the majority of white Americans who are English speaking, but many Black Americans were critical – if not hostile – to such an interpretation of their linguistic heritage.

The efforts by the Oakland School board to establish educational programs for their black students are similar to other efforts by applied linguists elsewhere in the world who coordinate explicit language planning and related policies.

Within the United States, however, language policies are somewhat ad hoc, which provided a sociolinguistic atmosphere that encouraged the extreme interpretations of Ebonics that were so strongly embraced in Oakland, but which were thoroughly rejected elsewhere. Part of the explanation for these capricious trends is the fact that the United States is a nation comprised of states that have differing language policies, and those policies change from time-to-time based on a combination of immigration trends, political fluctuations, differential educational opportunities and alternating economic circumstances (see the reviews by Ricento in Volume 1, and by Christian in Volume 4).

Many European nations, for example, are confronted with the fact that social and political changes in eastern Europe have had direct economic, educational, political, and linguistic consequences in western Europe, and various nations have reacted differently to the waves of immigrants that have either entered or vacated countries where matters of language and citizenship have become more pronounced. For linguists these trends are more than the bases of changing language demographics, they reflect the potentially important role that we must play in helping to formulate policies that can bolster prospects for improved communication and enhanced social harmony. It is toward this end that matters of child language acquisition and education in racially divided societies come, once again, to the fore.

Europeans have confronted racial barriers as part of these immigration trends, much of it owing to economic pressures and immigration from former colonies where European languages were imposed. Indian immigrants to England, or Algerian immigrants in France, or Turkish workers in Germany, all face racial problems that were unknown prior to the influx of nonwhite immigrants. The plight of Gypsies in many European countries reflect racial problems that are, in many ways, similar to those of African Americans in the U.S. Gypsies are often denied access to education, wealth, and positions of political influence; they often live in inferior housing, and when they do become more successful it often takes place in the fields of entertainment or through illicit economic activities. There are linguistic consequences to this trend (see the review by Skutnabb Kangas in Volume 1).

Conflicts between Arabs and Jews in the Middle East, and racial barriers that face Koreans who live in Japan, or Blacks who are now emerging from the overt consequences of racial apartheid in South Africa, all illustrate the fact that linguistic behavior is part of the 'racial tail' that is wagged by the body of the larger 'racist dog' in nations and communities where unequal opportunities are accentuated by race. Bortoni's (1985) studies of native (i.e. indigenous) populations in Brazil, as they migrate to the cities, is yet another example of how race and linguistic experience are intricately intertwined (see the review by Bortoni-Ricardo in this volume).

Brief global comparisons of Black English, that is, prior to the Ebonics controversy in the United States, serve to illustrate these research and racially charged social trends. Specifically, the birth and evolution of Black English in the Caribbean, England, South Africa, and the United States allow us to consider the sociology of language acquisition, as well as related educational implications and policies. Ironically, the original definition of Ebonics, as coined by Robert Williams (1975) includes this international orientation; that is, rather than a linguistic variety that is exclusive to the United States:

Ebonics may be defined as the linguistic and paralinguistic features which on a concentric continuum represents the communicative competence of the West African, Caribbean, and United States slave descendant of African origin. (Williams 1975, vi)

Black English research is also a good point of intellectual departure since many of Labov's early formulations for general sociolinguistic theory draw directly upon Black English data, albeit data drawn exclusively from American Blacks.

How is it that children of African descent have come to learn English, either as a first or second language, or through pidginization and creolization? The answers to these questions can be captured in a single word; "colonialism." The linguistic and educational consequences of colonialism, racism, and slavery still linger, and point to an observation, described by Baugh (1987), that racial groups and linguistic groups are not coincidental. England's conquests in Africa, Asia, India, and elsewhere coincided with a corresponding expansion of the English language. The conquests associated with the growth of the former British empire did not reflect enlightened language policies; that is, the indigenous languages were not nurtured under British rule, nor were they supported under contemporaneous colonial dominations by France, Portugal, or Spain.

The African slave trade fostered states of social inequality that are often difficult to comprehend. The overt subjugation of enslaved and colonized Africans gave rise to a host of religious, educational, and linguistic policies that diminished the value of African culture in favor of Britain's former military might. Slavery, by definition, does not foster humanitarian equality, and the involuntary transport of enslaved Africans throughout north and south America coincided with corresponding linguistic transformations, as European languages came to dominate and replace indigenous languages in Africa too (see the review by Egbo [on literacy in sub-equatorial Africa] in Volume 2). It is the combined linguistic legacy of colonization and the subjugation of people of African descent that inspired the coinage of the term Ebonics in the first place; however, its current controversial status in America and elsewhere grows directly from the political circumstances by which the term has been injected into the global lexicon.

Enslaved Africans in the United States and the Caribbean were initially denied access to education and literacy, which had direct consequences for their language acquisition. White immigrants to the US were typically provided access to public education, and it usually took three generations for the transition from the language of the old country to native acquisition of American English. Slaves, by the sharpest of contrasts, were denied access to literacy by law. Slaves were not allowed to attend school, nor did they have access to others who spoke their mother tongue. Slave traders engaged in the practice of isolating slaves upon capture, thereby limiting the prospect of revolts or other forms of insurrection. The linguistic isolation was an early form of "language planning," with the death of African languages as an indirect product of attempts to restrict communication among captured slaves.

This brings us back to Bickerton (1981), and to Mufwene (1983), Holms (1984), Rickford (1985), Singler (1991), Edwards (1991), Winford (1991), and others who have studied the pidginization and creolization processes that resulted from the African slave trade. Edwards (1986) and Sutcliffe (1982) have studied the ensuing impact of Black English as it eventually came to reside in England; that is, as Blacks who lived in the Caribbean and former British colonies migrated to England in search of jobs and other educational opportunities.

The situation in South Africa is quite different from that of Black English in all of the above situations in the sense that the African population in South Africa was subordinated, but indigenous. The colonization of South Africa by Europeans from different language backgrounds did not require the importation of slaves. Whites remain the minority population in South Africa, whereas Blacks remain as minorities in England and the US (see the reviews by Smit and by Rassool in Volume 1, and by Rodseth in Volume 4).

What, then, does race have to do with the acquisition of English among people of African descent? Race was a primary factor in the subordination of Africans on their home continent and elsewhere. Uriel Weinreich once defined a standard language as the language spoken by those who control the military, and vestiges of this observation hold true for the evolution of Black English in global perspective. While it is true that some former slave descendants, like this author, have come to master standard (American or British) English, we have done so through a secondary process that is more similar to the diglossic situations first described by Ferguson.

Black English tends not to be standard English; that is, the vast majority of Blacks who acquire English – either as their first or second language – do so through a dialect that differs from the dominant dialect spoken by members of the upper classes, who are typically White. Those Blacks who master dominant English norms, in speech or writing, are rare individuals who constitute a minority group within a minority group (indeed, we are currently engaged in experiments that seek to determine the extent to which one's racial background can be (in)accurately identified based on speech alone, Baugh, 1996); and those Blacks (and other minorities) who speak in a manner that is perceived to be "White" do so based on extensive contact with Whites, and, generally, greater access to the same educational institutions that serve most White students. This trend appears to be common for both British and American standard English.

Based on these collective observations we can offer some tentative generalizations about the socially and racially divided contexts of language acquisition and use: as human language first emerged, along with distinct racial groups, we know that languages changed more rapidly than did the racial groups – or tribes within those racial groupings. But, with the advent of advanced technology, colonial conquest, and slavery history, we witnessed a gradual change where linguistic expansion consumed peoples from many different racial backgrounds.

The methodological consequences of this reality, for linguists, educators, and others who seek to study language development among racially subordinate groups, are illustrated – to a large extent – in other reviews cited herein, but the most profound methodological change lies in the fact that decontextualized experimentation on child language development may be ill suited to scholars who hope to understand child language acquisition in natural social settings, particularly if the children who are the object of inquiry reside in communities that are marginal to the dominant or prevailing linguistic and cultural norms of the corresponding society.

PROMISING RESEARCH TRENDS

Studies of language in social context (Labov, 1994; Trudgill, 1986; Milroy, 1987) offer some of the most promising research trends for those who seek to resolve real or potential conflicts in speech communities that are divided by race. Language policy research also plays an important role in this regard, because language policies have often been designed to overcome some of the linguistic barriers that result from overt or covert racist policies (Crawford, 1993). Wiley & Lukes (1996) observe two significant ideological paths that are prevalent within the U.S.: the first stresses a monolingual ideology, grounded in an immigrant paradigm that affirms the importance of English as the single most important language in a nation of multilingual immigrants, the second is marked by a standard language ideology reflected in attitudes and behaviors which are biased against creolized or – allegedly less "literate" varieties of English, such as African American English, Appalachian English, and Hawaiian creole English. There are, of course, overt racial and linguistic biases that are more pronounced in the second scenario, but both traditions are firmly entrenched.

Many nations have official languages, as well as organizations that are intended to protect and preserve the purity of those official languages; other nations may not have official policies, but the social emergence of dominant languages will be clear to anyone with knowledge of the nation or community at issue.

It is partially for this reason that readers must consider these matters in terms of specific localities. Here we concentrate on linguistic divisions by race, and related consequences for language acquisition, but other speech communities that may not be divided by race are likely to be divided along other lines, such as religious differences, or regional differences, or social differences. Fishman (1972) has been the leading figure to explore linguistic aspects of social strife, and one of the promising research trends for the future would be to combine his studies of the Sociology of Language with classical analyses of child language acquisition.

As mentioned previously, the most influential studies of child language development tend not to look at race or social class because they have been primarily interested in universal aspects of language development that are not influenced by external factors. However, children who grow up in upper class families acquire dialects that allow them more ready access to positions of social privilege, and children who are poor tend to adopt speech patterns that are not standard. Although policy studies have not focused specifically on the nature of language acquisition, their work could provide a useful point of intellectual departure for others who would like to integrate analyses that connect the sociology of language with the development of children's language. Valdes (1996) offers some ethnographic insights along these lines in *Con Respeto*, where she looks at language among Spanish speakers in the U.S. who strive to survive in communities where English is dominant. Heath's (1983) study of Blacks and Whites in North Carolina offers similar ethnographic insights regarding uses of language and literacy that differ in adjacent racially divided communities. Bortoni's (1985) study of rural Indians who migrate to urban areas in Brazil takes into account not only regional prejudice (i.e. rural versus urban), but also racial differences (i.e. Indian versus non-Indian) and class segregation.

FUTURE DIRECTIONS

The challenges that lie before scholars who are interested in this topic center on coherent integration of diverse research trends. Language acquisition research has, here-to-fore, been driven by efforts to find commonalities among all normal children, while studies of social differences in speech communities have looked at characteristics that apply to subgroups within those speech communities. Chambers (1992) is nearly alone in exploring the impact of "second dialect acquisition" which is often implied (or explicit) in many language policies throughout the world, and Hakuta (1981) draws specific attention to stereotypes and benefits of bilingual competence.

Members of racial minorities may face a combination of linguistic barriers in societies that devalue them and their relative contributions, and often linguistic differences are the object of scorn and ridicule by uninformed elites who presume that their own dialects or languages, that is, the dialects or languages of institutional influence and social power, are inherently superior to minority dialects, or languages, spoken by members of racial and cultural groups who lack social power.

Even if linguists and educators can begin to provide empirical evidence that shows the value and linguistic integrity of minority dialects and languages that are not standard, there is a greater need to educate broader segments of the population to come to accept those who may not speak employing the dominant linguistic norms. As we have seen during the Ebonics controversy, the role of educating teachers in language diversity awareness is vital to this enterprise (see the reviews by Corson and by Wallace in Volume 6).

These are political matters that tend to be beyond the influence of scholars, but the absence of integrated analyses of language acquisition in racially divided communities could delay the eventual social equality that has long been denied to members of racially subordinated groups. Providing rigorous analyses of language development in racially divided speech communities may help to bridge the existing social abyss.

This review opened with some of the classical studies of race and language by Sapir (1921), and explored global differences in research on language, language policies, and language acquisition in communities that are divided by race. As of this writing few scholars have attempted to integrate these research trends for a combination of reasons: the methods and terminology used by policy analysts, child language researchers, and sociolinguists who have studied racially divided speech communities, does not yet mesh in ways that lend to coherent integration. There is another trend that leads sociolinguists, anthropological linguists, and ethnographers of communication, to evaluate the language of mature members of a speech community; older individuals are among the most competent members of their respective speech communities, while their children have yet to master that competency.

Several alternative research perspectives have been introduced here, many of which focus on matters of race and language in one form or another. This author brings a bias to the topic however, that is, as an African American seeking to employ social science in support of greater social equity, and it is presumed that readers of this review share the same desire to find innovative means to provide improved opportunities for members of subordinated racial groups around the world.

Stanford University
USA

REFERENCES

Baugh, J.: 1983, *Black Street Speech: Its History, Structure, and Survival*, University of Texas Press, Austin.

Baugh, J.: 1987, 'Language and race: Some implications for linguistic science', in F. Newmeyer (ed.), *Linguistics: The Cambridge Survey* (Vol. 4), Cambridge University Press, Cambridge.

Baugh, J.: 1996, 'Linguistic perceptions in black and white', in E. Schneider (ed.), *Perspectives on the U.S.A.* John Benjamins, Philadelphia.

Bickerton, D.: 1981, *Roots of Language*, Karoma, Ann Arbor.

Boas, F.: 1940, *Race, Language and Culture*, Macmillan, New York.

Bortoni, S.: 1985, *The Urbanization of Rural Dialect Speakers*, Cambridge University Press, Cambridge.

Chambers, J.K., 1992, 'Dialect acquisition', *Language* 68(4), 673–705.

Chomsky, N.: 1964, *Current Issues in Linguistic Theory*, Mouton, The Hague.

Clark, E.: 1993, *The Lexicon in Acquisition*, Cambridge University Press, Cambridge.

Crawford, J.: 1993, *Hold Your Tongue*, Addison-Wesley, Reading, MA.

Edwards, V.: 1986, *Language in a Black Community*, Multilingual Matters, Ltd., Clevedon.

Edwards, W.: 1991, *Verb Phrase Patterns in Black English and Creole*, Wayne State University Press, Detroit.

Fishman, J.: 1972, *Readings in the Sociology of Language*, Mouton, The Hague.

Fishman, J., Ferguson, C.A. & Das Gupta, J. (eds.): 1968, *Language Problems of Developing Nations*, Wiley, New York.

Gauchat, L.: 1905, 'L'unite phonetique dans le patois d'une commune', *Aus Romanischen Sprachen und Literaturen: Festschrift Heinrich Morf*, 175–232.

Gleitman, L. & Gleitman, H.: 1971, *Phrase and Paraphrase*, Norton, New York.

Gumperz, J.J.: 1971, *Language in Social Groups*, Stanford University Press, Stanford.

Hakuta, K.: 1981, *Mirror of Language*, Basic Books, New York.

Harris, Z.: 1951, *Methods in Structural Linguistics*, University of Chicago Press, Chicago.

Heath, S.B.: 1983, *Ways with Words*, Cambridge University Press, Cambridge.

Holms, J.: 1984, 'Variablity of the copula in Black English and its creole kin', *American Speech* 59(4), 291–309.

Hymes, D.: 1964, *Language in Culture and Society*, Harper and Row, New York.

Kroeber, A.L.: 1948, *Anthropology: Culture, Patterns, and Process*, Harcourt, Brace and World, New York.

Kurath, H.: 1949, *A Word Geography of the Eastern United States*, University of Michigan Press, Ann Arbor.

Labov, W.: 1966, *The Social Stratification of English in New York City*, Center for Applied Linguistics, Washington, DC.

Labov, W. et al.: 1968, *A Study of the Non-Standard English of Negro and Puerto Rican Speakers in New York City*. Cooperative Research Project No. 3288, Columbia University, New York.

Labov, W.: 1994, *Principles of Linguistic Change*, Blackwell, Oxford.

Martinet, A.: 1955, *Economie des changements phonetiques Francke*, Berne.

McDavid, R.: 1979, *Dialects in Culture*, University of Alabama Press, University.

Meillet, A.: 1921, *Linguistique historique et linguistique generale*, La Societe Linguistique de Paris, Paris.

Milroy, L.: 1987, *Observing and Analyzing Natural Language, Blackwell*, Oxford.

Mufwene, S.: 1983, 'Observations on time reference in Jamaican and Guyanese creoles', *English World-Wide* 4(2), 199–229.

Preston, D.: 1993, *American Dialect Research*, John Benjamins, Amsterdam.

Rickford, J.: 1985, 'Ethnicity as a sociolinguistic boundary', *American Speech* 60(2): 99–125.

Sapir, E.: 1921, *Language*, Harcourt, Brace and Company, New York.

Sapir, E.: 1949, *Culture, Language, and Personality*, University of California Press, Berkeley.

Singler, J.: 1991, 'Coula variation in Liberian Settler English and American Black English', in W.F. Edwards & D. Winford (eds)., *Verb Phrase Patterns in Black English and Creole*, Wayne State University Press, Detroit, 129–164.

Skinner, B.F.: 1969, *Contingencies of Reinforcement*, Appleton-Century-Crofts, New York.

Slobin, D.: 1967, *A Field Manual for Cross-Cultural Study of the Acquisition of Communicative Competence*, University of California, Berkeley.

Sutcliffe, D.E. (ed.): 1982, *British Black English*, Blackwell, Oxford.

Trudgill, P.: 1986, *Dialects in Contact*, Blackwell, Oxford.

Valdes, G.: 1996, *Con Respeto*, Teachers College Press, New York.

Weinreich, U.: 1953, *Languages in Contact*, Mouton, The Hague.

Wiley, T.G. & Lukes, M.: 1996, 'English-only and standard English ideologies in ths U.S.', *TESOL Quarterly* 30(3), 511–535.

Williams, R.: 1975, *Ebonics: The True Language of Black Folks*, Robert L. Williams and
Associates, St. Louis.
Winford, D.: 1991, 'Another look at the copula in Black English and Caribbean Creoles',
American Speech 67, 21–60.

Section 3

Language, Culture, and Education:
Recent Advances in Approaches, Methods, and Topics

IFFAT FARAH

ETHNOGRAPHY OF COMMUNICATION

The ethnography of communication is an approach to language research which has its origin in the development of a view in anthropology that culture to a large extent is expressed through language and of the view in linguistics that language is a system of cultural behaviors (Hymes, 1974; Geertz, 1973; Hymes, 1968). Hymes argued that the study of language must concern itself with describing and analyzing the ability of the native speakers to use language for communication in real situations (communicative competence) rather than limiting itself to describing the potential ability of the ideal speaker/listener to produce grammatically correct sentences (linguistic competence). Speakers of a language in particular communities are able to communicate with each other in a manner which is not only correct but also appropriate to the socio-cultural context. This ability involves a shared knowledge of the linguistic code as well as of the socio-cultural rules, norms and values which guide the conduct and interpretation of speech and other channels of communication in a community. The ethnography of speaking or the ethnography of communication, as it was later referred to, is concerned with the questions of what a person knows about appropriate patterns of language use in his or her community and how he or she learns about it.

EARLY DEVELOPMENTS

A main focus of the ethnography of communication is the speech community which defines the sample of description and is understood as "a community sharing rules for the conduct and interpretation of speech and rules for the interpretation of at least one linguistic variety" (Hymes, 1972, p. 54). Members of such a community belong to a common locality and are connected through a network of social roles and relationships which forms the basis of shared knowledge (of both the linguistic code and socio-cultural rules) (Gumperz & Hymes, 1972). The speech community may be as large as an entire country or village or as small as a class or a group of children within it.

In a speech community, communication is organized in terms of events. Hymes defines speech events as "activities or aspects of activities that are directly governed by rules or norms for the use of speech" (Hymes,

N.H. Hornberger and D. Corson (eds), Encyclopedia of Language and Education,
Volume 8: Research Methods in Language and Education, 125–133.
© *1997 Kluwer Academic Publishers. Printed in the Netherlands.*

1972, p. 56). The term communicative event is more appropriate for these activities because they include both oral and literate language and other channels. The term literacy events has also been introduced to refer to activities involving reading and writing (Basso, 1974; Heath, 1982, 1983). Some events have clearly defined boundaries. The boundaries may be recognized in various ways for example ritual opening and closing as in telephone conversations, change of topic or change of code such as switching from talking about official matters in English to talking about personal matters in a national language in several developing countries. Communicative events themselves are located in speech situations, a term which refers to the setting and context in which language or other channels of communication are being used. So for example, a speech event (private conversation or a grammar lesson) may be situated in a speech situation (a party or an ESL class).

Ethnography of communication involves describing a communication event in terms of the components which make up its content and context. Early work in the ethnography of communication (Hymes, 1964, 1972, 1974; Sherzer & Darnell, 1972; Blom & Gumperz, 1972; Ervin Tripp, 1972; Gumperz, 1982) identified and defined key units of analysis. Hymes (1972) suggests eight components for the analysis of speech events, mnemonically represented by SPEAKING: (S) Setting including the time and place, physical aspects of the situation such as arrangement of furniture in the classroom; (P) participant identity including personal characteristics such as age and sex, social status, relationship with each other; (E) end including the purpose of the event itself as well as the individual goals of the participants; (A) act sequence or how speech acts are organized within a speech event and what topic/s are addressed; (K) key or the tone and manner in which something is said or written; (I) instrumentalities or the linguistic code i.e. language dialect, variety and channel i.e. speech or writing; (N) norm or the standard socio-cultural rules of interaction and interpretation; and (G) genre or type of event such as lecture, poem, letter. These components are interrelated although some may be more significant than others in particular speech events. (Sherzer & Darnell, 1972; Saville-Troike, 1989).

Two other dimensions which have contributed towards comprehensive descriptions of language use in communities, especially multilingual communities, are speech repertoire and domain of use. Speech repertoire refers to the communicative resources (languages, varieties, styles or instumentalities) available to a person within a speech community. A person's own repertoire may contain the ability to use more than one language, dialect or style as well as the ability to read and write. On the other hand he or she may not possess these skills but can rely on the community repertoire i.e. the skills of the other individuals in the community (Gumperz, 1982, 1986).

A domain is defined as the "institutional context" such as the official or the educational (Fishman, 1972). The domain of language use affects the speaker's choice of language, style or channel and is an important concept in the description of patterns of communication in bilingual or multilingual societies. Mostly in bilingual situations, the choice of language or variety depends upon the domain in which the event is located. For example, the choice of language and tone of a conversation may depend upon whether it is taking place in the official domain or the personal domain. Blom & Gumperz (1972) provide an example of code switching associated with social significance of the situation. The residents of a Norwegian town whose repertoire includes both the dialect and standard choose the dialect to signify localness, however when switch (mainly phonologically) takes place it does so in accordance with the speaker's perception of the domain (informal conversation, topic related to a business, or conversation taking place in city as opposed to the village) and assertion of identity and role relationship. Blom and Gumperz's analysis of the shift in pronunciation, morphology and syntax as conveying social meaning is an example of the micro and macro level of analysis feeding into each other to create a complete picture of patterns of language use (Blom & Gumperz, 1972; Gumperz & Cook-Gumperz, 1981; Hornberger, 1989; Duff, 1995).

The early studies in sociolinguistics were criticized for limiting their analysis to data collected only through elicitation or naturalistic observation (often in experimental situations). These methods failed to obtain data for an account of the process of construction and interpretation of meaning in contexts. Such description must include not only linguistic and sociolinguistic data about the particular interactions but information about the social structures within which language is being used and the cultural norms being applied by the interlocutors (Hymes, 1970; Gumperz, 1972, 1986; Ervin Tripp, 1976; Heath, 1983).

Ethnography, an approach traditionally associated with anthropology, is valuable for its holistic approach (Agar, 1985). The goal of the ethnographer is to create "a whole picture of the particular cultural event under study – a picture that leaves nothing unaccounted for and that reveals the interconnectedness of all the component parts" (Hornberger, 1994, p. 688). In creating such a picture the ethnographer also aims to incorporate the perspective of the member of the community or what is referred to as the emic perspective.

PROBLEMS AND DIFFICULTIES

The basic methods of data collection within ethnography are participant observation, and formal and informal open ended interviews with community members. Participation in community interaction and activities is a critical element allowing the researchers to define and test out their hypothesis about boundaries of particular events and the norm applying to them. Participation requires that the researcher take on authentic roles and develop reciprocal relationships with the members of the community being researched and the opportunity to come close to the perspective of the insider who observes and experiences language use in real situations. The approach demands suspension of preconceived assumptions and involvement in an ongoing process of data analysis: drawing and redrawing hypotheses, constantly testing the validity of data and the researchers' interpretation of it against the understanding of the community members. Even when a researcher is working in her own community or one similar to it, she must take on the role of "an outsider" verifying her own perceptions and hypotheses with those of other members through observation and interviews.

However, the necessity to get to the participants' perspective also poses many dilemmas for the ethnographer who must maintain a balance between the insider and outsider perspective. First of all the "suspension of prior assumptions" is easier said than done; a researcher cannot shed his or her identity. Hornberger (1994) succinctly summarizes other dilemmas. Becoming too familiar with the culture one is studying may not allow us to notice its characteristics and distort interpretation. Being a stranger may restrict access to significant events as well as exclude the emic perspective. Too much participation may change the nature of the events whereas too little participation may mean that the researcher may not encounter them and lose important data.

The ethnographer of communication needs to obtain information about the larger context – social structures, cultural values, roles and relationships – as well as closely analyze the linguistic and non-linguistic features of interaction in a particular speech events. Thus, methods associated with ethnosemantics (Frake, 1972; Garfinkel, 1972) and interactional analysis are also considered useful for close analysis of the rules of interaction and interpretation being applied in speech events (Saville-Troike, 1989). Ethnosemantics is useful as it focuses upon the emic perspective and attempts to discover how community members themselves group speech events. One outcome of this approach is a taxonomy of events; another outcome is a close analysis of content of the event (Frake, 1972). Ethnomethodology is slightly different from the traditional ethnography of communication approach in that instead of looking for community wide agreed upon norms, it focuses on the ongoing process by which interlocutors in an interaction produce and interpret speech in particular contexts. The method involves describing the assumptions that interlocutors make and agree upon during an interaction in order to understand and respond to each other. These may be based upon shared cultural knowledge, or beliefs about the status, relationships, and intention of the speakers. This method of micro analysis of the process of meaning making in communicative events is not traditionally associated with ethnography but is useful to the ethnographer of communication in arriving at "clearer understandings of the processes by which members of a speech community actually use and interpret language especially in every day interaction – a vital aspect of their communicative competence" (Saville-Troike, 1989, p. 133, see also the reviews by Heap and by Garcez in this volume).

MAJOR CONTRIBUTIONS

The early studies classified as ethnography of communication and collected in the volume *Directions in Sociolinguistics: the Ethnography of Communication* provided descriptions of culturally significant speech events in different speech communities mostly in non western contexts undertaken with a comparative purpose (Gumperz & Hymes, 1972; also see Bauman & Sherzer, 1974). Albert (1972) for example, describes how the speech patterns in Burundi are shaped by the social position of the participants, the topic and the values associated with the art of rhetoric, truth, practicality and self preservation. Frake (1972) focuses upon the form and structure of litigation as a kind of Yakan talk; and Dundes, Leach and Özkök (1972) describe the genera of verbal dueling among Turkish boys.

Since the early seventies the ethnography of communication has also been used to understand the contexts of education and language learning for children. Several studies in North America have addressed such questions as: How are children socialized in the home and the school? What are the patterns of language use in these two settings? How do these differences affect children's performance in school (Philips, 1972; Au & Jordan, 1981; Michaels, 1981; Heath, 1983)? The studies question assumptions about the poor performance of minority children in schools. In her oft cited study of the Warm Springs Indian children's patterns of linguistic and non linguistic behavior in the community and school, Warm Springs Indian children were considered to be silent, inactive and unsuccessful in school. Through description and comparison of appropriate and acceptable patterns of interaction in the context of home, community and the classroom, Philips was able to show that Indian children's performance was not the result of poor second language ability but their unfamiliarity and discomfort with classroom norms of interaction. The classroom context which required individual students to interact with the teacher and which demanded and rewarded individual performance rather than peer interaction and group performance was alien to Indian children whose speech community valued group interaction and cooperation rather than individual performance and competition.

In the same tradition, Heath (1993) conducted research in three communities – a working class black community, a working class white community, and a white middle class community represented by the school teachers. She carried out participant observation spending time in homes and school, talking with children and mothers, carrying out errands, observing adults and children read, write, talk and play in various situations at home and in school over a period of ten years. Through detailed description of what she calls "literacy events" representing oral and literate behavior in these communities, Heath demonstrates that the patterns of language use and the habits of language learning that children develop are shaped by the social structures and cultural contexts. In the three communities these were sharply different even when the same linguistic code was used. The difference or similarity in the experiences of language use at home and those encountered in the classroom explain why children of black working class communities fail, those of the white working class communities barely survive, and those from the white middle class are prepared to succeed.

A number of studies have described the patterns of language use in school and community and the relationship between them in bilingual and multilingual contexts of education in North America and developing countries (Guthrie, 1985; Edelsky, 1986; Hornberger, 1988; Farah, 1992) and have been concerned with the domain and function specific distribution of languages in communities and schools. Hornberger conducted fieldwork over several years in Peru in three communities and bilingual and immersion schools located there. Using the framework of SPEAKING, Hornberger describes communication events in three domains highlighting the patterns of language choice in the physical contexts of the home and the school. The choice between Spanish and Quechua is based on the various SPEAKING components as well as the shared significance and values and domains associated with the two languages. This understanding leads her to raise questions about the impact of bilingual programs for the maintenance of the Quechua language. Farah (1992) describes the patterns of oral and literate uses of language in the religious and secular domains and in the contexts of the home, the school and the community in rural Pakistan through two events which the community identifies as the "Quranic lesson" and the "school lesson". The study shows first of all that traditional beliefs about rote reading of the Quran as meaningless activity do not hold in this community. The Quranic lesson has a symbolic religious meaning associated with it and also the literacy skills and behaviors learnt in these lessons are transferred to the school lessons as well as other situations. In fact, both the Quranic lesson and the school lesson have a similar social meaning and significance for the participants even though overt intentions of the two types of lessons are different.

In studying communication patterns in the ESL context and relating them to the larger societal goals and policy, Guthrie (1985) described language use in a bilingual school in a Chinese community in northern California and in the process revealed that the bilingual program with the intention of maintaining Chinese was actually serving transitional goals. Moll & Diaz (1985) studied patterns in English Reading Lessons in bilingual programs in southern California and argued that ESL reading lessons must draw on the L1 reading skills of the children. In a similar vein Edelsky described writing in a bilingual program in Southwestern U.S. to show how children applied their L1 knowledge in developing their writing skills in English.

In a recent ethnography of communication of an EFL classroom, Duff (1995) investigates the micro level changes in classroom discourse patterns as a result of a policy of introducing English immersion classes in some experimental dual language programs in Hungarian schools. Focusing upon the speech event of student lectures in the English medium history class, which have substituted the traditional event of recitation in the Hungarian medium classes in other subject areas, Duff shows that the use of English was also changing the participation patterns and discourse of learning and was bringing about a reconfiguration of the social organization of the classroom. She also questions the appropriateness and desirability of such change.

FUTURE DIRECTIONS

As is apparent from this review, the ethnography of communication has revealed important aspects of communicating in the worlds that children encounter in the school and at home. These studies have raised questions about traditional assumptions about language use in communities and schools and language programs. For example, studying community patterns has raised questions about beliefs about childrens' classroom performance. Studying bilingual programs within the ethnography of communication approach has revealed the mismatch between programs' intended goals and actual achievements. Description of traditionally significant literacy events such as the Quranic lesson has revealed that although thought of as a meaningless rote exercise by the outsider, it is meaningful to the insiders. The patterns of learning to read in this type of lesson are actually transferred to the context of "the school lesson". Thus, the ethnography of communication approach has usefully drawn attention beyond "interaction in the classroom" to the multilayered contexts in which it is embedded (including that of the classroom itself). Much needs to be learnt about what knowledge and experiences children bring to their classrooms, especially in bilingual situations. We know little about communication events in schools and other educational settings in non western societies, many of which are multilingual. Such studies can be helpful to both practice and policy making in these countries. However, ethnography is a time-consuming approach requiring intense work over a long period where the only tool the researcher has to depend upon is himself or herself. We cannot therefore anticipate that it will be undertaken very frequently.

Agha Khan University
Pakistan

REFERENCES

Agar, M.: 1985, *Speaking of Ethnography*, Sage, Beverly Hills, CA.

Albert, E.: 1986[1972], 'Culture patterning of speech behavior in Burundi', in J.Gumperz & D. Hymes (eds.), *Directions in Sociolinguistics: The Ethnography of Communication*, Basil Blackwell, New York.

Au, K. & Jordan, C.: 1981, 'Teaching reading to Hawaiian children: Finding a culturally appropriate solution', in G. Guthrie, H. Trueba & K. Au (eds.), *Culture and the Bilingual Classroom*, Newbury House, Rowley, MA.

Bauman, R. & Sherzer, J. (eds.): 1974, *Explorations in the Ethnography of Speaking*, Cambridge University Press, New York.

Basso, K.: 1974, 'The ethnography of writing', in R. Bauman & J. Sherzer (eds.), *Explorations in the Ethnography of Speaking*, Cambridge University Press, New York.

Blom & Gumperz, J.: 1986[1972], 'Social meaning in linguistic structures', in J. Gumperz & D. Hymes (eds.), *Directions in Sociolinguistics: The Ethnography of Communication*, Basil Blackwell, New York.

Duff, P.: 1995, 'An ethnography of communication in immersion classrooms in Hungary', *TESOL* (29), 505–536.

Dundes, A. Leach, J. & Özkök, B.: 1972, 'The strategy of Turkish boys' verbal dueling rhymes', in: J. Gumperz & D. Hymes (eds.), *Directions in Sociolinguistics: The Ethnography of Communication*, Basil Blackwell, New York.

Edelsky, C.: 1986, *Writing in a Bilingual Program: Habia Una Vez*, Ablex Publishers, Norwood, New Jersey.

Ervin Tripp, S.: 1986[1972], 'On sociolinguistic rules: Alternation and co-occurence', in J. Gumperz & D. Hymes (eds.), *Directions in Sociolinguistics: The Ethnography of Communication*, Basil Blackwell, New York.

Farah, I.: 1992, *Literacy Practices in a Rural Community in Pakistan*, Unpublished doctoral dissertation: University of Pennsylvania.

Fishman, J.: 1972, 'Domains and relationships between micro- and macro sociolinguistics', in J. Gumperz & D. Hymes (eds.), *Directions in Sociolinguistics: The Ethnography of Communication*, Basil Blackwell, New York.

Frake, C.: 1986 [1972], ' "Struck by Speech": The Yakan concept of litigation', in J. Gumperz & D. Hymes (eds.), *Directions in Sociolinguistics: The Ethnography of Communication*, Basil Blackwell, New York.

Garfinkel, H.: 1972, 'Remarks on ethnomethodology', in J. Gumperz & D. Hymes (eds.), *Directions in Sociolinguistics: The Ethnography of Communication*, Basil Blackwell, New York.

Geertz, C.: 1973, *The Interpretation of Cultures*, Basic Books, New York.

Gumperz, J.: 1972, 'Sociolinguistics and communication in small groups', in J.B. Pride & J. Holmes (eds.), *Sociolinguistics*, Penguin Books, Harmondsworth, Middlesex.

Gumperz, J.: 1982, *Language and Social Identity*, Cambridge University Press.

Gumperz, J.: 1986[1972], 'Introduction', in J. Gumperz & D. Hymes (eds.), *Directions in Sociolinguistics: The Ethnography of Communication*, Basil Blackwell, New York.

Gumperz, J. & Cook-Gumperz, J.: 1981, 'Ethnic difference in communicative style', in

C.A. Ferguson & S.B. Heath (eds.), *Language in the USA*, Cambridge University Press, Cambridge.

Gumperz, J. & Hymes, D. (eds.): 1986[1972], *Directions in Sociolinguistics: The Ethnography of Communication*, Basil Blackwell, New York.

Guthrie, G.P.: 1985, *A School Divided: An Ethnography of Bilingual Education in a Chinese Community*, Lawrence Erlbaum, Hillsdale, NJ.

Heath, S.B.: 1982, 'Protean shapes in literacy events: Ever shifting oral and literate traditions', in D. Tannen (ed.), *Exploring Literacy and Orality*, Albex, Norwood, NJ.

Heath, S.B.: 1983, *Ways with Words*, Cambridge University Press, New York.

Hornberger, N.: 1988, *Bilingual Education and Language Maintenance: A Southern Peruvian Quechua Case*. Dordrecht, Foris/Berlin, Mouton.

Hornberger, N.: 1989, 'Continua of biliteracy', *Review of Educational Research* 59(3), 271–296.

Hornberger, N.: 1994, 'Ethnography', in A. Cumming (ed.), *Alternatives in TESOL Research: Descriptive, Interpretive, and Ideological Orientations. TESOL Quarterly* 28, 688–690.

Hymes, D.: 1964, 'Introduction: Towards ethnographies of communication. *American Anthropologist* 66(6) (Part 2), 1–35.

Hymes, D.: 1968, 'The ethnography of speaking', in J. Fishman (ed.), *Readings in the Sociology of Language*, Mouton, The Hague, 99–138.

Hymes, D.: 1972, 'Models of the interaction of language and social life', in J. Gumperz & D. Hymes (eds.), *Directions in Sociolinguistics: The Ethnography of Communication*, Basil Blackwell, New York.

Hymes, D.: 1974, *Foundations in Sociolinguistics: An Ethnographic Approach*, University of Pennsylvania Press, Philadelphia.

Michaels, S.: 1981, ' "Sharing time": Children's narrative styles and differential access to literacy', *Language and Society* 10, 423–442.

Moll, L. & Diaz, S.: 1985, 'Ethnographic pedagogy: Promoting effective bilingual instruction', in E. Garcia & R. Padilla (eds.), *Advances in Bilingual Education Research*, University of Arizona Press, Tucson.

Philips, S.: 1972, 'Participant structure and communicative competence: Warm springs children in community and classroom', in C. Cazden, V.P. John & D. Hymes (eds.), *Functions of Language in the Classroom*, Teachers College Press, New York.

Saville-Troike, M.: 1989, *The Ethnography of Communication: An Introduction*, Basil Blackwell, New York.

Sherzer, J. & Darnell, R.: 1986[1972], 'Outline guide for the ethnographic study of speech use', in J. Gumperz & D. Hymes (eds.), *Directions in Sociolinguistics: The Ethnography of Communication*, Basil Blackwell, New York.

KAREN ANN WATSON-GEGEO

CLASSROOM ETHNOGRAPHY

Classroom ethnography refers to the application of ethnographic and socio-linguistic or discourse analytic research methods to the study of behavior, activities, interaction, and discourse in formal and semi-formal educational settings such as school classrooms, adult education programs, and day-care centers. In contrast to quantitative approaches to classroom research, classroom ethnography emphasizes the sociocultural nature of teaching and learning processes, incorporates participants' perspectives on their own behavior, and offers a holistic analysis sensitive to levels of context in which interactions and classrooms are situated. A spectrum of approaches have developed within classroom ethnography over the past 25 years, varying from purely naturalistic to partly statistical in method, and from focused studies using ethnomethodological, sociolinguistic, and/or discourse analytic methods to studies combining micro-macro analytic concerns within a critical framework.

EARLY DEVELOPMENTS

The important role that schools and classrooms play in cultural transmission, colonialism, and other socialization processes has long been recognized by anthropologists. Anecdotal ethnographic accounts and critiques of classroom processes occur in the work of many early American anthropologists, including Ruth Benedict, Margaret Mead & Jules Henry (1971). The 1950s saw the rise of the more structured and systematic 'ethnography of schooling' approaches of Solon Kimball (1974) and George and Louise Spindler (e.g., 1987). George Spindler's (1973) work in Germany was particularly important for its integration of schooling into a larger account of socialization.

Classroom ethnography, however, owes its primary impetus to historical and methodological developments that converged across the disciplines of anthropology, sociology, linguistics, and education in the U.S. and England during the late 1960s and early 1970s. The emergence of the 'ethnography of communication' in anthropological linguistics and of the interdisciplinary subfield of sociolinguistics coincided with a national crisis in the U.S. on how to overcome educational inequities for ethnic minority children. As attention turned to contrasting patterns of culture and language use in community and classroom settings, it became clear that quantitative and/or experimental research designs were inadequate for addressing culture and

N.H. Hornberger and D. Corson (eds), Encyclopedia of Language and Education,
Volume 8: Research Methods in Language and Education, 135–144.
© 1997 Kluwer Academic Publishers. Printed in the Netherlands.

moment-by-moment classroom interaction. The 1970s and 1980s saw a flowering of federally-funded studies using classroom ethnography, many of which focused on bilingual classrooms.

Similarly, in sociology and the sociology of education in the late 1960s, the turn towards qualitative research methods generally, and towards an ethnographic approach specifically, reflected a growing disillusionment with prevailing theory and method. Sociologists Howard Becker and Blanche Geer's (Becker, Geer et al., 1961) study of student culture in medical school and Philip Jackson's (1968) work on classroom life were influential sociological studies pointing the way to qualitative approaches in classroom research. Many sociologists, such as Ray Rist (1970) in the U.S. and Martyn Hammersley (1974), Andrew Hargreaves (1978), and Peter Woods (1975) in England, were frustrated with deterministic models of behavior that left little room for the creative agency of groups and individuals. They argued that quantitative methods relying on the correlation of input and output educational variables failed to encompass the complexity of classroom life or the perspectives of teachers and students.

MAJOR CONTRIBUTIONS

In the most general sense, ethnography is the long-term, holistic, intensive study of people's behavior in ongoing settings (typically, communities), a central aim of which is to understand the social organization and culturally-based perspectives and interpretations that underlie knowledge and guide behavior in a given social group (Watson-Gegeo, 1988).

Classroom ethnography involves the intensive, detailed observation of a classroom over the period of its duration (e.g., semester or year), recording a large sample of classroom activities on audio- or videotape. Observations are supplemented by interviews with teacher and students. The finished report includes: a description of the classroom setting; a statement of the principles underlying classroom social organization; and an account of the social norms guiding participants' behavior and shaping their interpretations of specific interactions (e.g., see Erickson, 1985). Although each study is guided by existing theory, analytic categories in classroom ethnography are in large part emic (derived from teachers' and students' own concepts and categories) rather than etic (imposed from the analytic language of the social sciences).

The four basic approaches to classroom ethnography – ethnography of communication, micro-ethnography, discourse analysis, and critical ethnography (cf. respectively, Farah, Garcez, Norton, and May, this volume) – vary with regard to topic of focus, analytic techniques, mix of micro- and macro-level contexts included, and intensity of data collection and analysis. However, considerable overlap occurs among the types of approaches. For instance, ethnography of communication and microethnography both draw heavily on sociolinguistics for theoretical perspectives and analytic techniques, and all four approaches focus primarily on culture and language data. School-community comparative studies are particularly associated with ethnography of communication and micro-ethnographic approaches. Many of these studies have been based on the 'cultural difference' explanation of school failure, i.e. that linguistic, cultural, and/or class differences in behavioral expectations between home and school influence children's classroom success or failure, and that classroom discourse should be altered in ways that bridge these differences.

Ethnography of communication studies are typically the most comprehensive in their treatment of community culture, values, and interactional norms. Dell Hymes (1980), John Gumperz (Gumperz & Cook-Gumperz, 1980), and their students (e.g., Cazden, John & Hymes, 1972) were the first to examine contrasting patterns of language use in American ethnic community and mainstream classroom settings, combining ethnographic and sociolinguistic research methods. The notion of 'participant structure' (patterns in the allocation of speaking rights and obligations associated with context or activity), which Susan U. Philips (1972) developed out of her study of Warm Springs' Indian children's contrasting behavior in differing classroom speech activities, has become a core analytic concept for examining classroom interaction in all four approaches to classroom ethnography. Based on classroom and community ethnography, the Kamehameha Early Education Program's success in raising Native Hawaiian children's reading scores by using local 'talk-story' routines in reading instruction was the first demonstration that bridging cultural differences in interactional rules and patterns can make a difference for minority children's classroom success (Au & Jordan, 1981; Boggs, 1985). Shirley Brice Heath's (1983) nine-year home/school study in the Piedmonts – which compared language socialization patterns in African American and white working-class communities with those expected by mainstream schools, and then detailed her collaboration with teachers in adjusting classroom discourse to take community patterns into account – set a high standard for comprehensiveness in data collection and analysis.

In the 1980s and 1990s, classroom studies in the ethnography of communication approach became increasingly rigorous in methodology and eclectic in techniques of data collection and analysis. The ethnography of communication/sociolinguistic approach has been used to study a variety of ethnic and mixed-ethnic classrooms around the world (e.g., Heltoft & Paaby, 1978; Malcolm, 1979; Spindler & Spindler, 1987; Hornberger, 1988; Jones, 1991)

Micro-ethnography, which draws on perspectives and methods in ethnomethodology, symbolic interactionism, and sociolinguistics, is concerned with the formal analysis of interactional events and with understanding how lessons, classroom organization, and school success or failure are jointly constructed by participants as interactional accomplishments. Key to this approach have been proxemic and kinesic techniques for analyzing video-recordings of interactions developed by Frederick Erickson and his students in the late 1970s. Hugh Mehan's (1979) study of the sequential structuring of lessons in a mainstream, mixed-ethnic third-grade classroom introduced the three-part I(nitiation)-R(esponse)-E(valuation) format associated with a dyadic participant structure common in American classrooms (see also Heap, this volume). Although Mehan's model has been used analytically in many studies to follow, other analysts (e.g., Sinclair & Coulthard, 1975) have suggested somewhat different models for lesson structure. Frederick Anderson's (1995) ethnographic/discourse analytic study of Japanese elementary classrooms found a four-part lesson structure of I(nitiation)-P(resentation)-Rx (Reaction)-E(valuation). Anderson argues that the four-part structure reflects an 'interactional umbrella' type of participant structure preferred in Japanese classrooms: multi-party interaction in which students react to (and evaluate) fellow students' Presentations (a more felicitous and accurate label for Mehan's Response category) prior to the teacher's offering of an Evaluation. Multi-party interaction, with reactions and evaluations coming from peers, reflects the Japanese cultural value placed on group authority and relationships.

Methodologically, micro-ethnographic studies have varied greatly with regard to rigor. Mehan's methodological recommendations for a 'constitutive' model for classroom ethnography provided stringent guidelines for micro-ethnographic classroom studies, especially in its requirement for comprehensive data treatment (inclusion of all instances of interaction in the analysis). In comparison to ethnography of communication's holistic examination of interactional patterns across many contexts in home/school comparisons, however, micro-ethnography involves a much narrower focus. A micro-ethnography may offer a detailed analysis of only one type of event or even a single instance of an event, perhaps contrasted with a second type or instance found in another context (e.g., Shultz, Florio & Erickson, 1982).

By the mid-1980s, most classroom ethnographies were taking a discourse analytic approach. In England, John Sinclair & Malcolm Coulthard (1975) developed a hierarchical model for discourse units in classroom lessons, based on speech-act theory and interactional data they collected from ethnically-mixed British primary classrooms. Conversational analysis and M.A.K. Halliday's (1976; Halliday & Hasan, 1976) systemic/functional linguistics are the discourse analysis approaches on which most classroom ethnographers have drawn. Jay L. Lemke's (1990) study of discourse in high school science classrooms was an influential substantive study of teaching-learning processes in science teaching as well as an important model for methodological rigor and analytical completeness. Himself a pioneer of ethnographic and discourse analytic techniques in classroom research, Hammersley (1990) has recently promoted the incorporation of quantitative techniques into classroom ethnography. (For a summary of work in mainstream and bilingual classroom discourse, see Cazden, 1986).

In the past decade, ethnography and discourse analysis have begun to be applied to second-language classrooms (e.g., van Lier, 1988; Bailey & Nunan, 1996), as well as to a variety of teaching-learning situations world-wide (e.g., Cook, 1996; Alton-Lee & Nuthall, 1991).

The critical approach to classroom ethnography has its roots in John Ogbu (1974) and Ray McDermott's (1976) work on American mixed-ethnic schools, and Basil Bernstein (1977), Paul Willis (1977), and Paul Corrigan's (1979) work on British working-class students and schools, all in the early and mid-1970s. Critical ethnography focuses specifically on the relations of power in language use, how social differentiation in the larger society is reproduced in the classroom through language and discourse, and the dialectical relationship between social structural con-straints and human agency (e.g., Okano, 1993, Watson-Gegeo & Gegeo, 1994). Critical ethnographers argue that oppressed peoples are not simply passive victims of a discriminatory social system, but are able to take action to improve their situation. The goal of critical classroom ethnography is empowerment for students and teachers, and many such studies involve collaborative relationships among teachers and researchers. The analy-tical framework for Peter McLaren's (1986) study of ritual processes in a Canadian parochial secondary school came from symbolic anthropology. However, most critical classroom ethnographies have used critical theory and discourse analysis. Robert Young's (1992) study of Australian class-rooms included a major methodological statement for critical ethnography, integrating a Hallidayan speech-act model with Jurgen Habermas' (1979) approach to analyzing communicative distortion. (For a review of critical ethnography in comparative studies, see Masemann, 1982.)

Classroom ethnographies have examined teaching styles, lesson struc-ture and other classroom speech activities (such as 'sharing time'), teacher and student discourse styles/registers, discourse tasks (questions, scaffold-ing, topic-setting, etc.), differential treatment of students by teachers, teacher expectations and idealizations of students, student resistance, teacher and student empowerment, and the teaching of classroom subjects (reading, writing, mathematics, science); these topics have been examined in both first and second language teaching situations. Although the major-ity of classroom ethnographies have focused on primary school classrooms, a few have addressed middle, secondary, and post-secondary classrooms.

PROBLEMS AND DIFFICULTIES

One of the continuing problems plaguing classroom ethnography is misapplication of the term 'ethnography' to work that is more correctly described as observational, naturalistic, or qualitative. Not all approaches that claim to be ethnographic in whole or part (e.g., Sarah L. Lightfoot's [1983] 'portraiture' approach) are ethnographic (as defined above). Approaches and individual studies labeled 'ethnographic' by their authors but actually involving impressionistic accounts and very short periods of observation, have been designated as 'blitzkrieg ethnography' by Rist (1980). The superficial nature of such studies, which caricature rather than characterize teaching-learning settings, has led to the misconception in some educational circles that ethnographic researchers are not accountable to rigorous methodological standards, and that ethnography is atheoretical.

A second problem in classroom ethnographies is within-data sampling to select instances of an event or interaction for analysis and to illustrate patterns or findings in the research report. Such choices need to be theory-driven, principled, and made on the basis of the entire data set (Mehan's 'comprehensive data treatment'). Ethnographers often feel constrained by the high cost in time and labor of collecting and analyzing large amounts of observational and recorded data: such costs are difficult to justify to granting agencies. Limitations on page-length for journal articles and books, and on complex discourse examples and models due to publishing costs further discourages comprehensive data treatment. Nevertheless, these difficulties do not justify the unprincipled selection of samples from data as found in some studies. When a single interactional event or type of event is selected from a child's home culture to be compared to a school lesson with regard to participant structure and other features, for instance, one must ask whether all contexts and activities in which the child participates at home were examined prior to the selection. At the least, the analyst must show whether the two events contrasted are actually comparable in *function* and *purpose*, whatever similarities or differences they may have in *form*. Otherwise, classroom ethnography is open to the criticism of being anecdotal rather than analytical.

Thirdly, a tendency towards reductionism and an avoidance of complexity have been noted in some studies that are identified asclassroom ethnographies. Michael Stubbs (1986) has taken analysts to task for reductionist descriptions of language use, that is, for ignoring complexity in favor of seizing on convenient surface features without locating these features in the explanatory context of the whole linguistic, discoursal, and sociolinguistic system. Finally, Douglas E. Foley (1991) has criticized classroom ethnographers for assuming within-group uniformity and failing to apply sophisticated techniques to examine within-group differences and variation.

FUTURE DIRECTIONS

Four current trends in classroom ethnography can be expected to intensify over the next few years. First, classroom ethnographers can be expected to incorporate quantitative techniques in their analyses more than they have in the past. Most classroom ethnographers already recognize the value of quantification (e.g., frequency counts, strength of association) in analyzing and displaying results from repeated observations and interviews, and in testing hypotheses. Probably not all would go so far as to agree with Hammersley (1990), however, that classroom ethnography will need to become more quantitative if it is to produce theory. Quantitative methods can usefully support ethnography's 'grounded theory' (theory based in data) approach to theory building, however (e.g. see Woods, 1985).

Secondly, ethnographic techniques will be applied to the study of an increasing range of second-language classrooms and community situations, with a focus on both second language acquisition and second language teaching. Although bilingual classrooms have been a major locus for classroom ethnography over the past 25 years, studies of second-language classrooms and second-language teaching that are fully ethnographic have been undertaken only in the past decade. Ethnographic techniques can also be usefully applied to the acquisition of communicative competence in a second language in both classroom and community contexts, following a language socialization approach.

Thirdly, teacher/researcher collaborative research is likely to expand and become a primary mode for classroom ethnography, especially for work done from a critical perspective. Teacher/researcher collaboration has a long history in 'action research,' where for nearly half a century researchers and practitioners have engaged in situationally-oriented research towards immediate intervention. To remain true to its goal of teacher and student empowerment, critical classroom research must engage teachers and students as research partners in designing and carrying out the research, as well as using the results to transform the classroom as a work place (see the review by McCarty in this volume). A good example is Stephen May's (1994) ethnographic study of critical practitioners in New Zealand, during the course of which he interacted with practitioners over his data to develop a theory of critical praxis.

Finally, we can expect to see the increasing application of classroom ethnography to settings in Europe, Japan, and other areas of the world beyond the U.S., Great Britain, Australia, and New Zealand, where classroom ethnography is well established.

University of California, Davis
USA

REFERENCES

Alton-Lee, A. & Nuthall, G.: 1991, *Understanding Learning and Teaching: Phase Two: Final Report to the New Zealand Ministry of Education*, Education Department, University of Canterbury, Canterbury.

Anderson, F.: 1995, *Classroom Discourse and Language Socialization in a Japanese Elementary-School Setting: An Ethnographic-Linguistic Study*, Unpublished Doctoral Dissertation, University of Hawai'i at Mānoa, Honolulu.

Au, K.H-P. & Jordan, C.: 1981, 'Teaching reading to Hawaiian children: Finding a culturally appropriate solution', in H.T. Trueba, G.P. Guthrie & K.H-P. Au (eds.), *Culture and the Bilingual Classroom: Studies in Classroom Ethnography*, Newbury House, Rowley, MA, 139–152.

Bailey, K.M. & Nunan, D.: 1996, *Voices from the Language Classroom; Qualitative Research in Second Language Education*, Cambridge University Press, London.

Becker, H.S., Geer, B. et al.: 1961, *Boys in White: Student Culture in Medical School*, University of Chicago Press, Chicago.

Bernstein, B.: 1977, *Class, Codes and Control*, Second Edition, Vol. 3 of *Towards a Theory of Educational Transmission*, Routledge & Kegan Paul, London.

Boggs, S.T.: 1985, *Speaking, Relating and Learning: A Study of Hawaiian Children at Home and at School*, with the Assistance of K.A. Watson-Gegeo & G. McMillen, Ablex, Norwood, NJ.

Cazden, C.B.: 1986, *Classroom Discourse: The Language of Teaching and Learning*, Heinemann, Portsmouth, NH.

Cazden, C.B., John, V.P. & Hymes, D. (eds.): 1972, *Functions of Language in the Classroom*, Teachers College Press, New York.

Cook, H.M.: 1996, 'The use of addressee honorifics in Japanese elementary school classrooms', in N. Akatsuka, S. Iwasaki & S. Strauss (eds.), *Japanese/Korean Linguistics*, Volume 5, Center for the Study of Language and Information, Stanford University, Stanford, 67–81.

Corrigan, P.: 1979, *Schooling the Smash Street Kids*, Macmillan, London.

Erickson, F.D.: 1985, 'Qualitative methods in research on teaching', in M.C. Wittrock (ed.), *Handbook of Research on Teaching* (third edition), Macmillan, New York.

Foley, D.E.: 1991, 'Reconsidering anthropological explanations of ethnic school failure', *Anthropology and Education Quarterly* 22, 60–86.

Gumperz, J.J. & Cook-Gumperz, J.: 1980, *Beyond Ethnography: Some Uses of Sociolinguistics for Understanding Classroom Environments*, Bilingual Education Paper Series 4,3, National Dissemination and Assessment Center, California State University at Los Angeles, Los Angeles.

Habermas, J.: 1979, *Communication and the Evolution of Society*, Beacon, Boston.

Halliday, M.A.K.: 1976, *System and Function in Language*, Oxford University Press, London.

Halliday, M.A.K. & Hasan, R.: 1976, *Cohesion in English*, Longman, London.

Hammersley, M.: 1974, 'The organisation of pupil participation', *Sociological Review* 22(3), 355–368.

Hammersley, M.: 1990, *Classroom Ethnography: Empirical and Methodological Essays*, Open University Press, Buckingham.

Hargreaves, A.: 1978, 'The significance of classroom coping strategies', in L. Barton & R. Meighan (eds.), *Sociological Interpretations of Schooling and Classrooms*, Nafferton, Driffield, England, 73–100.

Heath, S.B.: 1983, *Ways With Words: Language, Life, and Work in Communities and Classrooms*, Cambridge University Press, New York.

Heltoft, A.M. & Paaby, K.: 1978, *Tampen Braender: En Analyse af Undervisning Som Samtale*, Hans Reitsels, Copenhagen.

Henry, J.: 1971, *Essays on Education*, Penguin, Harmondsworth.

Hornberger, N.: 1988, 'Iman Chay?: Quechua children in Peru's schools', in H. Trueba
& C. Delgado-Gaitan (eds.), *School and Society: Teaching Content Through Culture*,
Praeger, New York, 99-117.
Hymes, D.: 1980, *Language in Education: Ethnolinguistic Essays*, Center for Applied
Linguistics, Washington, DC.
Hymes, D.: 1981, 'Ethnographic monitoring', in H.T. Trueba, G.P. Guthrie & K.H-P.
Au (eds.), *Culture and the Bilingual Classroom: Studies in Classroom Ethnography*,
Newbury House, Rowley, MA, 56–68.
Jackson, P.: 1968, *Life in Classrooms*, Holt, Rinehart & Winston, New York.
Jones, A.: 1991, *"At School I've Got a Chance": Culture/Privilege: Pacific Islands and
Pakeha Girls at School*, Dunmore, Palmerston North.
Kimball, S.T.: 1974, *Culture and the Educative Process: An Anthropological Perspective*,
Teachers College Press, New York.
Lemke, J.L.: 1990, *Talking Science: Language, Learning, and Values*, Ablex, Norwood,
NJ.
Lightfoot, S.L.: 1983, *The Good High School: Portraits of Character and Culture*, Basic
Books, New York.
Malcolm, I.: 1979, 'The West Australian aboriginal child and classroom interaction: A
sociolinguistic approach', *Journal of Pragmatics* 3, 305–320.
Masemann, V.: 1982, 'Critical ethnography in the study of comparative education',
Comparative Education Review 26(1), 1–15.
May, S.: 1994, *Making Multicultural Education Work*, Multilingual Matters, Clevedon.
McDermott, R.P.: 1976, *Kids Make Sense: An Ethnographic Account of the Interactional
Management of Success and Failure in One First Grade Classroom*. Unpublished
Ph.D. Thesis, Stanford University, Stanford.
McLaren, P.: 1986, *Schooling as a Ritual Performance: Towards a Political Economy of
Educational Symbols and Gestures*, Routledge & Kegan Paul, Boston.
Mehan, H.: 1978, *Learning Lessons: The Social Organization of Classroom Behavior*,
Harvard University Press, Cambridge.
Ogbu, J.U.: 1974, *The Next Generation: An Ethnography of Education in an Urban
Neighborhood*, Academic Press, New York.
Okano, K.: 1993, *School to Work Transition in Japan: An Ethnographic Study*, Multilingual
Matters, Clevedon.
Philips, S.U.: 1972, 'Participant structures and communicative competence: Warm Springs
children in community and classroom', in C.B. Cazden, V.P. John & D. Hymes (eds.),
Functions of Language in the Classroom, Teachers College Press, New York, 370–394.
Rist, R.: 1970, 'Student social class and teacher expectations: The self-fulfilling prophecy
in Ghetto education', *Harvard Educational Review* 40, 411–451.
Rist, R.: 1980, 'Blitzkrieg ethnography: On the transformation of a method into a move-
ment', *Educational Researcher* (9), 8–10.
Shultz, J.J., Florio, S. & Erickson, F.: 1982, 'Where's the floor?: Aspects of the cultural
organization of social relationships in communication at home and in school', in P.
Gilmore & D.M. Smith (eds.), *Children In and Out of School: Ethnography and
Education*, Center for Applied Linguistics, Washington, DC, 88–123.
Sinclair, J. McH. & Coulthard, M.: 1975, *Towards an Analysis of Discourse: The English
Used by Teachers and Pupils*, Oxford University Press, Oxford.
Spindler, G.D.: 1973, *Burgbach: Urbanization and Identity in a German Village*, Holt,
Rinehart & Winston, New York.
Spindler, G.D. & Spindler, L.: 1987, *Interpretive Ethnography of Education: At Home and
Abroad*, Lawrence Erlbaum Associates, Hillsdale, NJ.
Stubbs, M.: 1986, 'Scratching the surface: Linguistic data in educational research', in M.
Hammersley (ed.), *Controversies in Classroom Research*, Open University, Philadel-
phia, 62–103.

van Lier, L.: 1988, *The Classroom and the Language Learner: Ethnography and Second Language Classroom Research*, Longman, New York.

Watson-Gegeo, K.A.: 1988, 'Ethnography in ESL: Defining the essentials', *TESOL Quarterly* 22, 575–592.

Watson-Gegeo, K.A. & Gegeo, D.W.: 1994, 'Keeping culture out of the classroom in rural Solomon Islands schools: A critical analysis', *Educational Foundations* 8(2), 27–55.

Willis, P.: 1977, *Learning to Labour: How Working Class Kids Get Working Class Jobs*, Saxon House, Farnborough.

Woods, P.: 1975, 'Showing them up in secondary school', in G. Chanan & S. Delamont (eds.), *Frontiers of Classroom Research*, National Foundation for Educational Research, Slough, 122–145.

Woods, P.: 1985, 'Ethnography and theory construction in educational research', in R.G. Burgess (ed.), *Field Methods in the Study of Education*, Falmer Press, Lewes, 51–78.

Young, R.: 1992, *Critical Theory and Classroom Talk*, Multilingual Matters, Clevedon.

CASE STUDY METHODS IN RESEARCHING LANGUAGE AND EDUCATION

Case study research stems from a special interest in individual cases (Stake, 1994). In the field of language and education, case study methods of research have produced some important discoveries about (1) how children and adolescents learn oral and written language; (2) how language teachers draw on perspectives and assumptions to inform their practices, and (3) how what happens outside the classrooms in school settings interacts with the ways that children and adolescents learn and use oral and written language inside of classrooms.

EARLY DEVELOPMENTS

Case study methods have been used in social science research since the late 1940s (Llewellyn, 1948). Researchers in language and education began using them in the 1970s A feature common to all case study methods since their development as a research strategy is that they examine a specific phenomenon as a *bounded system* (Smith, 1978). A bounded system is one in which the unit of analysis has fairly clear-cut boundaries in the eyes of the researcher, such as a teacher, a home, a classroom, or a school (Johnson, 1992).

Two main types of case study methods are *interpretive* and *intervention*. Both types of methods rely on observation and reflection techniques for and during data collection. The analysis of the data entails figuring out the linkages between the context and the particular phenomenon of interest. Beyond reflection and analysis, both types can involve multiple sites, quantitative analysis and evaluation (Merriam, 1988). A key difference between the two methods is that in intervention case studies the researcher studies what effect an intervention has on participants in the case, while in interpretive case studies, there is no intervention. The case itself is the primary interest.

Data collection in both methods of case study can be done within the natural setting of the case, or it can involve elicitation of predetermined oral and written language information. Some studies use a combination of both. In language and educational settings for naturalistic purposes, researchers most often use note-taking, audio-recording, and/or video-recording to capture interactions and other information. Written language

N.H. Hornberger and D. Corson (eds), Encyclopedia of Language and Education,
Volume 8: Research Methods in Language and Education, 145–152.
© *1997 Kluwer Academic Publishers. Printed in the Netherlands.*

samples such as notes, journals and letters produced spontaneously for communicative purposes also qualify as naturalistic data. Some of the widely used techniques for elicitation of data are structured interviews, open-ended questionnaires, think-aloud protocols, stimulated recall, and interactive journal writing between the researcher and case study participants (Johnson, 1992). Teacher- and/or researcher-elicited writing activities are also examples of elicited data.

A major part of case study research is the report in which the researcher represents the case (Stake, 1994). The researcher seeks to provide a rich portrayal of what happened within the boundaries of the case by carefully selecting and presenting descriptions and analyses of discourse, scenes and other information derived from the entire data set. In this manner, the case study report, which can be written, oral or visual, ultimately depends on the researcher's interpretive and analytical judgments about what counts as valuable, defensible, and justifiable evidence (Merriam, 1988).

In language and education studies, written cases predominate. Written case studies typically include a statement about assumptions, a research question, a methodological section, descriptive information on the particulars of the case, and an analysis section where the story is told. A rich case study provides details not only about the phenomenon and its context, but also a discussion about how the conclusions were drawn, and the ways they relate to theoretical assumptions. This in turn helps the reader to draw conclusions based on the evidence and the researcher's defense of them. Finally, case study research in language and education often has implications for teaching. These are usually stated in terms of recommendations based upon what the researcher learned from the case study.

MAJOR CONTRIBUTIONS

Interpretive Case Studies. Interpretive case studies in language and education are analytical descriptions that illustrate, support or challenge existing theoretical assumptions about teaching and learning. Interpretive case studies necessarily involve attention to description and the interpretation of meaning. Beyond a description and discussion of the case, interpretive case study can vary in terms of the level of analysis used to interpret the events within the description. The level of analysis can range from exploring and asserting connections between context and phenomena to constructing theory. Pease-Alvarez & Winsler (1993) provide an example of an exploratory interpretive case study. In this study, the researchers focused on three fourth grade Mexican immigrant children's use of Spanish and English in a classroom where the teacher did not speak Spanish, but did everything he could to foster the maintenance and development of the students' native language, Spanish.

Many interpretive case studies in language and education begin with a set of assumptions about how or why a particular phenomenon of interest occurs, with an eye toward refining an existing theory constructed under different circumstances. One of the best and earliest examples of this approach is a study by Hakuta (1976) who conducted a case study of a 9 year old Japanese boy acquiring English as a second language (ESL) to determine whether the order of acquisition of certain morphemes for ESL was the same order as Brown (1973) had found and posited for English as a first language in his 3 year case study of three young children. Hakuta found that the child in his case study developed a different order of acquisition, leading him to assert that Brown's order did not apply to the acquisition of ESL. Both studies generated a host of new research, most of which no longer involved case study method, but rather used statistical correlation techniques.

In a case study of two bilingual early childhood teachers, Pease-Alvarez, García & Espinosa (1991) examined how the teachers' incorporation of certain pedagogical perspectives and practices helped young children become bilingual and biliterate. In Italy, Cicognani & Zani (1992) used an exploratory case study to focus on the verbal environment provided by nursery school teachers to the children.

Interpretive case studies have also been used to illustrate the connection between social factors and language in schools. Shannon (1995) conducted a case study of one bilingual teacher's resistance to the hegemony that English enjoys over other languages. She learned how the teacher's assumptions about language and literacy translated into practices that countered the power of English in her classroom as well as in and outside the school setting. In a similar vein, Escamilla (1995) presented a case study of a bilingual school to tell the story of how the use of Spanish and English in the larger community was reflected in bilingual classrooms. She found that English was the high status language, and like Shannon noted that English had hegemonic power over Spanish. Escamilla interpreted this to mean that for the children in bilingual classrooms, the sole purpose of using Spanish was to move them into English.

In Australia and New Zealand, Corson (1988, 1990) conducted a series of case studies of school-based planning for multilingual and multicultural schooling and used these to implement new programs to foster diversity (see the review by May in Volume 1). Cazden (1989) used a case study approach to understand how an educational leader in a New Zealand school engaged his staff in understanding his vision for creating a multiethnic school. Cazden studied how the principal embodied the vision in the organizational structures he jointly developed with staff, and through the patterns of interaction among the staff, children and the community.

Interpretive case study research has also led to important discoveries about how young children become literate. One of the first case studies on this phenomenon was conducted by Clay (1975). She sought to uncover how young children progressed from exploring the physical nature of letter shapes to gaining a sense of word-space-word in reading. Bissex (1980) studied how her own son acquired reading and writing understanding and abilities from ages 5 to 11. Calkins (1983) followed by studying one child as she developed into a reader and writer in a classroom that incorporated writer's workshop, an approach to literacy in which students read and write what is important to them. In a similar vein, Lyons (1988) used a series of personal letters as a case study to learn what a 9 year-old writer in England knew and needed to know about the English language.

Intervention Case Studies. In this method of case study, some type of intervention within the context occurs, and the researcher seeks to find out if and how the intervention had an effect on the phenomenon of interest. The methodology resembles what happens in experimental research, in that the goal is to explain behavior and/or meaning constructions on the basis of what happens as a result of the intervention. The difference is that experimental research uses quantitative (statistical) approaches and typically involves an experimental and control group without attention to context or boundaries. In contrast, intervention case studies focus on a single individual or site, and are expressly interested in understanding the contextual conditions under which the intervention operates or not.

The intervention case study method most often used in language and education cases typically involves a three-phase design. In phase 1, the goal is to establish through naturalistic and/or elicited data collection techniques a baseline against which future understandings and/or behaviors can be compared. This phase requires interpretation and analysis as in interpretive case studies, and may involve quantitative data collection as well. The researcher needs to understand and describe as accurately as possible the conditions and meanings that exist before the introduction of the intervention. In phase 2, the intervention begins, and the researcher again collects data to describe and interpret what happens, being careful not to attribute any changes in meanings or behaviors to the intervention. In the final phase, the intervention stops, and the researcher now focuses on the ways that the meaning and behaviors introduced in phase 2 remain or adjust over time. If there is a noticeable change from phase 1 to phase 3, the researcher may be justified in concluding that the intervention or parts of it were responsible for the change.

Intervention case studies are far less common in language and education than interpretive studies. In general, researchers who are interested in studying the effects of an intervention rely on a positivist experimental approach which requires a large sample size and uses inferential statistics.

In this type of research, if the results indicate that the intervention had a significant effect, the researcher feels justified in assuming that the results are reliable and thus, generalizable to similar populations. Intervention case studies make no such claim. Their purpose is to understand the phenomenon the way the participants interpret it within each of the phases of research. The researcher strives for internal validity, arguing that it is not possible to have internal validity without having reliability (Merriam, 1988).

In a tale of two children, Hudelson (1989) acted as a change agent and intervened in the ways that two Spanish-speaking children were invited to develop ESL writing abilities. Hudelson first studied how the two children were taught to write through exercises and teacher directed lessons. Hudelson was interested in how writing might develop differently after an intervention based on whole language principles of language and learning. After several months of intervention, the children progressed from viewing writing as copying workbook sentences to creating meaningful texts in English while they were still in the process of acquiring it orally. After the intervention ceased, Hudelson re-visited and found that both students continued to practice the kinds of writing that she had introduced to them.

Faltis (1994) conducted an intervention case study of two bilingual teachers who taught science and social studies in Spanish and English in a middle school. Both teachers used concurrent translation from English to Spanish, and tended to use Spanish for reprimands, and English for directions and summary explanations. Faltis taught the teachers to understand and use a non-translation concurrent approach (a variation of the New Concurrent Approach based on Jacobson, 1982). The approach uses a cue system for switching between languages during content teaching. In the final phase of the study, both teachers completely stopped using concurrent translation during teaching.

ISSUES AND PROBLEMS

A long-standing issue associated with case study methods is that their results are not generalizable to comparable settings or cases. The value of generalizability from a sample to a population is an artifact of positivist, statistically-driven research. Ending up with generalizable knowledge from case studies, however, is not a goal in interpretive research (Erickson, 1986). Nonetheless, case study methods do present evidence for readers to make their own generalizations based upon the particulars of the case. That is, each case has its own unique qualities manifested in concrete experiences, but within the case there are features and events that readers can find in similar settings, much in the same way that people transfer knowledge and meaning to newly encountered experiences on a daily basis (Merriam, 1988).

Beyond generalizability, case study researchers need to also address the issue of validity, i.e., how the findings match reality. Internal validity is the hallmark of well-done case-study. Without it, the conclusions the researcher draws are suspect, and reliability suffers as well. The problem researchers face is that they can never know if the reality they recon-struct is the reality that participants in the case study have. There are a number of ways researchers can minimize the difference between their own reconstructions and the constructions used by the participants in the case. Among the most popular ways of establishing internal validity in case study research are triangulation, long term observation at the case site, checking and re-checking assertions, and making assumptions and theoretical orientations known at the outset of the study.

Finally, there is the issue that Ragin & Becker (1992) bring out, which is that it is not an easy task to figure out what a case study is. They point out that there are many ways to conceptualize what is a case, depending on whether the researcher understands the case as being an existing reality to be discovered, described and verified, or as a theoretical construct that takes shape as the research progresses and a high level of internal validity is reached. Moreover, they point out that it is not always clear what a case study is a case of. For example, while a study may ostensibly be about how individual children learn to write in school (an empirical unit of analysis), it could also be that the study is a case of writing itself (a theoretical construct) or a case of how writing is socially constructed in one classroom setting (a collective theoretical construct).

FUTURE DIRECTIONS

In this post-modern era, increasing numbers of researchers in language and education are using case study methods to understand phenomena of interest. A number of critical case studies are starting to appear that chal-lenge assumptions about the neutrality of language and related educational issues. Critical case studies ask who benefits from certain policies and practices, and explore the issues of hegemony, silence, resistance, to name a few (Lemke, 1995). For example, case studies by Arthur (1996) and Lin (1996) echo Shannon's (1995) challenge of the assumption that dual lan-guage use in schools promotes bilingualism at the societal level. Arthur's study of Botswana and English medium schools in Botswana illuminates the power of English by studying students' as well as teachers' decisions to use one language or the other for classroom management and instructional purposes. Lin (1996) reports a case study of code-switching behaviors in a Hong Kong school to show how the school promotes English as a superior language to Cantonese, and how students use alternation strategies to resist efforts by the teacher to give instruction primarily in English.

Gender is also an issue that is showing up in critical case study research. Wolfe & Faltis (1997) conducted an exploratory case study of the same boys and girls across three high school bilingual classrooms to understand and illustrate how the teachers allocated talk, and the students participated in academic discussions. They found that allocation and participation varied in accordance with the discourse demands of classroom tasks and the teacher's ideological perspective.

Researchers are also starting to use case study methods to understand and refine theory about the nature of academic language and how students become members of the community of practice that uses academic language to make sense of knowledge systems. For example, Benson, Gurney, Harrison & Rimmershaw (1993) conducted a case study in England in the context of university students learning to write in the academic community. Students learned the differences between academic writing and their previous uses of writing. A related and critical issue for the future is understanding the needs of adolescent immigrant students who show up in secondary school with little or no academic and literacy experiences.

A promising theoretical perspective for understanding how students become acquired by academic discourses is the work of Lave & Wenger (1991) and Gee (1993). From this perspective, learning in school is a matter of being acquired by the discourse of the various academic subjects that students need to succeed in school (Lemke, 1995).

Arizona State University
USA

REFERENCES

Arthur, J.: 1996, 'Code switching and collusion: Classroom interaction in Botswana primary schools', *Linguistics and Education* 8, 17–34.

Benson, N., Gurney, S., Harrison, J. & Rimmershaw, R.: 1993, 'The place of academic writing in whole life writing: A case study of three university students', *Language and Education* 7, 1–20.

Bissex, G.: 1980, *Gnys at Wrk: A Child Learns to Read and Write*, Harvard University Press, Cambridge, Massachusetts.

Brown, R.: 1973, *A First Language: The Early Stages*, Allen and Unwin, London.

Calkins, L.: 1983, *Lessons for a Child: On the Teaching and Learning of Writing*, Heinemann, Melbourne, Australia.

Cazden, C.: 1989, 'Richmond Road: A Multilingual/Multicultural Primary School in Auckland, New Zealand', *Language and Education* 3, 143–166.

Cicognani, E. & Zani, B.: 1992, 'Teacher-children interactions in a nursery School: An exploratory study', *Language and Education* 6, 1–12.

Clay, M.: 1975, *What Did I Write?* Heinemann, Auckland, New Zealand.

Corson, D.: 1990, *Language Policy Across the Curriculum*, Multilingual Matters, Clevedon, Avon.

Corson, D.: 1988, 'Language policy across the curriculum (LPAC)', *Language and Education* 2, 61–63.

Erickson, F.: 1986, 'Qualitative methods in research on teaching', in M. Wittrock (ed.), *Handbook of Research on Teaching* (3rd edition), MacMillan, New York, 119–161.

Escamilla, K.: 1995, 'The sociolinguistic environment of a bilingual school: A case study introduction', *Bilingual Research Journal* 18, 21–48.

Faltis, C.: 1994, 'Doing the right thing: Developing a program for immigrant and bilingual secondary students', in R. Rodríguez & N. Ramos (eds.), *Compendium of Readings on Bilingual Education*, Texas Association for Bilingual Education, San Antonio, TX, 39–47.

Gee, J.: 1993, *The Social Mind: Language, Ideology, and Social Practices*, Bergin & Garvey, South Hadley, Massachusetts.

Hakuta, K.: 1976, 'A case study of a Japanese child learning English', *Language Learning* 26, 321–351.

Hudelson, S.: 1989, 'A Tale of two children: Individual differences in ESL children's writing', in D. Johnson & D. Roen (eds.), *Richness in Writing: Empowering ESL Students*, Longman, White Plains, NY, 84–99.

Jacobson, R.: 1982, 'The implementation of a bilingual instructional model – the new concurrent approach', in R. Padilla (ed.), *Ethnoperspectives in Bilingual Education Research* (Volume III), Eastern Michigan University, Ypsilanti, MI, 14–29.

Johnson, D.M.: 1992, *Approaches to Research in Second Language Learning*, Longman, New York.

Lave, J. & Wenger, E.: 1991, *Situated Learning: Legitimate Peripheral Participation*, Cambridge University Press, New York.

Lemke, J.: 1995, *Textual Politics: Discourse and Social Dynamics*, Taylor & Francis, Bristol, Pennsylvania.

Lin, A.M.Y.: 1996, 'Bilingualism or linguistic segregation? symbolic domination, resistance and code switching in Hong Kong schools', *Linguistics and Education* 8, 49–83.

Llewellyn, K.: 1948, 'Case method', in E. Seligman & A. Johnson (eds.), *Encyclopedia of Social Sciences*, Macmillan, New York.

Lyons, H.: 1988, 'Needing to know about language: A case study of a nine-year-old's usage', *Language and Education* 2, 175–188.

Merriam, S.: 1988, *Case Study Research in Education: A Qualitative Approach*. Jossey-Bass, San Francisco.

Pease-Alvarez, L. & Winsler, A.: 1994, 'Cuando El Maestro No Habla Español: Children's bilingual language practices in the classroom', *TESOL Quarterly* 28, 507–535.

Pease-Alvarez, L., García, E. & Espinosa, P.: 1991, 'Effective instruction for language minority students: An early childhood case study', *Early Childhood Research Quarterly* 6, 347–361.

Ragin, C. & Becker, H. (eds.): 1992, *What is a Case? Exploring the Foundations of Social Inquiry*, Cambridge University Press, Cambridge.

Shannon, S.: 1995, 'The hegemony of English: A case study of one bilingual classroom', *Linguistics and Education* 7, 175–200.

Smith, L.M.: 1978, 'An evolving logic of participant observation, educational ethnography and other case studies', in L. Shulman (ed.), *Review of Research in Education* (Volume 6), Peacock Itasca, IL, 326–377.

Stake, R.: 1994, 'Case studies', in N. Denzin & Y. Lincoln (eds.), *Handbook of Qualitative Research*, Sage, Thousand Oaks, CA, 236–247.

Wolfe, P. & Faltis, C.: 1997. 'Bilingualism, gender and academic language in a high school program', in C. Faltis & P. Wolfe (eds.), *So Much to Say: Adolescents, Bilingualism, and ESL in the Secondary School*, Teachers College Press, New York, 120–138.

OLGA G. RUBIO

ETHNOGRAPHIC INTERVIEW METHODS IN RESEARCHING LANGUAGE AND EDUCATION

Interviewing in the nineties has become a powerful form of communication in our society and in social scientific research. It is estimated that 90 percent of all social science research uses interview data (Briggs, 1992/1986). This review will provide a historical and current overview of the role of ethnographic interviews in language and education research. To successfully examine the role of interviews in language and education research it is imperative to understand the interview as an important tool of anthropologically grounded research. Ethnographic interviews are used by social scientists and educators today to get the informant's or interviewee's perspective on their beliefs, values, and understandings of life and other topics or cultural events. Interviews in language and education research are also seen as 'an information-providing speech exchange in which some of the knowledge of the consultant is given to the interviewer' Werner & Schoepfle (1987, p. 302). Erickson (1981) suggests that there are two main ways by which peoples' cultural knowledge can be studied, the first is by asking them, and the second, by watching them. He distinguishes between the different approaches based primarily on asking, such as questionnaires with their attendant technical problems involving possible sample and instrument bias, and formal and 'friendly conversations', as defined for example by Spradley (1979, pp. 3–55) and Erickson (1981, pp. 29–30).

Spradley (1979) published *The Ethnographic Interview*, a text widely cited in the eighties by educational anthropologists. Drawing on the use of semantic analysis as a way of understanding cultural meaning, the author describes the structure and the role of the interview in language and culture fieldwork. He notes that the interview is a speech event, one that may deal with at least two languages, the researchers' and the one spoken by informants'. Spradley separates the work of ethnography according to two major tasks, 'discovering' and 'describing'. He describes language as a 'tool for constructing realities'. To get at the various realities, the ethnographers' and the informants', Spradley suggests the need for the researcher to distinguish between the types of descriptions corresponding to 'outsiders' language' and 'insiders' language'. It is this task that remains at the heart of language and education research. One of the main challenges for the ethnographer is gaining access to the insider's communicative

N.H. Hornberger and D. Corson (eds), Encyclopedia of Language and Education,
Volume 8: Research Methods in Language and Education, 153–163.
© *1997 Kluwer Academic Publishers. Printed in the Netherlands.*

and metacommunicative competencies. Reaching a level of expertise in the language to conduct ethnographic interviewing requires a great deal of preparation and study. This review will summarize the origins of ethnographic interviewing in language and education research and situate it as a critical tool in getting at the cultural beliefs and values of people. It will also explore the problems and the limitations of this research tool. Finally, the review will end with an examination of the role of interviews in current and future language and education research.

EARLY DEVELOPMENTS

The sixties marks a critical juncture for the development of the interview as a tool for language and education research through the emergence of the new interdisciplinary fields sociolinguistics, linguistic anthropology and educational anthropology. Hymes edited a major anthology of scholarly works in 1964 where he problematized the articulation of 'language and culture' or 'language in culture'. The edition, *Language in Culture and Society: A Reader in Linguistics and Anthropology*, presented cogent, compelling cases to advance a new perspective that influenced anthropological, linguistic and later educational scholarly works. Given the basis of anthropologically grounded research in fieldwork, ethnography subsequently figured as essential in the examination of language in culture and society. Interviews, as part of other ethnographic research procedures, provided the social scientist with the tools to seek important information from the participants of such studies.

MAJOR CONTRIBUTIONS

Hymes, Gumperz and others continued to influence the field of language and education research in the mid-sixties and early seventies. Together, Dell Hymes and John Gumperz in 1964 edited another important text, *Directions in Sociolinguistics: The Ethnography of Communication*. The text raised the notion of society and its relationships to language and culture as a basis for the understanding of culturally discontinuous interaction by non-mainstream populations. In it the major components of the study of ethnography of communication were put forth. An 'ethnography of communication framework includes analysis of speech and of the situational contexts that invoke linguistic alternatives as well as the cultural norms used in 'everday talk' (Hymes, 1972; Bonvillain, 1993, p. 2). The ethnographic perspective provides researchers with critical links between language and culture (see the review by Farah in this volume).

In 1972, The *Functions of Language in the Classroom* edited by Courtney Cazden, Vera John, and Dell Hymes, focused on the results of sociolinguistic and linguistic anthropological works seeking to respond to the social problems of children underachieving in classrooms in the United States and in other countries. Concurrently, William Labov had been adamantly carving out social context and social variables as key in the study of linguistic theoretical problems. Labov's new methods featured the oral narrative elicited through the interview, as an important research tool to study everyday language use. It was finally suggested that the interdisciplinary approach could achieve unity 'through a common focus upon language behavior in the communication between teachers and students in classrooms' (Labov, 1972).

In all this work exploring the communication patterns of teachers and students in classrooms, interviews, formal, informal or casual, were used as a standard method of the ethnographic approach, along with participant-observation and document review. Yet, interviews themselves as a speech event, or genre, were not discussed or critically analyzed in the discussion of the methods used. These earlier works for example, presented compelling data drawn from informal conversations with informants, or from classroom recordings of the students in the study but cited these findings with little mention of how the interviews were conducted. Linguists, anthropologists and educators who used ethnographic research tools included excerpts from transcribed conversations between researchers and their informants; however, the methodology itself remained fairly unexamined until the mid eighties.

By 1983, Shirley Brice Heath's decade long research in rural Appalachian U.S. paved the way for the literature on socialization in language and education research. Building on the pioneer works of Elinor Ochs & Bambi Schieffelin (1979) in the socialization of language, Heath pursued the ethnography of communication approach in schools and community rural Appalachia. She had been asked by the communities to assist them in responding to the large number of African American children underachieving in the schools. Her extensive multiple year ethnography of interracial communities in the South, *Ways with Words*, marked a different theoretical trend in language and education research. In it, she reports on everyday life and language use at home and in school in two communities in the Piedmont, Carolinas: Trackton, the working class, African-American rural community, and Roadville, the predominantly European-white, working-class community. Heath's description of the important developmental links between the bicultural, biracial communities cited marked cultural differences between the two groups. The variation was captured in the systematic tape recordings and transcriptions of the Trackton and Roadville residents. The ethnography reported primarily on the face-to-face network in which children learned the "ways of acting, believing, and valuing" of the informants in the heterogeneous communities. Formal and informal interviewing techniques were used in the work. Interview chunks were used to illustrate the interracial norms of 'gettin' on in two communities' or 'learning how to talk in Trackton', 'teaching how to talk in Trackton', or to describe the 'types of uses of reading in Roadville' (pp. 19–72). Heath and her associates were able to confirm norms verbalized by the residents with their actual practices illustrating the relevance of recording and observing in conducting ethnographic research. Interview sections appear in a rich contextual manner to further illustrate Roadville and Trackton's ways of speaking. Significantly, the study marked the value of diachronic, cross-cultural, cross-class sociolinguistic analysis in studying the achieving and underachieving problems of marginalized children in a biracial setting.

No review of ethnographic interviewing can be complete without an examination of the sociolinguistic work of Susan Gal and Lesley Milroy. Susan Gal (1987, 1979, 1978) in her anthropological linguistic work builds on social network analysis to study linguistic variation in bilingual Austria, specifically, Oberwart, a primarily peasant community. Her approach to the study of linguistic variation in the Austrian/German community was to study the interviewee's social network as a structural unit of analysis. Gal argued that the 'speakers' linguistic behaviors are constrained and shaped by the sorts of social contacts they maintain' and suggests that their speech influences other people's perception of their status (p. 131). The Language Usage Interview she conducted included questions in whatever language the speaker chose, and it covered a wide range of public and personal domains. She included questions about the church, official business, work, shopping, school, kin, neighbors, pals (Kolegak), entertainment, and general attitudes (pp. 177–184). Thus the focus of the questions framed the kinds of network contacts in the multiple settings. Gal's work illustrates how social networks shape people's goals and their means of action.

Milroy's (1980/1989) sociolinguistic study of language use in Belfast was published in her text, *Language and Social Networks*. In it she provided an advancement to the earlier pioneer works of Blom & Gumperz in Hemnes, Norway and William Labov in Martha's Vineyard, the Lower East Side of New York City and Harlem on dialectal variation. Milroy explored the role of the 'observer's paradox' that Labov had posed as inevitable in studying language in natural settings. The insider/outsider paradigm that strongly characterizes field-grounded research was used by Milroy to further probe and extend this paradox discussed by earlier sociolinguists yet not applied to their own research methodologies. For example, Milroy points to how Blom and Gumperz used social networks to do their study, but did not examine their own role in collecting their data and how Labov worked with dialect proficient field-workers yet made little mention of their possible role in the interpretation of the linguistic variation data. Milroy took social analysis as an "analytic concept" and proposed a systematic use of Belfast's close networks to conduct her research. This particular approach positions the field-worker/ethnographer as a link in the network and as such, someone who could play an instrumental role in interpreting and understanding language use. The "basic postulate is that people interact meaningfully as individuals in addition to forming parts of structured, functional institutions such as classes, castes, or occupational groups" (Milroy, 1980/1989, p. 45–67).

The interview style described by Milroy in social network analysis is one where the interviewer acknowledges responsibility for asking and initiating the questions or topics. She goes on to distinguish between the interview that is spontaneous from the one that may be slower paced, punctuated with deliberate pauses. Milroy took social network analysis as the notion that speech events such as narrative, banter, or apology represent real challenges in distinguishing the community norm for the insider/outsider fieldworker. Finally, she argues that network analysis enables the researcher to 'define her/his relationship to the group systematically' (p. 69). Milroy found the Belfast community to be one characterized as low-status, and that subsequently social networks, or unfolding study through networks of family and friends could also facilitate scholarly works with other low-status, or working-class communities.

PROBLEMS AND DIFFICULTIES

As suggested earlier, the specifics about the use of interviews in the decades of the seventies and early eighties were barely explicitly mentioned in many of the earlier works, but a shift in reporting sociolinguistic data occurred in the mid eighties. Two works in particular explored the uses of interviewing as a research tool in the social sciences (Hill & Anderson, 1993, p. 111). Both were published in 1986, *Research Interviewing: Context and Narrative* (Mishler, 1986) and *Learning How to Ask: A Sociolinguistic Appraisal of the Role of the Interview in Social Science Research* (Briggs, 1986). The latter text focused on the author's own 'communicative blunders' committed in conducting research interviews among Spanish-speakers in northern New Mexico. He cautions scholars on the following: that non-native speakers need to be aware of the wide range of metacommunicative repertoires existent in all multilingual communities. Briggs' critical examination of his own methods provides researchers with the opportunity to reexamine and to rethink the role of the interview in social science research. He focuses on the importance that the social roles assumed by interviewer and respondent have for the success of the interview. Using what he calls his 'communicative blunders' he illustrates to the reader how a researcher's limited metacommunicative competence may lead to a misinterpretation of the realities and language the ethnographer is attempting to understand. He argues that by respondents not sharing in the communicative event 'interview' a limited indexical interpretation of speech may ensue. Problems of interpretation may evolve if the researcher does not understand the distinctions between indexical and referential meaning. He recommends that interviews once collected should be transcribed in their entirety, and that by chunking these, the ethnographer may overlook important contextual clues to more exhaustively interpret the speech collected. Procedurally, Briggs finds that 'the single most serious shortcoming relating to the use of interviews in the social sciences is the commonsensical, unreflective manner in which most analyses of interview data are conducted' (p. 2). Briggs goes on to argue that 'the communicative structure of the entire interview affects the meaning of each utterance' (pp. 102–103). This honest reflection invited a critique by all language and educational researchers to reexamine the role of interviews in linguistic and cultural research.

Mishler (1986) also focused his critique on the use of interviewing, working from 'within a psychological tradition' (Hill & Anderson, 1993, p. 111). Interviews for Mishler are 'speech events in which discourse is constructed jointly between the interviewee and the interviewer, the analysis and the interpretation of the results are based on a theory of discourse and meaning, and finally, the meanings of questions and answers are contextually grounded' (Mishler, 1990, p. 11) The author primarily concerned himself with the stimulus-response paradigm of the experimental laboratory (Mishler, 1986, p. 13) and proposed instead, the use of ethnographic methods, case studies or grounded-theory all belonging to what he calls 'inquiry-guided' research. Finally, Mishler raised three issues in evaluating different types of approaches to inquiry-method research, or narrative inquiry approaches, 1) How do we establish units of analysis, or in other words, when is it appropriate to use the whole interview, or a single narrative from it; 2) How do we define and use the terms, and what function should these play, 3) How do we evaluate the validity of varying interpretations of a single narrative. Mishler and Briggs (see also Briggs, 1983) both provided important critiques of interviews used in experimentally based research and suggested interviewing as a means of studying language. Yet, missing from their thoughtful suggestions are other questions. Hill and Anderson question Brigg's argument that the ethnographer should know all local norms of communication; the linguists counterpose a provocative question: 'Why does the interview, as a speech event, have to reflect the respondent's everyday norms of communication?' Hill and Anderson suggest that there could be a function and a role for an anthropologist violating norms as a way of testing local cultural knowledge, or to further understanding of deeper cultural values embedded in everyday speech. Yet other questions that emerge from these critiques include the probability of an outsider's mastering the community's total communicative repertoire, or culture. Can the outsider become an insider? How do questions shape the construction of realities between the interviewer and interviewee? Finally, how do these various roles influence language and education research?

The issue of validity in language and education research has been a consideration for a few, but not so overt an issue in the works of the sociolinguists and ethnographers to date. For the sociolinguist and the ethnographer it is the narrative and its performance, or the production of speech that becomes the purpose and objective of the study. Uncovering speech acts, events, and their linguistic, semantic or pragmatic function consequently take precedence in such research reports. Thus, the lingering question that emerges in this review is, to what extent does authenticity of the ethnographer's interpretations of the speech network or community matter? Do insider/outsider paradigms affect the presentation and the outcome of sociolinguistic and ethnographic research of communication networks in communities? In general, and in the conduct and interpretation of interviews in particular? Also, to what extent does the ethnographer's position in his/her study influence the interviews and their interpretation?

FUTURE TRENDS AND DIRECTIONS

Further examination of the "insider/outsider" paradigm (Delgado-Gaitan, 1993) and the role of the interview in it promises to continue as an important trend in language and education research. Rubio's (1994) microethnographic case study of Puerto Rican parents in a dual language school in Philadelphia provides a context for the exploration of these considerations as they arose in conducting spontaneous interviews in the course of doing ethnography of communication research in an urban setting. Specifically, Rubio's work raises the need for further probing on the repositioning of the ethnographer in fieldwork (Rosaldo, 1989).

The role of the interview may also play a significant part in another developing trend in ethnographic studies in language and education, namely the challenging/contesting of cultural difference and home school mismatch theories. Vasquez, Alvarez-Pease & Shannon (1994), in their co-authored book each report on their work with the Eastsiders, a Mexicano community in California. By studying the socialization of language patterns used within family networks, the ethnographers were able to uncover convergent ways in the use of everyday language. Vasquez et al. argue that ethnograpies of communication that also do not illustrate the continuous or cross-cultural contexts upon which the metacommunicative competence of language minority children are based are not adequately representing the cross-cultural variation involved in language socialization.

Another future direction in ethnographic research and education research with implications for ethnographic interviewing may be the incorporation of ever wider interdisciplinary approaches. Morgan (1994) like Gal, argues the need for sociolinguists to historicize their linguistic investigations. The historical context, she argues, can really shape the way a community is perceived. Her work with five generations of African-American women from Chicago revealed the significance of considering gender variation in sociolinguistic studies but she also demonstrates the need to historicize the linguistic analysis of the time to better understand the complex ways in which society constructs and communicates meaning through language.

Other ethnographers of language and education have also drawn from other disciplines. Hornberger's scholarly work in bilingual communities in Latin America (1988) was grounded in ethnography, sociology of language and policy studies. Her study of language use among the Quechua in Southern Peru drew from three main procedures, observations, interviews, and record-keeping. Through her careful journalizing of speech use she was able "to identify and to isolate speech events in terms of the message sender, message receiver, the setting, topic, code and channel of the general speech event; and the sender, receiver, school-talk category, content, code and channel of the classroom speech event" (p. 9). Hornberger goes into great lengths to describe her interviewing procedures. She conducted formal and informal interviews, using a Language Use/Language History interview guide with approximately twenty members in each of two communities, and impromptu, unrecorded, informal interviews on language related matters with several members of each of the two communities she studied, Kinschata and Visallani. What is important about the ethnographer's work is that she took care to interview and record in Quechua, and used Spanish only when the speaker insisted on switching to Spanish. Additionally important in the examination of the role of interviews in sociolinguistic data, she listed the criteria she used to ensure metacommunicative competence in the conduct and interpretations of the interviews. First, the interview was carried out only after the interviewee knew her quite well; second, the interview was entirely in Quechua, which put the interviewee at the greatest possible ease; and third, she cross-referenced the authenticity of the answers by triangulating with observations of the speakers with others in different sociolinguistic interactional contexts (p. 8). Ultimately, Hornberger's sociological profile of language use by the Quechua produced a rich and informative study that informs language policy planners in a significant way. This use of microlevel, school/community ethnographic research based on participant-observation and interviewing, to evaluate and inform macro-level policy making marks another developing trend in the use of ethnographic interview methods in language and education research.

Other sociolinguists have sought to integrate ethnography with discourse analysis. Freeman's (1993) sociolinguistic research is grounded on an ethnographic/discourse analytic approach. That is, she uses ethnography to study the sociopolitical context of a successful dual language program for language minority children, Public School 157 in the East Coast U. S.

Her focus was on documenting how the school successfully implemented a dual language policy. Using ethnographic approaches she drew heavily on observations of the school site and the key participants involved in the school, and extensive interviewing to get at the emic distinctions or the units of interaction germane to the school in question. Freeman's analysis provides the basis for cross-cultural or cross-situational comparisons in an urban school. Using discourse analysis, the sociolinguist interprets the texts of the interviews. By so doing, the researcher was able to provide an exhaustive analysis of the ways in which PS 157 met the linguistic and academic needs of the language minority children. This approach also provided an innovative way of studying language policies and the effects of their implementation with a great degree of empirical data gleaned largely from interviews. More recently, Freeman (1996) continues to draw on the intersection of ethnography and discourse analysis to better understand how the sociopolitical context interacts with every facet of language planning and implementation.

Future research promises to frame and recast interviews in greater historical and diachronic perspective. Interviews must be carefully examined and constructed to allow for authentic interpretation of the interviewees. To get at their own metacommunicative competence ethnographers and sociolinguists must continue to grapple with insider/outsider/insider questions. Such acknowledgments by scholars will contribute to deeper interpretations of the lives and vernaculars of members of marginalized communities at home and in schools in different contexts and across generations, gender, and class. Presentation of future findings must seek to find ways that further authenticate the voices of the people in such studies while maintaining their focus on the research goals to examine multidimensional contexts of language use, in individual and social network settings. Such works will continue to bear compelling results to transform existing mainstream, unidimensional schooling practices.

Columbia University,
USA

REFERENCES

Blom, J.P. & Gumperz, J.J: 1974, 'Social meaning in linguistic structures: Codeswitching in Norway', in J.J. Gumperz & D. Hymes (eds), *Directions in Sociolinguistics*, Holt, Rinehart & Winston, 407–444.

Bonvillain, N.: 1993, *Language, Culture, and Communication: The Meaning of Messages*, Vol. 2, Prentice Hall, Englewood Cliffs, 89–111.

Briggs, C.: 1986/1992, *Learning How to Ask: A Sociolinguistic Appraisal of the Role of the Interview in Social Science Research*, Cambridge University Press, New York.

Briggs, C.: 1983, 'Questions for the ethnographer: A critical examination of the role of the interview in fieldwork', *Semiotica* 46(2/4), 233–261.

Cazden, C., Hymes, D. & Vera, J. (eds.): 1972, *Functions of Language in the Classroom*, Teachers College Press, New York.

Delgado Gaitan, C.: 1993. 'Researching change and changing the researcher', *Harvard Educational Review 63,4, Winter 1993, 389-411.*

Erickson, F.: 1981, 'Some approaches to inquiry in school-community ethnography', in H. Trueba, G. Guthrie & K. Au (eds.), *Culture and the Bilingual Classroom: Studies in Classroom Ethnography*, Newbury House Publishers, Rowley, Massachusetts, 17–35.

Freeman, R.: 1993, *Language Planning and Identity Planning for Social Change: Gaining the Ability and the Right to Participate*, Unpublished doctoral dissertation, Georgetown University.

Freeman, R.: 1996, 'Dual language planning at Oyster Bilingual School: It's much more than language', *TESOL Quarterly* 30(3), 557–582.

Gal, S.: 1978, 'Peasant men can't get wives: Language change and sex roles in a bilingual community', *Language in Society* 7, 1–16.

Gal, S.: 1979, *Language Shift: Social Determinants of Linguistic Change in Bilingual Austria*, Academic Press, New York, 97–184.

Gal, S.: 1987, 'Codeswitching and consciousness in the European periphery', *American Ethnologist*.

Gumperz, J. & Hymes, D. (eds.): 1972, *Directions in Sociolinguistics: The Ethnography of Communication*, Holt, Rinehart and Winston, New York.

Heath, S.: 1983, *Ways with Words*, Cambridge University Press, New York.

Hill, C. & Anderson, L.: 1993, 'The interview as a research tool', *New Ideas in Psychology* 11, 111–125.

Hornberger, N.: 1988, *Bilingual Education and Language Maintenance: A Southern Peruvian Quechua Case*, Foris Publications, Dordrecht-Holland.

Hymes, D.: 1972, 'Models of the interaction of language and social life', in J. Gumperz & D. Hymes (eds.), *Directions in Sociolinguistics: The Ethnography of Communication*, 35–71.

Hymes, D.: 1972, 'Introduction', in C. Cazden, V.P. John & D. Hymes (eds.), *Language in Education: Ethnolinguistic Essays*, Center for Applied Linguistics, Washington, DC, xi–lvii.

Hymes, D. (ed.): 1964, *Language In Culture and Society: A Reader in Linguistics and Anthropology*, Harper & Row, Publishers, New York.

Labov, W.: 1972, *Language in the Inner City: Studies in the Black English Vernacular*, University of Pennsylvania Press, Philadelphia.

Labov, W.: 1972, 'On the mechanism of linguistic change', in J. Gumperz & D. Hymes (eds.), *Directions in Sociolinguistics: The Ethnography of Communication*, 512–538.

Milroy, L.: 1980/1989, *Language and Social Networks*, Second Edition. Basil Blackwell, Great Britain, 45–69.

Mishler, E.G.: 1986/1991, *Research Interviewing: Context and Narrative*, Harvard University Press, Cambridge.

Mishler, E.G.: 1990, 'Validation in inquiry-guided research: The role of Exemplars in narrative studies', *Harvard Educational Review* 60(4), 415–442.

Morgan, M.: 1994, 'The African-American speech community: Reality and sociolinguistics', in M. Morgan (ed.), *Language & the Social Construction of Identity*, Center for Afro-American Studies, UCLA, Los Angeles.

Ochs, E. & Schieffelin, B. (ed.): 1979, *Developmental Pragmatics*, Academic Press, New York.

Rosaldo, R.: 1989/1993, *Culture and Truth: The Remaking of Social Analysis*, Beacon Press, Boston.

Rubio, O.: 1994, *Una buena educacion: A Study of Parental Values, Beliefs, and Aspi-*

rations in a Dual Language School, Unpublished doctoral dissertation, University of Pennsylvania.

Schieffelin, B.: 1996, Review of *Pushing Boundaries: Language and Culture in a Mexicano Community, Language in Society* 25(2), 325–327.

Spradley, J.: 1979, *The Ethnographic Interview*, Holt Rinehart & Winston, New York.

Vasquez, O., Alvarez-Pease, L. & Shannon, S.: 1994, *Pushing Boundaries: Language and Culture in a Mexicano Community*, Cambridge University Press.

Werner, O. & Schoepfle, M.: 1987, *Systematic Fieldwork*. Volume I. *Foundations of Ethnography and Interviewing*, Sage Publications, Newbury Park, 291–353.

SARAH H. NORGATE

RESEARCH METHODS FOR STUDYING THE LANGUAGE OF BLIND CHILDREN

Although the theoretical and practical significance of studying language development in blind children is well documented (Fraiberg, 1977; Urwin, 1978; Mulford, 1988), a number of methodological issues make this field challenging to researchers. This section identifies such issues and the ways they have been handled since the 1940's. In particular: concerns surrounding the comparison of language functioning between blind and sighted groups; the difficulties in comparing outcomes between different studies; the way theoretical frameworks and techniques used with sighted children have been applied to the study of blind children; and the issues around establishing knowledge about patterns of language development from studies based on small samples. Ways in which future developments in methodology may best advance knowledge about language acquisition in blind children are discussed.

EARLY DEVELOPMENTS

Between 1940 and 1954, the number of babies who were born prematurely and subsequently blinded by an overexposure to oxygen increased substantially, drawing clinicians and educators to the study of these children (Stone & Church, 1957). The first reports of language development relied predominantly upon methods involving direct comparisons between the development of blind children and their sighted peers. Some took a psychoanalytic perspective and compared blind and sighted children in terms of how language functioning was thought to be disturbed by the parents' inevitable reaction to the blindness (e.g. Burlingham 1961, 1965). Others made comparisons on the basis of how individual children or groups of children performed on various developmental schedules (e.g. Norris, Spaulding & Brodie, 1957). By documenting the age at which children attained such milestones as comprehending requests for games such as 'patacake' and achieving vocabularies of various sizes the assumption made was that blind children followed the same developmental routes into language as sighted children, albeit at a slower rate.

During this period, in contrast to clinicians and educators, linguists largely disregarded the relationship between visual information and language functioning and interest in this remained, at most, largely specula-

N.H. Hornberger and D. Corson (eds), Encyclopedia of Language and Education,
Volume 8: Research Methods in Language and Education, 165–173.
© *1997 Kluwer Academic Publishers. Printed in the Netherlands.*

tive. Some have interpreted this disregard as implying that linguists viewed blindness as having only limited negative consequences on language development (McGinnis, 1981; Dunlea, 1989). Indeed, Miller (1963) predicted that an absence of visual information would result in faster language learning on the grounds that blind children depend on language as a form of communication. Such a claim implied that there is a single route into language development. The disadvantage of relying on methods which make direct comparisons between the rate at which sighted and blind children acquire language is that the qualitative aspects of individual differences in the acquisition process tend to be ignored.

MAJOR CONTRIBUTIONS

By the end of their pre-school years, many blind children are reported to have achieved communicative competence (Reynell, 1979). However, reports suggest that before this time, developmental setback may occur in around a third of blind two- or three-year olds initially judged to be of normal cognitive potential (e.g. Cass, Sonksen & McConachie, 1994). Researchers have therefore focused on the ways in which language development may go off-course during this period.

During the 1980's, the majority of research projects focused on developing methods to study different aspects of language functioning: phonological development (Mills, 1983); syntactical development (Wilson, 1985); morphological development (Miecznikowski & Andersen, 1986); lexical development (Bigelow, 1983); semantic development (Dunlea, 1989) and pragmatic development (Dunlea, 1989). Small groups of children were typically tracked longitudinally using observational methods. The benefits of using longitudinal rather than cross-sectional designs are particularly highlighted in the study of blind children since longitudinal studies provide a greater opportunity to investigate the role of vision in particular stages of the acquisition process. Researchers frequently rely on video and audio recording to learn about different aspects of language development in these children. To date, most studies have focused on early patterns of communication between young blind children and their parents. Interactions are video-recorded between blind children and their families in an environment familiar to a blind child usually around every two to three months. It is common for researchers to formulate research questions about aspects of the acquisition process after making a video recording since there are few theoretical accounts of the role of vision in language development available to direct research. Observational methods are usually supplemented by asking parents to keep a report of their child's language development (e.g. early vocabulary usage using a word-diary).

One criticism made by Warren (1994) of methods used in some of the early studies was that researchers often failed to acknowledge the heterogeneity of the population by not publishing information about the factors which distinguish between blind children. By documenting information about the age of onset, aetiology and extent of blindness, prematurity and the existence of any additional disabilities, the studies completed during this period aided comparison of findings between studies and also contributed to knowledge about the way in which these different factors contributed to the course of acquisition. For example, it has been demonstrated that having even a small amount of vision increases the likelihood that the course of language development will more closely resemble that of a sighted child (McConachie & Moore, 1994). Furthermore, particular conditions of blindness can be associated with particular patterns of language functioning. The condition *retionopathy of prematurity* (ROP) is often associated with particular clusters of social-emotional difficulties, manifested by presence of speech which is repetitive (echolalic) and difficulties in using language appropriately to respond to others (Keeler, 1958).

Visual impairment is often associated with prematurity and presents a further complication in trying to elucidate the extent to which a visual deficit alone contributes to particular patterns of language functioning. In line with developmental research with sighted children, researchers typically report chronological age corrected for prematurity.

Typically, most studies have included children who are congenitally blind. Indeed, documenting the age of onset of visual impairment is particularly relevant in the case of language development since the period before the onset of speech offers opportunities for infants to gain an understanding the ways adults refer to actions, objects and events in the environment through their use of gestures, sounds and direction of gaze. It is probable that the mechanisms of language development are substantially affected by the age difference in the onset of sight loss.

During the 1980's, researchers not only started to report more information about the children participating in the research but also tightened up their use of terminology, subsequently enabling opportunities to make comparisons between findings from different studies. Whereas previously, the word 'blind' was often used to describe individuals who had various levels of visual impairment, advances in pediatric ophthalmology made it possible to assess levels of visual impairment more accurately. Theoretically, a child who exhibits no visual response is the ideal case to study since an absolute deficit creates the opportunity for determining the role of vision in different aspects of language development. This view is reflected in much of the literature, where most researchers aim to establish a sample which include children with as little vision as possible. Crucially, however, this raises the issue of the extent to which findings can inform practical strategies generalisable to the rest of the blind population. More recent studies have frequently involved groups of infants and children who are classified as either 'blind ' or 'severely visually impaired' (SVI) (Dunlea, 1989). In these studies, 'blind' is defined as either having no vision or vision which is limited to light perception. SVI is defined as a minimal amount of form vision such that the infants can usually detect movement and might be able to use their residual vision to help them move around their environment. Support for separating groups with different degrees of visual impairment comes from studies which detect a difference in language functioning between groups (Dunlea, 1989; McConachie & Moore, 1994).

WORK IN PROGRESS

Recent research into language development in this population has raised concern over the extent to which it is appropriate to include a sighted control group and/or to rely on research strategies which borrow from approaches commonly used with sighted children (Warren, 1994; Landau, 1995; Norgate, 1996; Lewis & Collis, in press). For example, the literature on language development in typical children has focused on children's understanding of objects and their understanding of actions/events has been neglected (Merriman & Tomasello, 1995). Conclusions about language development in blind children have been influenced by a bias existing in the literature on sighted infants towards language functioning defined in terms of object understanding and noun usage. Many studies of language development have largely been preoccupied with infants' production of words and with their use of words for objects. Merriman and Tomasello argue that these preoccupations lead to an unbalanced view of the nature of language development. This research bias towards objects has also been reflected in the literature on blind infants. Norgate (1996) has argued that this bias has led researchers to conclude that an absence of visual information results in a cognitive deficit (e.g. Dunlea, 1989). Individuals who are blind predominantly have access to temporal, rather than spatial information and so are better able to process information about actions and events rather than objects. It is therefore crucial to view language development in blind children in relation to the sensory information to which they do have access. Studies of language development in blind children need to pay attention to the way these children make sense of actions/events as well as objects.

Particular methodological techniques used with sighted children have often been directly applied for use with blind children. For example, in looking at pre-language skills Dunlea (1989) remarked that the four blind infants in her study were unable to sort a set of same and different class objects, and on this basis concluded that they have difficulties treating category members as the same sort of thing. However, Dunlea had transferred a *sequential analysis* technique used with sighted children to the study of object manipulations in blind children. This analysis technique is inappropriate for use with blind children because it makes no allowance for object manipulations which function as haptic scans (use of touch to explore objects) in these children (Norgate, 1996). This view is consistent with a point made by Landau (1995) who remarked that this method was inappropriate because blind children would have difficulty keeping track of which objects they had or had not explored. Findings suggest that if haptic scans are taken into account then blind children can demonstrate the ability to treat category members as the same sort of thing (Norgate, 1996).

Another domain where it has been problematic to apply methods used with sighted children directly to those of blind is in the detection of particular phenomena of early language development. When children use words referentially to talk about new referents in their environment, their speech often contains errors, in the form of overextensions (Anglin, 1977). Overextensions concern the way in which a child will use a referential word for the appropriate standard adult usage as well as for additional objects and entities which would normally be referred to by another word in adult usage. For instance, a child might say 'cup' to refer to cups as well as other bowls, egg-cups and vases.

For a number of reasons, it is likely that researchers would tend to underestimate the extent to which blind infants overextend their words to other referents. First, as is often the case with sighted children, it is important to note that scope for extensions often depend upon the emergence of a particularly suitable referent. Bigelow's (1982) point that blind infants have less immediate access to the environment means that it is not surprising that they are not often observed to extend the words they use to other referents. Second, the absence of visually based communicative strategies for joint attention also makes it likely that the frequency of overextensions will be underestimated in blind infants. When a sighted or a blind child has an object in their hands it is easy to detect whether or not they are using a word appropriately (i.e. overextending) or not. However, for an object which is in close proximity, but not in contact with the child (but that the blind child knows is present), it is more difficult to establish whether a blind child is overextending. Sighted children are likely to isolate the target referent by engaging in pointing and shared gaze. In this way, the caretaker is likely to identify which referent the child is referring to and is in a position to detect if the child is using the appropriate word. In contrast, blind children do not use gestures like pointing and it seems likely that the cues that they do use (e.g. orientation of body) are not powerful enough for them to isolate an object/action from competing ones.

It would also seem that blind children have fewer words in their vocabularies which readily lend themselves to overextension. The most frequently cited examples of overextension in sighted children's speech are based on words which refer to concrete, discrete entities which are typically learnt in 'point and label' activities such as picture book reading. Blind infants have been demonstrated to produce significantly fewer words referring to concrete, discrete objects than their sighted peers and, further, it has been shown that the proportion of these words does not increase with increasing vocabulary size (Norgate, 1996). Taken together, these points demonstrate that we must be cautious before automatically gauging the language development of blind children against that of sighted children. The very absence of vision may directly be confounded with the search for the phenomena being detected.

PROBLEMS AND DIFFICULTIES

The low incidence of blindness makes it difficult to establish sizeable samples with which to track language development. A recent survey by Walker, Tobin & McKennell (1992) estimates that in the UK around 1 in 1000 children are registered blind, of whom about 70% are likely to have an additional handicap. Similarly, estimates in the USA suggest that 10 per 10,000 school age children are blind (Garwood, 1983). Given that most studies of blind infants are based on single case studies or three or four children at most, the problem remains of how researchers can be certain that the findings are typical of blind children. This particular problem has frequently arisen in studies of the age of onset of first word production when there has been disagreement over the extent to which blind infants are delayed in the production of their lexical milestones. One of the reasons for this concerns the issue of making comparisons between measures of central tendency where samples are based on small numbers of children. When measures of central tendency are used, these tend to produce discrepancies between studies. However, when studies of the range in age at which blind and SVI infants achieve their milestones are reviewed, these indicate that these infants are no different from sighted children.

It is possible that blind infants vary in the age at which they produce their first words as much as the sighted population. In light of the impracticability of ever establishing large samples of blind/SVI infants to examine the variation in the age at which first words are produced it would seem crucial to explain differences in the age of onset of first words as well as focusing on any measure of central tendency. Although current trends in research into language functioning in sighted children suggest that estimations of variability require a substantial sample size and researchers have started to study language development in sample sizes of over 1,800 children (e.g. Fenson et al., 1993) we are reminded by Peters (1994) that by focusing on a single child, the researcher has time to discover 'rich and unanticipated detail' which provides the opportunity to explore new methods for understanding what drives developmental change.

FUTURE DIRECTIONS

Findings indicate that once research strategies take into account the different perceptual information available to blind children, their language development is viewed more positively. Future studies of language development must ensure that the abilities of blind children are not underestimated. It is important to devise special techniques which take into account the temporal basis of the perceptual information available to these children. The design of new approaches which take into account the reliance blind children have on temporal information may lead to new ways of understanding language development. Recent research demonstrating that blind children can make their way into language through a reliance on non-object-focused information suggests that in the absence of gaining access to the same environmental supports as children with sight, blind children are able to rely predominantly on temporal information in order to build up information about objects in their environment. On this basis, it is worth considering the extent to which blind children make their way into language using a route which is merely one end of a spectrum of routes used by sighted children.

The use of a sighted control group with which to gauge the rate and nature of language development in blind children is often of limited value. Linguistic differences between children need to be explained and differences between blind children are best not seen as noise in average developmental trends but rather as one of the phenomena to be explained. As Plomin (1995) has pointed out, explanations of normative development bear no necessary relationship to those of an individual's position. This point is supported by Warren (1994) who suggests that many of the differences between blind children can be attributed to environmental variables that tend to accompany visual impairment. Blindness may assume any one of a number of aetiologies, have a varied age of onset, co-occur with additional handicaps and prematurity. In addition, the parental expectations and the emotional climate of the blind child's family will make each child's experiences distinct. Since the emergence of the ability to talk is an important developmental step for the parent of any child, but particularly for parents of blind children since it provides new channels for communication, it is important that information be available to parents about what blind children can achieve linguistically.

The Open University
England

REFERENCES

Anglin, J.M.: 1977, *Word, Object and Conceptual Development*, Norton, New York.
Bigelow, A.E.: 1982, 'Early words of blind children', *Paper presented at the International Conference on Infant Studies*, Austin, Texas, March.
Bigelow, A. E.: 1983, 'Development of the use of sound in the search behavior of infants', *Developmental Psychology* 19, 317–321.
Burlingham, D.: 1961, 'Some notes on the development of the blind', *Psychoanalytic Study of the Child* 16, 121–145.
Burlingham, D.: 1965, 'Some problems of ego development in blind children', *Psychoanalytic Study of the Child* 20, 194–208.
Cass, H.D, Sonksen, P.M. & McConachie, H.R.: 1994, 'Developmental setback in severe visual impairment', *Archives of Disease in Childhood*, 70, 192–196.
Dunlea, A.: 1989, *Vision and the Emergence of Meaning*, Cambridge University Press, Cambridge.
Fenson, L., Dale, P.S., Reznick, J.S., Bates, E., Hartung, J., Pethick, S. & Reilly, J.: 1993, *The MacArthur Communicative Development Inventories: User's Guide and Technical Manual*, Singular Publishing Group, San Diego.
Fraiberg, S.: 1977, *Insights From the Blind*, Basic Books, New York.
Garwood, S.: 1983, *Educating Young Handicapped Children: A Developmental Approach* (second edition), Aspen systems Cooperation, Rockville, Maryland.
Keeler, W.R.: 1958, 'Autistic patterns and defective communication in blind children with retrolental fibroplasia', in P.H. Hoch & J. Zubin (eds.), *Psychopathology of Communication*, Grune and Stratton, New York, 64–84.
Landau, B.: 1995, *Language and Experience in Blind Children: Retrospective and Prospective*, Paper presented at the Mary Kitzinger Trust Symposium, Blindness and Psychological Development, 0–10 years. September 5–6th, University of Warwick, UK.
Lewis, V. & Collis, G.M.: in press, *Blindness and Psychological Development in Young Children*, British Psychological Publications, Leicester.
McConachie, H.R. & Moore, V.: 1994, 'Early expressive language of severely visually impaired children', *Developmental Medicine and Child Neurology* 36, 230–240.
McGinnis, A.: 1981, 'Functional linguistic strategies of blind children', *Journal of Visual Impairment and Blindness* 75(5), 210–214.
Merriman, W.E. & Tomasello, M.: 1995, 'Introduction: Verbs are words too', in M. Tomasello & W.E. Merriman (eds.), *Beyond Names for Things*, Lawrence Erlbaum Associates, Hillsdale, NJ.
Miecznikowski, A. & Andersen, E.: 1986, 'From formulaic to analysed speech: Two systems or one?', in J. Connor-Linton, C.J. Hall & M.McGinnis (eds.), *Southern California Occasional Papers in Linguistics, Volume 11*, University of Southern California Department of Linguistics, Los Angeles.
Miller, G.A.: 1963, *Language and Communication* (revised edition), McGraw-Hill Book Co., New York.
Mills, A.: 1983, 'Acquisition of speech sounds in the visually handicapped child', in A. Mills (ed.), *Language Acquisition in the Blind Child*, Croom Helm, London.
Mulford, R.: 1988, 'First words of the blind child', in M.D. Smith & J.L. Locke (eds.), *The Emergent Lexicon: The Child's Development of a Linguistic Vocabulary*, Academic Press, London.
Norgate, S.H.: 1996, *Conceptual and Lexical Functioning in Blind, Severely Visually Impaired and Sighted Infants*, Unpublished PhD doctoral dissertation, Warwick University.
Norris, M., Spaulding, P.J. & Brodie, F.H.: 1957, *Blindness in Children*, University of Chicago Press, Chicago.

Peters, A.M.: 1994, 'The interdependence of social, cognitive, and linguistic development: Evidence from a visually impaired child', in H. Tager-Flusberg (ed.), *Constraints on Language Acquisition*, Lawrence Erlbaum, London.

Plomin, R.: 1995, Editorial comment in C.M. Shore, *Individual Differences in Language Development*, Sage, London.

Reynell, J.: 1979, *Manual for the Reynell-Zinkin Scales*, NFER, London.

Stone, L.J. & Church, J.; 1957, *Childhood and Adolescence: A Psychology of the Growing Person*, New York, Random House.

Urwin, C.: 1978, *The Development of Communication Between Blind Infants and Their Parents: Some Ways into Language*, Unpublished PhD doctoral dissertation, University of Cambridge.

Walker, E., Tobin, M. & McKennell, A.: 1992, *Blind and Partially Sighted Children in Britain: the RNIB Survey*, Volume 2, HMSO, London.

Warren, D.H: 1994, *Blindness and Children: An Individual Differences Approach*, Cambridge University Press, Cambridge.

Wilson, R.B.: 1985, *The Emergence of Semantics of Tense and Aspect in the Language of a Visually Impaired Child*, Unpublished DPhil doctoral dissertation, University of Hawaii.

JAN BRANSON AND DON MILLER

RESEARCH METHODS FOR STUDYING THE LANGUAGE OF THE SIGNING DEAF

The natural sign languages of Deaf communities are fully-fledged languages like any other languages, and are mutually unintelligible in normal discourse. Sign languages differ from each other as much as sound-based languages. There are families of sign languages (Woodward, 1977) and there are no necessary syntactical relationships to surrounding sound-based languages. Sign languages, like oral languages, also only manifest themselves in practice. They are unwritten face-to-face languages. While, as indicated below, there have been scholars in previous centuries who have acknowledged that the natural sign languages of Deaf communities are languages, it is only since the 1960s that modern linguistics has even begun to see sign languages as languages worthy of their attention. The development of research methods for the study of sign languages has been particularly influenced by two central qualities of sign languages:

- The mode of sign language – i.e. that it excludes the very basis of so much linguistics, sound, but rather uses a range of conventions to generate meaning based on handshapes, the use of space, the face and body. The mode has also required that linguistics has had to focus on an aspect of language so often ignored, namely the non-oral aspects, the bodily hexis.
- The fact that sign languages are unwritten languages and that they must be approached in a way akin to oral languages without the aid of phonetically-based scripts. The development of notation systems for recording sign languages has therefore been an important aspect of linguistic research. More recently, the use of video-based materials in research has become particularly important.

The impact of these features of sign language on the development of methodologies for the study of sign languages will be explored further below in relation to the directions that research has taken, is taking and might take in the future. The impact of wider social and cultural orientations towards the Deaf, particularly in relation to education, on the development of sign language research will also be explored (also see the review by these authors in Volume 1; and by Gibson, Small and Mason in Volume 5).

N.H. Hornberger and D. Corson (eds), Encyclopedia of Language and Education,
Volume 8: Research Methods in Language and Education, 175–184.
© *1997 Kluwer Academic Publishers. Printed in the Netherlands.*

EARLY DEVELOPMENTS

The earliest recorded studies of sign language, like so many that come afterwards, are directly associated with one or both of the following issues:
- the education of the deaf;
- and the link between language and humanity.

There is evidence of the Deaf being taught through the medium of natural sign languages to read and write, first in Latin and later in the languages of everyday life, from well before the so-called Enlightenment, but it is from the beginning of the sixteenth century that educators emerge throughout Europe intent on teaching the deaf and dumb (the privileged children of merchants and the nobility) not only to read and write but to speak. Most paid little attention to existing sign languages but rather developed systems of fingerspelling designed for the purposes of speech training. There was, however a heightened consciousness of manually-based languages, and of the potential for communication through signs. This came to the fore as the education of the deaf moved beyond the very exclusive instruction of the nobility to the development of education for the poor deaf. In the mid-eighteenth century, in 1755, the Abbé de l'Epée established a school for poor deaf children in Paris. While teaching the deaf children to speak was one of his educational aims, particularly in the beginning, he moved away from speech training as central to the education of the deaf towards the use of signing as a means for teaching the deaf pupils to read and write. But he did not use the two-handed alphabet in use among the Parisian Deaf communities and did not use existing sign languages with their distinctive syntax as the language of instruction. Rather he used the one-handed alphabet and developed a system of signed French, a manual code, not a fully-fledged language.

The development of his "System of Methodological Signs", while linked to his involvement with the philosophical issues discussed below regarding the nature of language, steered attention away from the natural sign languages of Deaf communities. It was, however, one of his successors, Bébian, who laid the ground for the methodological study of natural sign languages. Bébian was dedicated to the study and recognition of natural sign language (see Fischer, 1995). Bébian's work is exceptional; of particular significance, both methodologically and in terms of its impact on contemporary sign language studies, was his detailed development of a notation system for the recording of sign languages, his "mimographie" (Bébian, 1825; Fischer, 1995). Much research remains to be done on the early work of the educators of the deaf in relation to the study of sign languages, for example of Castberg in Denmark and Villabrille in Spain (Rodríguez-González, 1993, plus other articles in Fischer & Lane, 1993).

The sixteenth century also saw the burgeoning of interest in the very nature of language itself and of its link to the creative potential of human beings. The mysteries of language, of secret codes and their creative potential, led some philosophers to consideration of manually coded systems, thus also focusing some attention on the natural sign languages of Deaf communities. These interests are reflected in particular in the work of Bulwer and Wallis in England. The links between their philosophical works and their knowledge of and research into the natural sign languages of Deaf people remains to be explored. Bulwer's 1644 book, *Chriologia, or the naturall language of the hand . . .*, makes no mention of the deaf but four years later, in 1648, his *Philophocus, or the deafe and dumb man's friend*, specifically sees the manual alphabet as of particular significance for the deaf. By the mid 1600s we know that Wallis was using a two handed alphabet very similar to the current British and Australian two-handed alphabet in the education of deaf people (see Defoe, 1720), and the *Digiti Lingua*, the first surviving published two-handed alphabet, is also oriented specifically to the deaf (see Branson, Toms et al., 1995). As mentioned above, de L'Epée's work on sign languages was also spurred on by philosophical concerns with the nature of language. It was in the school established by de L'Epée that the physician Itard explored the links between language and humanity, especially in relation to the linguistic abilities of the wild boy of Aveyron (see Lane, 1976, 1988).

This flurry of interest in sign systems, and to a lesser extent in the natural sign language of Deaf communities, waned dramatically in the late nineteenth century as educational policies with regard to the deaf focused almost totally and worldwide on the use of therapies for the teaching of speech and lip reading. The use of sign language or signing of any kind was in many cases banned. Oralism dominated the education of the deaf, and where signing was used at all, hearing educators constantly tampered with the signing traditions of their pupils, subordinating and severely restricting its lexicon to the demands of spoken and written languages, some insisting on the possibility of signing and speaking at the same time. The rebirth of signing in the education of the deaf in the late 1960s involved, in the main, the development of manually coded versions of the dominant spoken and written language, akin to de L'Epée's signed French. Manually coded versions of national spoken and written languages – such as Signed English, Signed Swedish or Signed French – are neither fully fledged languages of communication nor natural languages but rather manual codes based on written forms of language, using "frozen signs" – a single unchanging sign for each word or morpheme – and thus making little use of the dynamic and creative features of sign languages. It is worth noting here that the development of Signed English in the 1970s coincided with a stage of linguistic theory that laid emphasis on the role of syntax in language. But the 1960s also saw the fruit of Bébian's heritage with the re-emergence of the serious linguistic study of the natural sign languages of Deaf communities.

MAJOR CONTRIBUTIONS

Comprehensive research into sign languages is relatively recent, dating from the work of Stokoe in the United States and Tervoort in Holland in the 1960s, Hansen in Denmark and Bergman in Sweden, in the early 1970s (see Boyes Braem & Kolb, 1990; Bergman & Wallin, 1990; Hansen, 1990), and Brennan (Brennan et al., 1980), Deuchar (1984), Kyle and Woll (Kyle & Woll, 1983) in Britain in the late 1970s. A comprehensive international bibliography focussing on research into sign languages is produced by the University of Hamburg as both a book and a CD Rom, with the CD Rom constantly updated (Joachim & Prillwitz, 1993; see also Lucas, 1990a). Sign language research itself has a strong international focus with a small but very active body of researchers taking every opportunity to meet through international conferences. The proceedings of these conferences provide an up-to-date record of current research (see Ahlgren & Bergman, 1980; Kyle & Woll, 1983; Tervoort 1986; Prillwitz & Vollhaber 1990a,b; Ahlgren, Bergman & Brennan, 1994; Bos & Schermer, 1995). The sociolinguistic study of sign languages within their community contexts is a relatively new field of research. Current progress in the field is well documented in Cucas 1990b, 1995 and 1996.

Current linguistic research focuses in the main on two areas: on the one hand, the morphology and phonology of sign languages; and on the other, lexicography, centering on the production of sign language dictionaries in both print and video-based formats. The study of syntax and semantics is less developed, with major contributions coming from the work of Ceil Lucas at Gallaudet University in Washington, DC.

As indicated above, research into sign languages re-emerged in the 1960s. The first International Symposium on sign language research was held in Sweden in 1979. This relatively recent sign language research focussed on two linked issues:

1. The need to prove that sign languages were indeed languages, especially in countries such as America and Europe where, after the general acceptance that oral educational methods were best for deaf children, sign language was denigrated by teachers. It was seen by many as merely a system of gestures which could convey limited information and therefore was inappropriate as a mode of educational instruction. In challenging these views of sign languages linguistics also saw sign languages as presenting an interesting challenge to the notion of language universals.

2. The low educational standards of deaf students at that time, giving rise to new interest in the potential role of sign language in deaf education.

In response to the first issue, the need to prove that sign languages were indeed bona fide languages, early linguistic research studied sign languages in the same way as other languages were studied, using traditional linguistic approaches. Wilbur (1987) identifies three key problems with regard to these early studies. Firstly, the borrowing of methods directly from oral languages led to a bias in the interpretation of research. Secondly, the research failed to take into account the educational experiences of the subjects, thus failing to take note of the signer's language background, particularly with regard to competency skills. Fluent first language signers were often not included in the research. Thirdly, assumptions taken from oral languages were made about the nature of sign languages, such as linearity, thus resulting in misleading research conclusions.

One of the key methodological problems these researchers had to deal with was the question of how to describe or write down the language to allow for research and comparison. This led to a number of notation systems being developed, in the same way as Bébian had developed a system 150 years earlier. Numerous countries throughout the world tried to develop transcription systems including England, America, Germany, Spain, Japan, Sweden and Denmark. The two most well known notation systems are the one developed by Stokoe (1965 – also Wilbur, 1987: 19ff) in America and the HamNoSys developed in Hamburg at the Zentrum für Deutsche Gebärdensprache (Prillwitz & Zienert, 1990). The main problem that arises with these notation systems is the tendency towards oversimplification of the three dimensional and temporal aspects of sign formation. In some cases this resulted in crucial linguistic features being excluded.

In response to the second issue, the link between their language of instruction and the low educational standards of deaf students, research into the mode of langauge to be used in educational settings was split between:
- the oralists, who believed that the primary role of education was to teach deaf children to speak;
- those who believed that a manually coded version of the dominant spoken language should be used;
- advocates of total communication (the use of speech and signing at the same time);
- and those who, in the 1970s, argued for the reintroduction of natural sign languages and a bilingual education system.

Educational research in this area was often carried out by teachers or teacher trainers hoping to establish that their method was correct. Results were usually presented at conferences of teachers of the deaf rather than in academic refereed journals. A notable exception was the work of Kyle and Woll in Bristol (Kyle & Woll, 1985).

WORK IN PROGRESS

The stress on proving the validity of sign as a true language led initially to a focus on descriptions of signs, a marked exception being Liddle's work on ASL syntax (brought together in Liddle, 1977). In 1960 Stokoe coined the word "cherology" (Greek "kheir"–"hand") as an alternative to phonology, and the word "chereme" to refer to elements making up a sign. The use of these terms has not continued and "phonology" is used to describe the linguistic study of the internal structure of a sign (see Wilbur, 1987: 19ff). Phonology is still one of the major areas of sign language research, but by now there has been work in all the major linguistic areas, and an increasing focus on morphology and syntax (see e.g. Padden, 1988; Wilbur, 1987: 139ff).

All the basic processes that occur in sound-based languages also occur in sign languages. Current developments in sign language linguistics therefore go hand in hand with developments in linguistics in general. General references have been outlined above but some examples of current work in different areas are: work on sign modification – i.e. how signs change depending on their structural context (e.g. Lucas, 1995; Johnston, 1991; Endberg-Pedersen, 1993); work on the order of the production of signs, focussing in particular on whether production is linear or non-linear (e.g. Brennan & Turner, 1994); the use of classifiers (e.g. Supalla, 1986); the use of space (e.g. Endberg-Pedersen, 1993); and stylistics (e.g. Valli, 1994).

Sign language acquisition studies have made an important contribution to the debate about the link between on the one hand, early gestural communication and sign, and on the other, spoken language acquisition, in both deaf and hearing children (e.g. Volterra & Erting, 1990). Also important as an on-going area of research is neuro- and psycho-linguistic work examining language development. Here the work of Bellugi and her colleagues at the Salk Institute in San Diego continues to lead the field. Bellugi's work dates back to the early 1970s and covers a vast terrain (see Poizer, Klima & Bellugi, 1990).

Much research continues to focus on lexicology, particularly on the production of sign language dictionaries. Two of the latest and most linguistically informed are by Johnston (1989) for Auslan and Brien (1992) for British Sign Language.

PROBLEMS AND DIFFICULTIES

The focus of writings on research methodology has been on the problem of transcription, notation and sign writing as discussed above. Recently researchers have looked for new ways to deal with this problem through the use of computer technology using gesture recognition techniques, or data gloves which record the movement and shape of the hands. Far less attention has been paid to the actual process of language collection for analysis and to the issues of sample selection, to sociolinguistic features affecting signing variation among informants, as well as to the impact on the research of the fact that most of the researchers studying the sign language are members of the dominant group which traditionally has suppressed sign languages.

Additional difficulties arise in terms of the perception of sign languages by researchers working in similar fields in relation to other languages. Sign language is rarely on the agenda of mainstream conferences, and in some instances major writers, such as Walter Ong (1982, p. 7), still deny their existence as bona fide languages.

FUTURE DIRECTIONS

We are seeing an increasing spread of sign language research beyond Western countries into African, South American and Asian countries, as evidenced by entries in Lucas (1996). This shift is accompanied by a shift towards the recognition of the multiplicity of sign languages, of moving beyond the concept of national sign languages to recognise regional differences (see the review by Branson & Miller in volume 1). These processes are also highlighting the vital importance of sociolinguistic work on sign languages, linking sign language research to other work on minority languages and linguistic rights. These moves are giving added weight and substance to more conventional linguistic areas such as semantics, pragmatics and discourse analysis, which have so far received less attention than phonology, syntax and lexicology.

Of particular importance to sign language research has been the development of computer-based use of video materials through rapidly improving digitising processes. The analysis of video-based research data, the development of improved teaching programs and the development of better, more dynamic "dictionaries", all involve the use of interactive CD ROM technology.

Of particular importance for the development of an effective research process and environment has been the increasing involvement of Deaf researchers and of Deaf communities in research as researchers and not simply as informants, and indeed the increasing tendency for Deaf communities to take control of research into their own languages and cultures (e.g. Zienert, 1994). This has become increasingly possible as educational opportunities and better support services have given Deaf people access to education through sign languages. Also associated with increasing educational opportunities, and with increasing bilingualism in education, is the development of effective sign language curricula for the teaching of sign languages in schools and universities (e.g. Branson, Miller et al., 1995).

La Trobe University
Australia, and
Monash University
Australia

REFERENCES

Ahlgren, I. & Bergman, B. (eds.): 1980, *Papers from the First International Symposium on Sign Language Research, June 10–16, 1979 Skepparholmen, Sweden*, Sveriges dövas riksförbund, Leksand.

Ahlgren, I., Bergman, B. & Brennan, M. (eds.): *Proceedings of the Fifth International Symposium of Sign Language Research, Durham*, isla, Durham.

Bébian, A.: 1825, *Mimographie, ou Essai d'écriture mimique, propre à régulariser le langage des sourds-muets*. Paris.

Bergman, B. & Wallin, L.: 1990, 'Sign language research with the deaf community', in S. Prillwitz & T. Vollhaber (eds.), *Sign Language Research and Application: Proceedings of the International Congress, Hamburg, 1990*, Signum Press, Hamburg, 187–214.

Bos, H. & Schermer, T. (eds.): 1995, *Sign Language Research 1994: Proceedings of the 4th European Congress on Sign Language Research, Munich, September 1–3, 1994*, Signum Press, Hamburg.

Bourdieu, P.: 1991, *Language and Symbolic Power*, Polity Press, Cambridge.

Boyes Braem & Kolb, A.: 1990, 'An introduction to sign language research', in S. Prillwitz & T. Vollhaber (eds.), *Sign Language Research and Application: Proceedings of the International Congress, Hamburg, 1990*, Signum Press, Hamburg, 97–113.

Branson, J. & Miller, D.: 1993, 'Sign language, the deaf, and the epistemic violence of mainstreaming', *Language and Education* 7(1), 21–41.

Branson, J., Miller, D., Bernal, B., Toms, J., Adam, R. & Rado, M.: 1995, *National Auslan Curriculum for First and Second Language Learners*, NID & DEET, Bundoora.

Branson, J., Toms, J., Bernal, B. & Miller, D.: 1995, 'The history and role of fingerspelling in Auslan', in H. Bos & T. Schermer (eds.), *Sign Language Research 1994: Proceedings of the 4th European Congress on Sign Language Research, Munich, September 1–3, 1994*, Signum Press, Hamburg.

Brennan, M.: 1990, *Word Formation in BSL*, University of Stockholm.

Brennan, M., Colville, M. & Lawson, L.: 1980, *Words in Hand: A Structural Analysis of the Signs of British Sign Language*, Moray House College of Education, Edinburgh.

Brennan, M. & Turner, G.: 1994, *Word Order Issues in Sign Language: Working Papers*, International Sign Linguistics Association, Durham.

Brien, D.: 1992, *Dictionary of British Sign Language*, Faber & Faber, London.

Bulwer, J.B.: 1644, *Chirologia, or the naturrall language of the hand*, London.

Bulwer, J.B.: 1648, *Philophocus, or the deafe and dumb man's friend: exhibiting the philosophicall verity of that subtile art, which may inable one with an observant eie, to heare what any man speaks by the moving of his lips: upon the same ground . . . that a man borne deafe and dumbe, may be taught to heare the sound of words with his eie, & thence learne to speake with his tongue*, London.

Defoe, D.: 1720, *The History of the Life and Adventures of Mr. Duncan Campbell*, London.

Deuchar, M.: 1984, *British Sign Language*, Routledge and Kegan Paul, London.
Endberg-Pedersen, E.: 1993, *Space in Danish Sign Language. The Semantics and Morpho-syntax of the Use of Space in a Visual Language*, Signum, Hamburg.
Fischer, R.: 1995, 'The notation of sign languages: Bébian's *Mimographie*', in H. Bos & T. Schermer (eds.), *Sign Language Research 1994: Proceedings of the 4th European Congress on Sign Language Research, Munich, September 1–3, 1994*, Signum Press, Hamburg.
Fischer, R. & Lane, H. (eds.): 1993, *Looking Back: A Reader on the History of Deaf Communities and Their Sign Languages*, Signum Press, Hamburg.
Hansen, B.: 1990, 'Trends in the progress towards bilingual education for deaf children in Denmark', in S. Prillwitz & T. Vollhaber (eds.), *Sign Language Research and Application: Proceedings of the International Congress, Hamburg, 1990*, Signum Press, Hamburg, 51–62.
Joachim, G. & Prillwitz, S.: 1993, *International Bibliography of Sign Language*, Signum Press, Hamburg.
Johnston, T.: 1989, *A.U.S.L.A.N. Dictionary. A Dictionary of the Sign Language of the Australian Deaf Community*, Deafness Resources, Sydney.
Johnston, T.: 1991, 'Spatial syntax and spatial semantics in the inflection of signs for the marking of person and location in Auslan', *International Journal of Sign Linguistics* 2(1), 29–62.
Kyle, J. & Woll, B. (eds.): 1983, *Language in Sign: An International Perspective on Sign Language (Proceedings of the Second International Symposium of Sign Language Research in Bristol, July, 1981)*, Croom Helm, London.
Kyle, J. & Woll, B.: 1985, *Sign Language: The Study of Deaf People and Their Language*, Cambridge University Press, Cambridge.
Lane, H.: 1976, *The Wild Boy of Aveyron*, Harvard University Press, Cambridge, Mass.
Lane, H.: 1988, *When the Mind Hears: A History of the Deaf*, Penguin Books, Harmonds-worth.
Liddle, S.: 1977, *An Investigation into the Syntactic Structure of ASL*, U.M.I., Ann Arbor.
Lucas, C. (ed.): 1990a, *Sign Language Research: Theoretical Issues*, Gallaudet University Press, Washington DC.
Lucas, C. (ed.): 1990b, *The Sociolinguistics of the Deaf Community*, Academic Press, New York.
Lucas, C. (ed.): 1995, *Sociolinguistics in Deaf Communities*, Gallaudet University Press, Washington DC.
Lucas, C. (ed.): 1996, *Multicultural Aspects of Sociolinguistics in Deaf Communities*, Gallaudet University Press, Washington DC.
Ong, W.: 1982, *Orality and Literacy: The Technologizing of the Word*, Routeledge, London.
Padden, C.: 1988, *Interaction of Morphology and Syntax in American Sign Language*, Garland, New York.
Poizner, H., Klima, E. & Bellugi, U.: 1990, *What the Hands Reveal about the Brain*, MIT Press, Cambridge, Massachusetts.
Prillwitz, S. & Vollhaber, T. (eds.): 1990a, *Current Trends in European Sign Language Research: Proceedings of the 3rd European Congress on Sign Language Research, Hamburg July 26–29, 1989*, Signum Press, Hamburg.
Prillwitz, S. & Vollhaber, T. (eds.): 1990b, *Sign Language Research and Application: Proceedings of the International Congress, Hamburg, 1990*, Signum Press, Hamburg.
Prillwitz, S. & Zienert, H.: 1990, 'Hamburg notation system for sign language devel-opment of a sign writing with computer application', in S. Prillwitz & T. Vollhaber (eds.), *Current Trends in European Sign Language Research: Proceedings of the 3rd European Congress on Sign Language Research, Hamburg July 26–29, 1989*, Signum Press, Hamburg.
Rodríguez-González, M.A.: 1993, 'Francisco Fernàndez Villabrille (1811–1864) and "el

lenguaje de signos" ', in R. Fischer & H. Lane (eds.), *Looking Back: A Reader on the History of Deaf Communities and Their Sign Languages*, Signum Press, Hamburg.

Stokoe, W.: 1960, *Sign Language Structure: An Outline of the Visual Communication System of the American Deaf*, Studies in Linguistics Occasional Paper, No. 8, University of Buffalo.

Supalla, T.: 1986, 'The classifier system in American sign language', in C. Craig (ed.), *Noun Classes and Categorization*, Benjamins, Amsterdam, 181–214.

Tervoort, B.T. (ed.): 1986, *Signs of Life: Proceedings of the Second European Congress of Sign Language Research, Amsterdam, July 14–18, 1985*, University of Amsterdam, Amsterdam.

Thompson, J.B.: 1991, 'Editor's introduction', to P. Bourdieu, *Language and Symbolic Power*, Polity Press, Cambridge.

Valli, C.: 1994, 'Linguistic features of ASL poetry', in Ahlgren, I., Bergman, B. & Brennan, M. (eds.), *Proceedings of the Fifth International Symposium of Sign Language Research, Durham*, ISLA, Durham.

Volterra, V. & Erting, C.: 1990, *From Gesture to Language in Hearing and Deaf Children*, Springer, Berlin.

Woodward, J.: 1977, 'All in the Family: Kinship lexicalization across sign languages', *Georgetown Roundtable on Language and Linguistics*, Washington DC.

Zienert, H.: 1994, 'The centre for German sign language in Hamburg: Deaf people doing research on their language with video and computers', in C. Erting, R. Johnson, D. Smith & B. Snider (eds.), *The Deaf Way: Perspectives from the International Conference on Deaf Culture*, Gallaudet University Press, Washington DC, 394–398.

Section 4

**Language, Interaction, and Education:
Recent Advances in Approaches, Methods, and Topics**

PEDRO M. GARCEZ

MICROETHNOGRAPHY

Microethnography is concerned with the local and situated ecology obtaining among participants in face-to-face interactional engagements constituting societal and historical experience. *Ethnographic microanalysis of interaction*, as microethnography is also known, aims at descriptions of how interaction is socially and culturally organized in particular situational settings. Microethnographers typically work with audiovisual machine recordings of naturally occurring social encounters to investigate in minute detail what interactants do in real time as they co-construct talk-in-interaction in everyday life. As such, microethnography offers a methodology for the investigation of face-to-face interaction and a particular point of view on language in use in complex modern societies (McDermott, Gospodinoff & Aron, 1978; Erickson, 1992). This view stresses that the social and cultural organization of human communicative action (Erickson & Shultz, 1982) involves conversationalists contained in physical bodies, occupying space in simultaneously constraining and enabling social situations, who must reflexively make sense of each others' actions as they act, without the benefit of an interpretive system that is shared completely between interlocutors.

EARLY DEVELOPMENTS

An interdisciplinary research approach, microethnography has intellectual origins in distinct research traditions that converge in their interest in various aspects of the organization of social interaction. Among early influences is *context analysis*, the collaborative work of a multi-disciplinary research group, including Gregory Bateson and Ray Birdwhistell, that pioneered the use of audiovisual records as primary sources of research data to study communicative interaction (see Kendon, 1990, chapter 2). Their work fundamentally shaped microethnography's commitment to the examination of nonverbal behavior and the unspoken activities of listenership in the study of face-to-face interaction (e.g., Erickson & Shultz, 1977/1981; McDermott & Gospodinoff, 1979/1981; Streeck, 1983). A second intellectual root is *the ethnography of communication* (see the review by Farah in this volume), from which microethnography inherited a linguistic anthropological concern with culturally appropriate forms of talk and with variation in the function-and-form relationship in language use within and across speech communities (e.g., Michaels, 1981; Shultz,

N.H. Hornberger and D. Corson (eds), Encyclopedia of Language and Education,
Volume 8: Research Methods in Language and Education, 187–196.
© *1997 Kluwer Academic Publishers. Printed in the Netherlands.*

Florio & Erickson, 1982). Yet a third source of insight are Goffman's studies on the 'situational' (Goffman, 1981, p. 84) character of *the interactional order*. Based on the view that social interaction occurs within constraints of what participants agree is the situation they are currently in, microethnographies demonstrate empirically the subtle ways in which participants (re-)arrange their alignments toward one another and (re-)frame their communicative actions accordingly. Significant for the analysis of the organization of communicative actions in face-to-face encounters (e.g., Shultz & Florio, 1979; Streeck, 1983), these observations also help explain key interactional mechanisms in phenomena such as interethnic miscommunication (e.g., McDermott & Gospodinoff, 1979/1981; Erickson & Shultz, 1982).

Ethnographic microanalysis of interaction has also profited from contemporary studies in *conversation analysis* about the real-time sequential organization of conversation (see the review by Heap in this volume). Given the shared methodological stance of privileging the participants' recognizable sense-making perspectives in the analysis of talk and social interaction, the conversation analytic and microethnographic perspectives often display close affinity (cf. Mehan, 1979; Goodwin, 1981).

Similar influences have also marked research in *interactional sociolinguistics* (Gumperz, 1982), with which microethnography shares most concerns and assumptions. Considerable overlap and cross-fertilization therefore exist between the two approaches (cf. Tannen, 1992) to the extent that they are often not differentiated.

MAJOR CONTRIBUTIONS

Initial microethnographic work began in the 1970's through an interest in examining processes of mutual social influence among face-to-face interactants, particularly in terms of how participants create context and *make sense* during their activities together in educational environments. This early work, led by Frederick Erickson and Ray McDermott, carried the hallmarks of the microethnographic contribution to the study of language and social interaction in educational settings (cf. Trueba & Wright, 1981). Among its features are, first, methodical attention to nonverbal and listener behaviors *simultaneously* with the (traditionally studied) verbal behaviors of speakers, including the noting of interactional rhythm and cadence; and, second, a thematic focus on mutual, simultaneous and successive influences among participants in interaction, the construction of labile situated social identities, and the management of culture difference.

In a seminal contribution, Erickson & Shultz (1977/1981) ask the crucial microethnographic question – 'when is a context?' Searching for a methodological approach that would incorporate contemporary advances in the understanding of human social interaction to the analysis of social competence in naturally occurring scenes in everyday life, Erickson and Shultz draw attention to aspects of interactional behavior whose meaning may be redundant across the different communicative channels. They show that this redundancy – easily mistaken for interactional noise – is in fact essential for face-to-face interactants to be able to gauge what and 'when' the context is in order to act in socially appropriate ways. Moreover, they argue, appropriate displays of this ability can be a determining factor in judgments made about social competence, an issue of paramount importance in educational encounters.

In a series of classroom studies investigating how teacher and minority children learning to read organized their activities and time together, McDermott (e.g., McDermott, Gospodinoff & Aron, 1978) builds a solid case for the microethnographic notion that 'people constitute environments for each other' (McDermott, 1976, p. 27, cited in Erickson & Shultz, 1982, p. 7). In the situational ecologies where discourse is produced in face-to-face interaction, it is through the monitoring of the effects of her/his performance on the listener that the speaker can see how effectively s/he is interacting, and where s/he must change according to the continuously emerging context. McDermott (1977), for example, focuses on systematic postural shifts in relation to bids for the floor in a reading group ecology to show how the participants' actions made sense in the local environment they created together – even if that meant more time working on 'relational struggles' and less on learning to read, which in and of itself may not make good educational sense.

In another study, McDermott & Gospodinoff (1979/1981) puzzle over the conflicting interaction between a white teacher and her Puerto Rican kindergarten student. The boy conspicuously flouted culture-specific social etiquette norms for address, bodily touch, and interactional space in the classroom until the teacher joined him in creating an incident which disrupted her work session with the bottom reading group. Combining careful scrutiny of the participants' verbal and nonverbal behaviors with attention to the micropolitics of the interaction, McDermott and Gospodinoff show that student and teacher are engaged in *border work*, that is, they are adding a socio-political layer onto cultural identity markers. McDermott and Gospodinoff posit that participants often exploit cultural differences – simple *boundaries* of identity which can be crossed over and do not intrinsically constitute impediments to optimal communication, such as norms for bodily touch in interaction – as convenient tools to deal with immediate interactional pressures or to communicate conflicting interests over resources. In the short run, the researchers point out, the classroom incident described above was 'to everyone's advantage' (1981, p. 224). The boy secured the teacher's attention to what he had bothered her about, while 'the teacher and the children in the bottom group

[got] a brief rest from their intense organizational negotiations' (p. 224). In the long run, however, occurrences of interactional conflict due to the micropolitical exploitation of small cultural differences sediment what would otherwise be passable *boundaries* of identity into insurmountable interactional *borders*, with lifetime consequences for those like the student mentioned above, as these borders serve as cultural trenches for societal struggle among individuals in competing identity groups.

Erickson & Shultz' (1982) detailed microanalysis of interethnic counseling interviews in junior colleges is a classic microethnographic investigation of participation structure, interactional rhythm, and listening behavior in relation to speaking. It shows how the local interdigitation of concerted action – the interlocking of interactional gears – enters into the achievement of critical gatekeeping decisions which are consequential in terms of access to social opportunity. Highly significant to the study of cross-cultural communication is Erickson & Shultz' (1982) empirical finding that, despite the clear relation between culture difference and interactional trouble, when culturally dissimilar student and counselor managed to activate particular 'attributes of shared status' (p. 35), or *comembership* (e.g., common interest in Catholic high school sports), their interactions were observed to be significantly less uncomfortable. In addition to providing evidence of the dynamically emergent nature of context in everyday interaction, Erickson & Shultz (1982) bring forth the social-scientific relevance of examining the real-time organization of verbal and nonverbal activities of speakers and listeners. They discuss these issues in terms of *reciprocity* (i.e., 'the interdependence of actions taken successively across moments in time') and *complementarity* (i.e., 'interdependence of actions taken simultaneously in the same moment,' p. 71), thus emphasizing the microethnographic view that face-to-face interaction is built on actions in physical time and space, rather than simply on the exchange of meaningful utterances.

A concern with real-time, locally appropriate ways of making sense in embodied interaction is also the focus of Shultz & Florio (1979). They show how a teacher's routine verbal and nonverbal behaviors – outside her own or the students' conscious awareness – are critical to the organization of classroom life, regulating the timing and social space for appropriate student contributions. Learning how to make sense of these contextualization cues (Gumperz, 1982; Dorr-Bremme, 1990), they show, enables students to navigate across the classroom environment appropriately and ultimately reflects on their perceived interactional competence.

Concerned with child-child interaction, Streeck (1983) examines linguistic and kinesic features composing the ecology of communicative processes in 'peer teaching' events in a group of five minority schoolchildren. He describes in concise detail the procedures by which the children organize their interaction frame by frame to achieve and sustain a consensus of what their activity is, and to seal off their interactional space from the surrounding world, a process in which they 'thereby contextualize the linguistic process of giving and receiving instructions' (p. 2).

Shultz, Florio & Erickson (1982) investigate the contrastive social organization of different participation structures for conversation that Italian-American students encountered at home and at school. While some social participation structures found in the classroom resemble the structure and timing for appropriateness of those in the children's homes, mismatches were observed. Participation structures in which the speaker-audience relationships allow for the simultaneous occurrence of more than one *floor* (i.e., access to a turn at speaking that is attended to by others) were routinely found to be sanctioned at home. However, when students produced them at school, the same participation structures constituted reason for reproach by the teacher. This analysis suggests that floor, as an aspect of the ecology of interaction, is not necessarily a unitary phenomenon, as previous work had proposed. In addition, it shows how small children may find it difficult to know what constitutes appropriate communicative behavior at school.

A number of microethnographic studies focus closely on such (mis)matches between home and school cultural norms for communicative behavior. Among them, Au (1980) and Au & Mason (1983) argue that cultural congruence in the rules governing participation in classroom activities may facilitate academic learning. These studies show how native Hawaiian children were more comfortable in a classroom ecology where participation structures similar to the ones they were familiar with at home were used in reading lessons, resulting in improved reading scores in the long run. Michaels (1981) analyzes 'sharing time' in an ethnically mixed first-grade classroom and argues that the observed mismatches in teacher/student culturally-based discourse strategies and prosodic conventions for giving narrative accounts have potentially adverse effects on the minority students' access to key literacy-related experiences.

WORK IN PROGRESS

Microethnographic studies are thus deeply concerned with the elusive nature of context in social interaction (Erickson & Shultz, 1977/1981), and the role it may play in the interpretation of utterances and other communicative behavior. Having offered early evidence for the understanding of context as the on-line and embodied creation of co-present interactants, microethnographers have also provided useful heuristics for its analysis in face-to-face interaction (Erickson & Shultz, 1977/1981; McDermott, Gospodinoff & Aron, 1978; Erickson, 1992). Theirs has been a significant contribution to unravel what constitutes social and communicative competence – especially in interaction in institutional settings and among socio-culturally dissimilar interactants – and to connect these interactional processes to societal issues such as social opportunity and cultural politics.

The main empirical concerns of early microethnographic work – the relationship of listening behavior in relation to speaking, the nature of contextualization processes in interaction, the construction of situated social identities and the lability in the foregrounding of aspects of social identity in everyday face-to-face interaction – continue to be the focus of current work (Dorr-Bremme, 1990; Fiksdal, 1990; Erickson, 1996; O'-Connor & Michaels, 1996). In addition, insights from that early work have also been taken in many new directions.

One such direction is current research on *the language and culture of classrooms* conducted by the Santa Barbara Classroom Discourse Group, which congregates researchers with special interest in issues of classroom interaction and reading and writing instruction, learning and practice (see contributions in Green & Dixon, 1994). An example of such focus is Tuyay, Jennings & Dixon's (1995) examination of how groups of students in a bilingual classroom made particular situated sense of a story-writing task. They thus show how one same task may lead to different learning opportunities as students shape and reshape the text they are composing through collaborative interaction with peers and others.

Similar research concerns are also present in the work of David Bloome and his associates on *literacy practices*. Bloome & Egan-Robertson (1993), for example, microanalyze a first-grade classroom reading event to show the moment by moment emergence of intertextuality as a social construction that can be 'located in the material of people's social inter-action' (p. 330). In demonstrating this, moreover, this microethnographic study aids the interpretation of an event in which two students resisted full participation in a reading lesson and seemed off-task, when in fact they were making relevant intertextual links, though using intertextuality differently from the rest of the class to 'define themselves as readers outside the definition of being students' (p. 330). Contemporary work on face-to-face interaction and literacy thus takes the initial microethnographic methods and point of view to the specific understanding of how reading and writing are constructed as integrally social processes.

Recent applications of microethnographic analytic perspectives have also contributed to new vistas on social competence in *communicative interaction in institutional settings* beyond schools. Ribeiro (1994), for example, analyzes psychiatric interviews, and provides a new lens for us to see a psychotic patient's discourse incoherence, at the level of referential topic, as coherent at the level of the frame for the situation the patient (believes she) finds herself in. Issues of foreign language use and cross-cultural communication in business situations have also been investigated from a microethnographic point of view. Miller (1991), for example, describes how different conventions regarding form, sequential position and timing of listening behavior can result in interactional trouble among Japanese and American co-workers in Japan, while Garcez (1993) describes how Brazilian manufacturers' and U.S. importers' different point-making conventions may conflict in a business negotiation. Additional microethnographic studies, including numerous dissertations, offer new angles for insight on a wide range of institutional practices and issues of professional education.

PROBLEMS AND DIFFICULTIES

The insights and contributions of ethnographic microanalysis of interaction to the fields of education, cross-cultural communication and the organization of face-to-face interaction have long been recognized (Trueba & Wright, 1981), and microethnography remains a productive research approach. Yet the relatively limited additional microanalytic work with 'the same sort of intensive videotape analysis that was the hallmark of the early research' (Shultz personal communication) bespeaks of difficulties in its wider application as a research method.

As Erickson (1992) points out, ethnographic microanalysis of interaction is labor intensive, and 'should not be used unless it is really needed' (p. 204). It is especially appropriate when one is interested in investigating social interaction in face-to-face events that are 'rare or fleeting in duration or when the distinctive shape and character of such events unfolds moment by moment, during which it is important to have accurate information on the speech and nonverbal behavior of particular participants in the scene' (pp. 204–205).

The very strengths of microethnography – a research method which permits investigation of the full range of variation and the determination of the typicality or atypicality of event types, modes and interactional organization – are indicative of how onerous it is. Despite improvements in technology which have greatly facilitated the collection and handling of video records of interaction, still the benefits of microethnographic research can only be fully achieved through careful and continued revisitation of these records in a long process of reviewing the whole event numerous times, identifying its major constituent parts and the aspects of organization within them, then focusing on the actions of individuals and finally comparing instances of the phenomenon of interest across the research corpus. This process of 'considering whole events, . . . analytically decomposing them into smaller fragments, and then . . . recomposing them into wholes' (Erickson, 1992, p. 217) demands great attention and time, inevitably limiting the amount of data that can be processed (thus the case-study nature of microethnographies). Nonetheless, it remains a distinctive strength of microethnography that it can produce deep analysis of phenomena which may be impossible to perceive in real time observation and which may be too heavily laden with common-sense perceptions for participant-observers to see through them.

Moreover, in its focus on complete analysis of audiovisual records of naturally occurring interaction, ethnographic microanalysis has the potential to reduce the analyst's limitation to the investigation of frequently occurring events and his/her dependence on premature interpretation of interactional phenomena. It thus offers tools 'to identify subtle nuances of meaning that occur in speech and nonverbal action – subtleties that may be shifting over the course of activity that takes place' and whose verification may enable us to see *'experience in practice'* more clearly (p. 205). Recent work on technology tools to support video analysis promises to facilitate and enhance this process, and also to enable participants to join the analytic task more closely.

The laborious quality of microethnography – as the methodological pursuit of a comprehensive point of view on social interaction – makes it an especially apt qualitative method for examining micro social processes and establishing their connection to more encompassing processes that ultimately constitute society and history (Giddens, 1984). It is in this light that microethnographers refer to the inadequacy of 'micro' as the label for their research work, which can in fact be quite macro (cf. Erickson, 1992, pp. 222–223; Bloome & Egan-Robertson, 1993, p. 331). Since the microethnographic approach to data analysis is largely inductive, *a priori* concerns with macro-structural formations (e.g., power and ideology) do not drive the analytic process (cf. Gumperz, 1982; Erickson, 1992). Though such issues often do emerge from the participants' observable behavior, it is only when substantial emic evidence warrants their treatment, in later stages of the research process, that they become analytically foregrounded. As a result, microethnographers may be seen as ignoring the wider social contexts that shape the interactants' displayed stances. However, in showing the subtle ecologies that participants create in face-to-face interaction, as social actors who are both reproducing and altering their macro social structures in situated talk-in-interaction, microethnographies in fact describe the co-construction, in and through discourse, of joint social realities which are intimately connected to wider societal processes such as, for example, interethnic struggle and social opportunity (e.g., Erickson & Shultz, 1982).

FUTURE DIRECTIONS

Recent advances in social theory have restored the notion that the situated communicative activities of flesh-and-blood interactants are critical to the constitution of society and historical experience (Giddens, 1984). In that it offers a consistent methodological framework for the investigation of video records of everyday face-to-face interaction as well as a broad theoretical basis guiding its practice (Erickson & Shultz, 1977/1981; McDermott, Gospodinoff & Aron, 1978; Erickson, 1992), microethnography stands as a discourse-and-interaction analytic research method that can in fact support the empirical characterization of what people do when they interact face to face in everyday life. With video becoming a common and accessible data collection resource, and with the increasing realization that verbal/speaker discourse is but one aspect of what needs to be attended to for the comprehensive understanding of the embodied and situated activities of human communicative behavior, we should therefore expect microethnography to offer increasingly significant contributions to the description of societal-historical processes constituted in the situated reflexive practice of social agents.

University of Santa Catarina
USA

REFERENCES

Au, K.H.: 1980, 'Participation structures in a reading lesson with Hawaiian children: Analysis of a culturally appropriate instructional event', *Anthropology and Education Quarterly* 11(2), 91–115.

Au, K.H. & Mason, J.M.: 1983, 'Cultural congruence in classroom participation structures: Achieving a balance of rights', *Discourse Processes* 6(2), 145–167.

Bloome, D. & Egan-Robertson, A.: 1993, 'The social construction of intertextuality in classroom reading and writing lessons', *Reading Research Quarterly* 28(4), 303–334.

Dorr-Bremme, D.: 1990, 'Contextualization cues in the classroom: Discourse regulation and social control functions', *Language in Society* 19, 379–402.

Erickson, F.: 1992, 'Ethnographic microanalysis of interaction', in M.D. LeCompte, W.L. Millroy, & J. Preissle (eds.), *The Handbook of Qualitative Research in Education*, Academic Press, New York, 201–225.

Erickson, F.: 1996, 'Going for the zone: The social and cognitive ecology of teacher-student interaction in classroom conversations', in D. Hicks (ed.), *Discourse, Learning and Schooling*, Cambridge University Press, Cambridge, 29–62.

Erickson, F. & Shultz, J.: 1977, 'When is a context? Some issues and methods in the analysis of social competence', *The Quarterly Newsletter of the Institute for Comparative Human Development* 1(2), 5–10. Also in J.L. Green & C. Wallat (eds.), *Ethnography and Language in Educational Settings*, Ablex, Norwood NJ, 1981, 147–160.

Erickson, F. & Shultz, J.: 1982, *The Counselor as Gatekeeper: Social Interaction in Interviews*, Academic Press, New York.

Fiksdal, S.: 1990, *The Right Time and Pace: A Microanalysis of Cross-Cultural Gatekeeping Interviews*, Ablex, Norwood, NJ.

Garcez, P.M.: 1993, 'Point-making styles in cross-cultural business negotiation: A microethnographic study', *English for Specific Purposes* 12(2), 103–120.

Giddens, A.: 1984, *The Constitution of Society*, University of California Press, Berkeley CA.

Goffman, E.: 1981, *Forms of Talk*, University of Pennsylvania Press, Philadelphia.

Goodwin, C.: 1981, *Conversational Organization: Interaction Between Speakers and Hearers*, Academic Press, New York.

Green, J.L. & Dixon, C.N. (eds.): 1994, Santa Barbara Classroom Discourse Group [Special Issue], *Linguistics and Education* 5(3/4).

Gumperz, J.J.: 1982, *Discourse Strategies*, Cambridge University Press, Cambridge.

Kendon, A.: 1990, *Conducting Interaction: Patterns in Focused Encounters*, Cambridge University Press, Cambridge.

McDermott, R. P.: 1977, 'Social relations as contexts for learning in school', *Harvard Educational Review* 47(2), 198–213.

McDermott, R.P. & Gospodinoff, K.: 1979, 'Social contexts for ethnic borders and school failure', in A. Wolfgang (ed.), *Nonverbal Behavior: Applications and Cultural Implications*, Academic Press, New York, 175–195. Also in H.T. Trueba, G. Guthrie & K.H. Au (eds.), *Culture and the Bilingual Classroom*, Newbury House, Rowley MA, 1981, 212–230.

McDermott, R.P., Gospodinoff, K. & Aron, J.: 1978, 'Criteria for an ethnographically adequate description of concerted actions and their contexts', *Semiotica* 24(3/4), 245–275.

Mehan, H.: 1979, *Learning lessons: Social Organization in the Classroom*, Harvard University Press, Cambridge MA.

Michaels, S.: 1981, ' "Sharing time": Children's narrative styles and differential access to literacy', *Language in Society* 10, 423–442.

Miller, L.: 1991, 'Verbal listening Behavior in conversations between Japanese and Americans', in J. Blommaert & J. Verschueren (eds.), *The Pragmatics of International and Intercultural Communication*, Johns Benjamins, Amsterdam/Philadelphia, 111–130.

O'Connor, M.C. & Michaels, S.: 1996, 'Shifting participant Frameworks: Orchestrating thinking practices in group discussion', in D. Hicks (ed.), *Discourse, Learning and Schooling*, Cambridge University Press, Cambridge, 63–103.

Ribeiro, B.T.: 1994, *Coherence in Psychotic Discourse*, Oxford University Press, New York.

Shultz, J.J., Florio, S. & Erickson, F.: 1982, 'Where's the floor? Aspects of the cultural organization of social relationships in communication at home and at school', in P. Gilmore & A.A. Glatthorn (eds.), *Ethnography and Education: Children in and out of School*, Center for Applied Linguistics, Washington DC, 88–123.

Shultz, J. & Florio, S.: 1979, 'Stop and freeze: The negotiation of social and physical space in a kindergarten/first grade classroom', *Anthropology and Education Quarterly* 10(3), 166–181.

Streeck, J.: 1983, *Social Order in Child Communication: A Study in Microethnography*, John Benjamins, Amsterdam/Philadelphia.

Tannen, D.: 1992, 'Interactional sociolinguistics', in W. Bright (ed.), *International Encyclopedia of Linguistics, Vol. 4*, Oxford University Press, New York, 9–12.

Trueba, H.T. & Wright, P.G.: 1981, 'On ethnographic studies and multicultural education', *NABE Journal* 5(2), 29–56.

Tuyay, S., Jennings, L. & Dixon, C.: 1995, 'Classroom discourse and opportunities to learn: An ethnographic study of knowledge construction in a bilingual third-grade classroom', *Discourse Processes* 19(1), 75–110.

STEPHEN A. MAY

CRITICAL ETHNOGRAPHY

Critical ethnography is a relatively recent development in social science research methodology. Situated within the broad ethnographic tradition, it reflects many of the characteristics of conventional ethnography. For example, it shares with much ethnography a reliance on the qualitative interpretation of data – examining particular social, cultural, or organisational settings from the perspectives of the participants involved. It also adheres to many of the core tenets of ethnographic methods, particularly the use of participant observation, where the researcher is both a participant and observer in the research setting.

However, critical ethnography also departs markedly from previous ethnographic approaches in a number of key ways. Firstly, as its name suggests, it is specifically 'critical' in its intent. With its antecedents in Marxism, neo-marxism, and the Frankfurt school of critical theory, critical ethnography adopts a perspective of social and cultural relations which highlights the role of ideology in sustaining and perpetuating inequality within particular settings. Secondly, and relatedly, the aim of critical ethnography is not simply to *describe* these settings as they appear to be – as in conventional ethnography – but to *change* them for the better. As Thomas observes, 'critical ethnography emerges when members of a culture of ethnography become reflective and ask not only "What is this?" but also "What could this be?"' (1993, p. v). Critical ethnography is thus simultaneously hermeneutic and emancipatory. Its overriding goal is to free individuals from sources of domination and repression, particularly those characteristic of late capitalism.

Critical ethnography arises then out of a specific concern to combine a critical conception of social and cultural reproduction with the study of particular organisational or social settings. What follows in this review is an analysis of the development of critical ethnography within educational research. The impact of critical ethnography – both on the research methodology of ethnography itself, and on the educational settings in which it has been employed – will also be examined.

EARLY DEVELOPMENTS

In order to discuss effectively the development of critical ethnography, it is first necessary to rehearse briefly the development of the ethnographic tradition within social science research. Ethnography first emerged

N.H. Hornberger and D. Corson (eds), Encyclopedia of Language and Education,
Volume 8: Research Methods in Language and Education, 197–206.
© *1997 Kluwer Academic Publishers. Printed in the Netherlands.*

as a research methodology within anthropology in the early part of this century and was perhaps most prominently associated with the work of Malinowski in the 1920s. The aims of ethnography, in this classic sense, are interpretive; one's goal as an ethnographer is to focus on a setting and discover what is going on there (Wilcox, 1982). This can be achieved by describing the norms, rules and expectations which identify people with a particular culture, setting, or institution. However, if the ethnographer wants to ascribe meaning to behaviour in a fuller sense, she or he needs to *share* in the meanings that participants take for granted in informing their behaviour, and to *describe* and *explain* these meanings for the benefit of the reader. Geertz (1973) has described this process as 'thick description' which seeks to discover the important and recurring variables in a setting – as they relate to one another, and as they affect or produce certain results and outcomes within it. This process of thick description is usually accomplished within a 'realist narrative' account (van Maanen, 1988; Hammersley, 1992). Through their involvement as 'disinterested' participant-observers, ethnographers recount the story of the research setting, and the multiple stories of the participants within it, for the benefit of the reader. In so doing, meaning is allowed to 'emerge' from the data; a key hallmark of the interpretive and naturalistic ethnographic account.

Conventional ethnography, as described above, has contributed much to the qualitative tradition of research, and ethnography and ethnographic methods have become increasingly popular with researchers in the social sciences as a result. This enthusiasm has been very apparent within educational research where, from the late 1960s and early 1970s, an ethnographic 'movement' began to emerge in the study of schools (see, for example, Jackson, 1968; Smith & Geoffrey, 1968; Smith & Keith, 1971; Rist, 1973; Wolcott, 1973). Employing the thick description and narrative realism characteristic of ethnography, these micro-level accounts provided rich and detailed examinations of what actually went on in school settings. Subsequent research along these lines has burgeoned within education, particularly through the use of the smaller-scale 'case study' approach.

However, critical ethnography has also subsequently emerged from this ethnographic tradition to challenge some of its central tenets. For example, critical ethnographers have rejected the abrogation of a theoretical perspective for the 'open-ended' collection of data, characteristic of conventional ethnography. This attempt to divorce theory from data collection is specious, critical ethnographers argue, since all research is theory laden. As such, no researcher can be wholly disinterested. A researcher *must* begin from a theoretical position of some description – whether this is articulated or not in the ensuing study (Angus, 1986; see also, Hughes, 1990).

Relatedly, critical ethnography specifically acknowledges, as its starting point, its indebtedness to critical theory. As Masemann – one of critical ethnography's early proponents – summarises it:

'Critical ethnography' refers to studies which use a basically anthropological, qualitative participant observer methodology but which rely for their theoretical formulation on a body of theory deriving from critical sociology and philosophy. (1982, p. 1)

For the critical ethnographer, the interpretative concern with 'describing' a social setting 'as it really is' assumes an objective, 'common sense' reality where none exists. Rather, this 'reality' should be seen for what it is – a social and cultural *construction*, linked to wider power relations, which privileges some, and disadvantages other, participants. Critical ethnographers are particularly dismissive here of what they perceive to be the narrow focus of micro-level ethnographic accounts of schooling. Such descriptions, they argue, often fail to shed light on the more complex issues that account for much of what goes on in schooling and in the wider society. As Lutz comments, 'the narrower the focus of a study of schooling processes, the more likely important, perhaps necessary, variables are to be unseen and unaccounted for' (1984, p. 110; see also, Ogbu, 1987).

Given this, critical ethnography attempts to move beyond the accounts of participants in particular settings to examine the ideological premises and hegemonic practices which shape and constrain these accounts. Critical ethnographers argue that the 'common sense' views which underpin participant accounts, and the settings in which these are expressed, contribute to the unequal distribution of power and control in these settings. The critical perspective brought to the research is thus linked to a general theory of society and a concept of social structure which exists beyond the actors' perceptions of it (Masemann, 1982; Angus, 1987). As Angus describes it, critical ethnography aims 'to develop an understanding of the processes and mechanisms by which macro forces are mediated [through human actors] at the level of a single institution' (1988, p. 4).

In this way, 'critical ethnographers seek research accounts sensitive to the *dialectical* relationship between the social structural constraints on human actors *and* the relative autonomy of human agency' (Anderson, 1989, p. 249; my emphases). This emphasis on the dialectical relationship between human agency and institutional structure enables a critical ethnography to explore the nature of the intersection between choice and constraint, and to centre on questions of power (Lather, 1986a). As such, it is ideally suited to exploring questions of educational inequality in relation to social class, gender and/or ethnicity, and to relate such questions to practice – particularly, to political and emancipatory practice.

MAJOR CONTRIBUTIONS

There have been, over the years, some notable examples of critical ethnography in the educational field. Willis (1977) and Corrigan (1979) provide two early examples, within a neo-Marxist framework. These two studies have proved extremely influential subsequently because of the powerful ways in which they combine critical theory production with ethnographic accounts; in both cases, exploring the alienation from schooling of working class young people in Britain. More recently, Weis (1985) and Fine (1991) have employed critical ethnography in exploring the positioning, marginalisation, and resistance of black and other ethnic minority students within, respectively, an urban community college and an urban high school in North America. Likewise, Angus (1988) provides an excellent critical ethnographic account of an Australian Catholic boys' high school in which he highlights the discontinuities between the historical working class location and ethos of the school and its traditional, academic curriculum. May (1994) combines many of these concerns in his critical ethnography of a New Zealand urban elementary school, exploring how the particular school – in consultation with its community – reformed its organisation, curriculum and pedagogy to the benefit of its predominantly working class and ethnic minority children. Other examples of critical ethnographic, and related, studies include work on student subcultures (Humphries, 1981; Jenkins, 1983; Macpherson, 1983; Aggleton, 1987); teacher education (Ginsburg & Newman, 1985; Kanpol, 1988; Smyth, 1989, 1991); curriculum (Anyon, 1981; Everhart, 1983; Bennet & Sola, 1985); school policy (Everhart, 1988); private schools (McLaren, 1993); and parental and community involvement (Connell et al., 1982; Carspecken, 1991).

Alongside these critical ethnographic projects, a range of useful commentaries has also been provided on ongoing methodological developments within critical ethnography (see Masemann, 1982; Simon & Dippo, 1986; Lather, 1986a, 1986b; Angus, 1986, 1987; Anderson, 1989; Gitlin et al., 1989; Thomas, 1993; Jordan & Yeomans, 1995; Carspecken, 1996). In addition to the characteristics outlined above, these studies highlight a number of emergent features within the tradition. For example, a key theme to emerge in these methodological discussions is the centrality of 'critical reflexivity' – the ability to critically reflect on the research process. Reflexivity is not to be misunderstood here as the mere self-reflection of the researcher. Rather, reflexivity involves a complex dialectic between the researcher, the research process, and the research outcome(s). Specifically, a critical ethnography needs to engage with (a) the researcher's constructs, (b) the informants' 'common sense' constructs, (c) the research data, (d) the researcher's ideological biases, and (e) the structural and historical forces that inform and shape the social setting under study (Anderson, 1989).

A related trend within critical ethnography concerns the democratisation of the research process. As in conventional ethnography, methodologies employed within critical ethnography tend to be eclectic. Along with the use of participant observation, for example, other methods such as document collection, field note taking and the use of interviews are also commonly used. However, there is an added recognition within critical ethnography of the need to *negotiate* meaning with all research participants and, in so doing, to question and critique the power relations between researcher and researched in the research setting. This has led to the increasing adoption of democratic research strategies which emphasise researcher/practitioner collaboration and participant empowerment. Examples of such strategies include oral life history methods (Weiler, 1988; Casey, 1993), and the use of informant narratives (Mishler, 1986; Brodkey, 1987).

These developments in critical ethnography within education have been complemented by similar developments elsewhere. In what has come to be known as 'postmodern ethnography' (Clifford & Marcus, 1986; Marcus & Fischer, 1988; Gitlin, et al., 1989; van Maanen, 1995), literary techniques associated with postmodernism have been used increasingly as a basis for ethnographies concerned with broader questions of cultural analysis. Within this approach, the notions of 'discourses', 'polyphonic texts' and 'reflexivity' have been drawn upon, usually in contrast to the 'narrative realism' associated with more conventional ethnographic accounts.

Critical ethnography has also been closely linked with recent developments in feminist ethnographic research (see Roberts, 1981; Lather, 1986a, 1986b; Weiler, 1988; Stanley, 1990; Arnot & Weiler, 1993; Casey, 1993; David, 1993). Feminist ethnographic research has been concerned to explore the structural subordination of girls and women – both within and beyond education – and their resistance to these positionings (see the review by Freeman in this volume). Weiler (1988), for example, uses the life histories of female teachers, and classroom observation, to explore the possibilities of a 'feminist counter-hegemony' in schools. Casey (1993) employs life histories and discourse analysis to similar ends. Both approaches are clearly consonant with the aims of critical ethnography.

PROBLEMS AND DIFFICULTIES

By attempting to add prediction and explanation to thick description, critical ethnography can be regarded, admittedly, as 'openly ideological research' (Lather, 1986a, 1986b). This raises specific concerns about the 'validity' of critical ethnography, particularly in its explicit use of *a priori* theory. As Anderson concedes, critical ethnography's 'agenda of social critique, [the] attempt to locate ... respondents' meanings in larger impersonal systems of political economy, and the resulting "front-endedness" of much of [the] research raises validity issues beyond those of mainstream naturalistic research' (1989, p. 253).

Given this, some critics have argued that critical ethnography adopts a teleological view of history; both in its use of critical theory, and in its pursuit of political and emancipatory practices (Hammersley, 1992). Relatedly, critical ethnographers are criticised for simply replacing the supposedly 'false' perspectives which they critique with their own, equally contestable, perspectives. The use of the emancipatory effectiveness of the research as a means of testing, or attesting to, its validity – what Lather (1986a, 1986b) terms 'catalytic validity' – is also problematic here. As Hammersley (1992) argues, such a criterion presupposes that successful practice must be based on 'correct' theoretical assumptions (and unsuccessful practice on 'false' assumptions). He goes on to suggest that this overstates the role of theory in influencing practice (for a response to Hammersley's position see, May, 1994; Jordan & Yeomans, 1995).

To counter these concerns with validity, and with the specific use of critical theory, a number of research characteristics are regularly employed in critical ethnography. There are the emphases on democratic research practices and critical reflexivity, already discussed. These provide a sophisticated account of the research process, and the roles and relationships of researcher and researched within it. Standard research procedures such as member checking, and triangulation of data sources and methods, are also applied to ensure the research reaches the accepted standards of qualitative research (Thomas, 1993).

More crucially, however, critical ethnographers reject the criticism of theoretical piety levelled at them by critics. They argue that the goal of critical ethnography is not to replace one particular ideology with another but to highlight the *role* of ideology in the construction of social and organisational settings. As Thomas argues, the goal of critical ethnography 'is not to create like-minded ideologues or to recreate the world in one's own image. Rather it challenges the relationship between all forms of inquiry and the reality studied and sustained' (1993, pp. 17–18). Brodkey argues, along similar lines, that critical ethnographers are 'narrators whose self-consciousness makes it necessary to point out that all stories, including their own, are told from a vantage point, and to call attention to the voice in which the story is being told' (1987, p. 71).

However, this brings us to a related criticism of critical ethnography, albeit one that comes from a different direction. As Anderson observes, educational critical theory has often been criticised for 'its tendency toward social critique *without developing a theory of action* that educational practitioners can draw upon to develop a "counter-hegemonic" practice in which dominant structures of classroom and organisational meaning are challenged' (1989, p. 257; my emphasis). Most critical ethnographies simply critique the malign influence of unequal power relations in education and consequently give little practical advice, or much hope for change, to practitioners. Jordan & Yeomans (1995) highlight this concern with their observation that, for all its democratising intentions, critical ethnography still invariably involves a relationship between an *academic* researcher and *non-academic* research participants; a distinction that continues to perpetuate an implicit power imbalance between the two. Rather, as Jordan

& Yeomans assert, the aims of critical ethnography should be redirected away from the privileged role of the academic researcher to facilitating the active engagement of the participants themselves. There is a need not only for critical research narration but for critical *practice* as well. As Anderson argues, along similar lines:

Although many critical ethnographies have attempted to address implications for practitioners . . . few have taken critical practitioners as objects of study . . . if educational critical ethnography shares with applied educational research the goal of social and educational change, then it must address its impact on educational practitioners. (1989, pp. 257, 262)

A final limitation of critical ethnography – at least, at this point in its development – is that, as yet, very few studies have explored the role of language in legitimating power relations in schooling (Anderson, 1989). This is surprising on two counts: the amount of sociolinguistic work already undertaken in this area (see below); and the centrality of the relationship between language, power and ideology to the overall concerns of critical ethnography. Neither of these has been extensively drawn upon within critical ethnography until recently (May, 1994). However, recent developments suggest that this is about to change.

FUTURE DIRECTIONS

The aims of critical ethnography are clearly complementary with those of postmodern ethnography and feminist ethnographic research (see above). However, critical ethnographers are also now beginning to establish additional alliances with other associated research traditions – particularly, those of action research and critical pedagogy (see May, 1994; Jordan & Yeomans, 1995; also the review by Goldstein in this volume). The tenets of action research and critical pedagogy, for example, accord with the critical reflexivity and ethnographic praxis of critical ethnography but extend these to include practitioners in the active formulation of, and engagement with, critical practice (see, for example, Carr & Kemmis, 1986, 1993; Elliott, 1991; Smyth, 1991; McLaren, 1995; Sleeter & McLaren, 1995). When applied to critical ethnography, the dual emphases of practitioner involvement and critical practice address its previous limitations as a methodology associated principally with critique rather than action.

Relatedly, sociolinguistic research within education is also belatedly being recognised as useful to critical ethnography. For example, despite the scepticism of critical ethnographers towards micro-ethnographic accounts of schooling, sociolinguistically informed ethnographic research in schools has increasingly adopted a critical perspective in its examination of the interrelationship between language, education, and wider social relations. Such research includes the traditions of micro-ethnography, ethnographies of communication and interactional sociolinguistics (for a useful overview of these approaches, and their distinctions, see Hornberger, 1995; see also,

Mehan, 1995). However, critical linguistics – the most recent variant of this tradition of sociolinguistic research – is seen as closest to critical ethnography in its theoretical and methodological concerns (Fairclough, 1995; May, 1995). Critical linguistics, and the associated methodology of critical discourse analysis, combine a close analysis of written and spoken discourses with an informed critical perspective on their role in reproducing or contesting dominant social structures and ideologies within schooling (see, Clark et al., 1990, 1991; Young, 1992; Fairclough, 1989, 1992, 1995; also the review by Gee, 1996; Norton in this volume). Linking critical linguistics with critical ethnography would thus facilitate the foregrounding of language and its role in sustaining and reinforcing unequal power relations within schools; an important focus which has hitherto not been prominent in critical ethnographic accounts.

Admittedly, these developments are still at a formative stage and they are also situated within a current educational climate which militates against critical and participatory forms of research. However, these caveats notwithstanding, the extension of critical ethnography along these lines suggests that the approach has much yet to offer the field of language and education.

University of Bristol
England

REFERENCES

Aggleton, P.: 1987, *Rebels Without a Cause*, Falmer Press, London.
Anderson, G.: 1989, 'Critical ethnography in education: Origins, current status, and new directions', *Review of Educational Research* 59, 249–270.
Angus, L.: 1986, 'Research traditions, ideology and critical ethnography', *Discourse* 7, 61–77.
Angus, L.: 1987, 'A critical ethnography of continuity and change in a Catholic school', in R. MacPherson (ed.), *Ways and Meanings of Research in Educational Administration*, University of New England Press, Armidale, 25–52.
Angus, L.: 1988, *Continuity and Change in Catholic Schooling: An Ethnography of a Christian Brothers College in Australian Society*, Falmer Press, Lewes.
Anyon, J.: 1981, 'Social class and school knowledge', *Curriculum Inquiry* 11, 3–41.
Arnot, G. & Weiler, K.: 1993, *Feminism and Social Justice in Education: International Perspectives*, Falmer Press, London.
Bennett, A. & Sola, M.: 1985, 'The struggle for voice: Narrative, literacy and consciousness in an East Harlem school', *Journal of Education* 167, 88–110.
Brodkey, L.: 1987, 'Writing critical ethnographic narratives', *Anthropology and Education Quarterly* 18, 67–76.
Carr, W. & Kemmis, S.: 1986, *Becoming Critical: Education, Knowledge and Action Research*, Falmer Press, Lewes.
Carr, W. & Kemmis, S.: 1993, 'Action research in education', in M. Hammersley (ed.), *Controversies in Classroom Research* (second edition), Open University Press, Milton Keynes.

Carspecken, P.: 1991, *Community Schooling and the Nature of Power: The Battle for Croxteth Comprehensive*, Routledge, New York.

Carspecken, P.: 1996, *Critical Ethnography in Educational Research: A Theoretical and Practical Guide*, Routledge, New York.

Casey, K.: 1993, *I Answer with my Life: Life Histories of Women Teachers Working for Social Change*, Routledge, New York.

Clark, R., Fairclough N, Ivanic, R. & Martin-Jones, M.: 1990, 'Critical language awareness, part I: A critical review of three current approaches to language awareness', *Language and Education* 4, 249–260.

Clark, R., Fairclough N, Ivanic, R. & Martin-Jones, M.: 1991, 'Critical language awareness, part II: Towards critical awareness', *Language and Education* 5, 41–54.

Clifford, J. & Marcus, G. (eds.): 1986, *Writing Culture: The Poetics and Politics of Ethnography*, University of California Press, Berkeley.

Connell, R., Ashenden, D., Kessler, S. & Dowsett, L.: 1982, *Making and Difference: Schools, Families and Social Division*, Allen & Unwin, Sydney.

Corrigan, P.: 1979, *Schooling the Smash Street Kids*, Macmillan, London.

David, M.: 1993, *Parents, Gender and Education Reform*, Polity Press, Oxford.

Elliott, J.: 1991, *Action Research for Educational Change*, Open University Press, Milton Keynes.

Everhart, R.: 1983, *Reading, Writing and Resistance*, Routledge & Kegan Paul, London.

Everhart, R.: 1988, *Practical Ideology and Symbolic Community: An Ethnography of Schools of Choice*, Falmer Press, New York.

Fairclough, N.: 1989, *Language and Power*, Longman, London.

Fairclough, N. (ed.): 1992, *Critical Language Awareness*, Longman, London.

Fairclough, N.: 1995, *Critical Discourse Analysis: The Critical Study of Language*, London, Longman.

Fine, M.: 1991, *Framing Dropouts: Notes on the Politics of an Urban Public High School*, SUNY Press, Albany.

Gee, J.: 1996, *Social Linguistics and Literacies: Ideology in Discourses* (2nd edition), Falmer Press, London.

Geertz, C.: 1973, *The Interpretation of Cultures*, Basic Books, New York.

Ginsburg, M. & Newman, K · 1985, 'Social inequalities, schooling, and teacher education', *Journal of Teacher Education* 36, 49–54.

Gitlin, A., Siegal, M. & Boru, K.: 1989, 'The politics of method: From leftist ethnography to educative research', *Qualitative Studies in Education* 2, 237–253.

Hammersley, M.: 1992, *What's Wrong with Ethnography*, London, Routledge.

Hornberger, N.: 1995, 'Ethnography in linguistic perspective: Understanding school processes', *Language and Education* 9, 223–248.

Hughes, J.: 1990, *The Philosophy of Social Research* (second edition), Longman, London.

Humphries, S.: 1981, *Hooligans or Rebels?*, Martin Robertson, Oxford.

Jackson, P.: 1968, *Life in Classrooms*, Holt Rinehart & Winston, New York.

Jenkins, R.: 1983, *Lads, Citizens and Ordinary Kids: Working-Class Youth Lifestyles in Belfast*, Routledge & Kegan Paul, London.

Jordan, S. & Yeomans, S.: 1995, 'Critical ethnography: Problems in contemporary theory and practice', *British Journal of Sociology of Education* 16, 389–408.

Kanpol, B.: 1988, 'Teacher work tasks as forms of resistance and accommodation to structural factors of schooling', *Urban Education* 23, 173–187.

Lather, P.: 1986a, 'Research as praxis', *Harvard Educational Review* 56, 257–277.

Lather, P.: 1986b, 'Issues of validity in openly ideological research: Between a rock and a soft place', *Interchange* 17, 63–84.

Lutz, F.: 1984, 'Ethnography: The holistic approach to understanding schooling', in R. Burgess (ed.), *Field Methods in the Study of Education*, Falmer Press, Lewes, 107–119.

Macpherson, J.: 1983, *The Feral Classroom*, Routledge & Kegan Paul, London.

Marcus, G. & Fischer, M.: 1986, *Anthropology as Cultural Critique: An Experimental Moment in the Cultural Sciences*, University of Chicago Press, Chicago.
Masemann, V.: 1982, 'Critical ethnography in the study of comparative education', *Comparative Education Review* 26, 1–15.
May, S.: 1994, *Making Multicultural Education Work*, Multilingual Matters/OISE Press, Clevedon/Toronto.
May, S.: 1995, 'Deconstructing traditional discourses of schooling: An example of school reform', *Language and Education* 9, 1–29.
McLaren, P.: 1993, *Schooling as Ritual Performance* (2nd edition), Routledge & Kegan Paul, Boston.
McLaren, P.: 1995, *Critical Pedagogy and Predatory Culture: Oppositional Politics in a Postmodern Era*, Routledge, New York.
Mehan, H., Lintz, A., Okamoto, D. & Wills, J.: 1995, 'Ethnographic studies of multicultural education in classroom and schools', in J. Banks & C. Banks (eds.), *Handbook of Research on Multicultural Education*, Macmillan, New York.
Mishler, E.: 1986, *Research Interviewing: Context and Narrative*, Harvard University Press, Cambridge MA.
Ogbu, J.: 1987, 'Variability in minority school performance: A problem in search of an explanation', *Anthropology and Education Quarterly* 18, 312–334.
Rist, R.: 1973, *The Urban School: A Factory for Failure*, MIT Press, Cambridge MA.
Roberts, H.: 1981, *Doing Feminist Research*, Routledge & Kegan Paul, London.
Simon, R. & Dippo, D.: 1986, 'On critical ethnographic work', *Anthropology and Education Quarterly* 17, 195–202.
Sleeter, C. & McLaren, P.: 1995, *Multicultural Education, Critical Pedagogy and the Politics of Difference*, SUNY Press, Albany.
Smith, L. & Geoffrey, W.: 1968, *The Complexities of an Urban Classroom*, Holt, Rinehart & Winston, New York.
Smith, L. & Keith, P.: 1971, *Anatomy of Educational Innovation*, Wiley, New York.
Smyth, J.: 1989, *Critical Perspectives on Educational Leadership*, Falmer Press, London.
Smyth, J.: 1991, *Teachers as Collaborative Learners: Challenging Dominant Forms of Supervision*, Open University Press, Milton Keynes.
Stanley, L. (ed.): 1990, *Feminist Praxis: Research Theory and Epistemology in Feminist Sociology*, Routledge & Kegan Paul, New York.
Thomas, J.: 1993, *Doing Critical Ethnography*, Sage, Newbury Park.
van Maanen, J.: 1988, *Tales of the Field: On Writing Ethnography*, University of Chicago Press, Chicago.
van Maanen, J.: 1995, *Representation in Ethnography*, Sage, London.
Weiler, K.: 1988, *Women Teaching for Change: Gender, Class and Power*, Bergin & Garvey, South Hadley, MA.
Weis, L.: 1985, *Between Two Worlds: Black Students in an Urban Community College*, Routledge & Kegan Paul, Boston.
Wilcox, K.: 1982, 'Ethnography as a methodology and its application to the study of schooling', in G. Spindler (ed.), *Doing the Ethnography of Schooling: Educational Anthropology in Action*, Holt Rinehart & Wilson, New York.
Willis, P.: 1977, *Learning to Labour*, Saxon House, Farnborough.
Wolcott, H.: 1973, *The Man in the Principal's Office: An Ethnography*, Holt Rinehart & Wilson, New York.
Young, R.: 1992, *Critical Theory and Classroom Talk*, Multilingual Matters, Clevedon.

BONNY NORTON

CRITICAL DISCOURSE RESEARCH

Educational researchers active in the critical study of language as 'discourse' are interested in language as a social practice. In other words, they investigate the way language constructs and is constructed by a wide variety of social relationships. These relationships might be as varied as those between writer and reader; teacher and student; test maker and test taker; school and state. What makes the researchers 'critical' is the shared assumption that social relationships are seldom constituted on equal terms. Social relationships may reflect and constitute inequitable relations of power in the wider society, on terms that may be defined, amongst others, by gender, race, class, ethnicity, and sexual orientation. For this reason, critical discourse research is centrally concerned with the way language is implicated in the reproduction of and resistance to inequitable relations of power in educational settings. It is important to note, however, that there is no coherent 'field' of critical discourse research. Although critical discourse researchers share a common interest in language, power, and social justice, they are associated with a wide variety of fields, including linguistics, education, anthropology, sociology, psychology, and philosophy. The purpose of this review is to identify some of the important themes associated with critical discourse research in education, in particular (see reviews by May in this volume; by Janks in Volume 1; and by Clark and Ivanić, and by Wallace in Volume 6).

EARLY DEVELOPMENTS

There is a dramatic irony in tracing the origins of critical discourse research in education. What is evident in this genealogical search is that critical discourse research itself reflects a discursive relationship among established scholars and their students and supporters. Some of these students have themselves become energetic scholars who, in turn, have influenced yet another generation of critical scholars. These relationships have not been static ones. New generations of scholars have brought different perspectives and theories to their work, and in doing so, have contributed to the evolution of critical discourse research.

Contemporary critical discourse researchers in education have tended to draw, in particular, on the work of one or more of the following scholars: Bakhtin (1981), Bourdieu (1977), Foucault (1980), Freire (1970), Gumperz

N.H. Hornberger and D. Corson (eds), Encyclopedia of Language and Education,
Volume 8: Research Methods in Language and Education, 207–216.
© *1997 Kluwer Academic Publishers. Printed in the Netherlands.*

(1982), Halliday (1978), Hymes (1974), Saussure (1959), and Weedon (1987). Not all of these scholars frame their work with reference to educational settings or address questions of power and inequality; nevertheless, their supporters have extended their work to critical discourse research in education.

The above scholars have influenced a second generation of scholars who are interested in the relationship between language, power, and education. These scholars include Corson (1993), Cummins (1996), Edelsky (1996), Giroux (1992), Gee (1990), Heller (1994), Kress (1989), Lemke (1995), Luke (1988), and Simon (1992). Other influential scholars, such as Fairclough (1992a) and Wodak (1996), whose work has not necessarily focussed on educational practice, have nevertheless had an important influence on contemporary critical discourse research in education. There is, in addition, an emerging group of critical discourse researchers who have benefitted from the work of the more established researchers cited above. These researchers are associated with work in feminist pedagogy, anti-racist education, critical pedagogy, and cultural studies. Their work will be discussed in greater detail below.

MAJOR CONTRIBUTIONS

Two important contributions of critical discourse research in language and education have been in extending and redefining theories of language and in reconceptualizing theories of identity.

With reference to theories of language, many critical discourse researchers have framed their work with reference to poststructuralist theories of language. In doing so, they have extended and reconceptualized the structuralist theories of language associated with the work of Saussure (1959). Saussure argued that language is an arbitrary system of differences in which elements gain their meaning only from their relation to all other elements. For structuralists, the building blocks of language structure are signs that comprise the signifier (or sound-image) and the signified (the concept or meaning). For structuralists, it is the linguistic system itself that guarantees the meaning of signs, and Saussure asserts that each linguistic community has its own set of signifying practices that give value to the signs in a language. Critical discourse researchers, in contrast, argue that structuralist theories of language cannot account for the conflicting struggle over the meanings that can be attributed to signs. Poststructuralists argue that linguistic communities are not homogeneous, consensual spaces in which language use is predictable and conventional. For poststructuralists, linguistic communities are perceived to be heterogeneous arenas in which language is implicated in struggles over meaning, access and power.

Thus the theory of 'discourse' that is central to critical discourse research represents a departure from notions of discourse (units of language larger than the sentence) associated with much traditional sociolinguistic research. In critical discourse research, discourses are the complexes of signs and practices that organize social existence and social reproduction. The discourses of the family, the school, the church, the corporation are constituted in and by language and other sign systems. Discourses delimit the range of possible practices under their authority and organize how these practices are realized in time and space. A discourse is thus a particular way of organizing meaning-making practices. However, because the social meanings of any given discourse are open to contestation, language itself becomes a site of struggle.

The following critical discourse researchers are amongst a growing number of researchers who conceptualize language as a site of struggle. In the 1970's, Fowler, Hodge, Kress & True (1979), in extending the work of Halliday, argued that theories of discourse must be understood with respect to larger, frequently inequitable, social and economic processes. In the 1980's and 1990's, the work of Bakhtin, Bourdieu, and Foucault became particularly influential in redefining theories of language in the field of language and education: Bakhtin has helped to reconceptualize notions of 'voice' in language and education (Morgan, 1996; Sola & Bennett, 1985; Walsh, 1987); Bourdieu's conception of 'legitimate language' has been used to frame innovative sociolinguistic research (Martin-Jones & Heller, 1996; May, 1994); and Foucault has become influential in research in language arts (Gilbert, 1991; Hardcastle, 1985; Luke, 1988), textual analysis (Kress, 1989; Lemke, 1995), and second language teaching (Bourne, 1988; Peirce, 1989; Pennycook, 1994a). The common thread in the work of Bakhtin, Bourdieu, and Foucault is that language is not only an abstract structure; it is a practice that constitutes and is constituted by complex and unequal sets of social relationships.

Given the centrality of poststructuralist theories of language to critical discourse research, it is perhaps not surprising that there has been a concomitant interest in investigating and redefining theories of identity in language and education. As Weedon (1987, p. 21) argues, 'Language is the place where actual and possible forms of social organization and their likely social and political consequences are defined and contested. Yet it is also the place where our sense of ourselves, our subjectivity, is constructed.' While critical discourse researchers draw on diverse theorists in investigating identity in their research studies (see for example Heller, 1987; Willinsky & Hunniford, 1986), feminist poststructuralism offers a particularly articulate conception of the relationship between the individual and the social world. Drawing on the work of Foucault, Lacan, Derrida, Kriteva and Althusser, feminist poststructuralists (Henriques et al., 1984;

Weedon, 1987) link individual experience and social power in a theory of subjectivity.

The terms 'subject' and 'subjectivity' signify a different conception of the individual from that associated with humanist conceptions of the individual dominant in Western philosophy. Three defining characteristics of subjectivity are as follows: First, whereas humanist conceptions of the individual presuppose that every person has an essential, unique and coherent core, feminist poststructuralism depicts the individual as diverse, contradictory and dynamic; multiple rather than unitary; decentered rather than centred. Second, subjectivity is produced in a variety of social sites, all of which are structured by relations of power in which the person takes up different 'subject positions' – teacher, mother, friend, critic – some positions of which may be in conflict with others. For this reason, subjectivity is conceptualized as a site of struggle. Third, a logical extension of the assumption that subjectivity is multiple and conflicted is that it is subject to change. This is a crucial point for educators as it opens up possibilities for educational intervention.

Feminist poststructuralism has been particularly powerful in recent studies of the way in which children – and girls in particular – engage with texts. For example, both Davies (1989) and Harper (1995) draw on feminist poststructuralism to demonstrate how girls of different age groups are invested in a particular vision of themselves and the future that must be understood in relation to powerful discourses on gender – discourses that often produce disruptive and contradictory responses to texts. In a different context, Peirce (1995) draws on feminist poststructuralism to understand the extent to which the immigrant women in her research created, responded to, and sometimes resisted opportunities to speak English. McKay & Wong (1996) draw on feminist poststructuralism to theorize their research on the second language learning experiences of adolescent Chinese immigrant students in the USA. Feminist poststructuralism offers great theoretical promise to research on language, identity, and learning.

WORK IN PROGRESS

It is difficult to do justice to the quantity and quality of educational research in progress that is investigating the relationship between language, power and education. In some contexts, this research is collaborative and interdisciplinary, and is represented by collected works with a particular theoretical focus. In other contexts, the research is topic specific, and attempts to grapple with the particularities of language and power in a given educational setting. What follows is a partial representation of some of this work.

With reference to collected works, van Dijk's new journal, *Discourse*

& *Society*, established in 1990, and published in Amsterdam, has as its central mandate 'to bridge the well-known gap between micro- and macro-analyses of social phenomena' (van Dijk, 1990, p. 8). Van Dijk argues that because discourse and communication have both micro and macro dimensions, their analysis offers new ways of analysing complex social and political processes. Janks (1993) edits a series on critical language awareness which explores language practices in a changing South Africa, while Cope & Kalantzis (1993) have edited a collection that addresses the innovative research on genre and the teaching of writing in the Australian context. Mitchell & Weiler (1991) have edited a collection of articles that problematizes traditional conceptions of literacy and seeks to link fields as diverse as linguistics, anthropology, education, and reading and writing theory. Green's book series, 'Language and Educational Processes', published by Ablex, seeks to investigate language and learning across a variety of educational sites, while Luke's book series, 'Critical Perspectives on Literacy and Education' published by Falmer Press, focuses on approaches to literacy education that directly address issues of access and equity. This series includes Gee's (1990) innovative sociolinguistic research, which draws on interdisciplinary perspectives on language and literacy.

Special journal editions on critical discourse research have increased in number. Martin-Jones & Heller (1996) have edited two special editions of *Linguistics and Education* titled, 'Education in Multilingual Settings: Discourse, Identities and Power'. The impetus for this special edition is the growing international research on the relationship between structures of power and bilingual discourse practices, both inside and outside classrooms. In a similar spirit, Sarangi & Baynham have edited a double special issue of *Language and Education* (1996) on 'Discursive Construction of Educational Identities.' In the field of English second language teaching, Norton (1997) has edited a special edition of *TESOL Quarterly* on 'Language and Identity', which incorporates innovative research in the international community on language, identity, and learning.

With reference to critical discourse research in given educational settings, the following work is indicative of the range of research in progress: In *higher education:* Pennycook (1996) draws on research on writing with undergraduate Chinese students in Hong Kong to argue that Western understandings of plagiarism and text ownership need to be problematized; Starfield (1995) draws on her ethnographic research on the development of academic literacy in a South African university to raise important questions about whose knowledge counts in tertiary education. In *multilingual education*: Goldstein (1997) draws on her research with immigrant women in Canada to argue that language choice in multilingual workplaces must be understood with reference to questions of power and access; Schenke (1991) brings insights from feminist pedagogy to bear

on her classroom research. In *language arts*: Delpit (1988) contributes
to the debate on process-oriented versus skills-oriented writing instruction, arguing that teachers must teach all students the implicit and explicit
rules of power in order to address the educational needs of black students;
Fairclough (1992b) edits a collection that addresses ways in which critical
language awareness can be applied in diverse educational contexts.

In the field of *assessment*: Holland, Bloome & Solsken (1994) offer critical perspectives on the assessment of children's language and literacy by
drawing on diverse research in anthropology, sociopsycholinguistics and
reader response theory; Morgan (1996) explores the intersection between
assessment, critical language awareness, and subjectivity; Peirce & Stein
(1995) draw on Kress's theory of genre to understand students' contradictory responses to a reading test. In the field of *second language acquisition*
(SLA): Rampton (1991) draws on his research with Panjabi adolescents to
argue that SLA research needs greater social and ethnographic contextualization; Peirce (1995) draws on her research with immigrant women in
Canada to propose a theory of 'investment' that frames motivation with
respect to the complex and changing identities of language learners. In *applied linguistics:* Corson (1997) stresses the need for a critically real
ontology/epistemology that underpins research, while Lantolf (1996)
celebrates diversity of research and theory.

PROBLEMS AND DIFFICULTIES

While critical discourse researchers have great interest in rapidly evolving theories of language and identity, this is not always shared by an
equally passionate commitment to the complexities of classroom practice.
Students' voices are sometimes little more than a backdrop to discussions
on the development of theory and teachers sometimes feel disempowered
by abstract notions that appear unrelated to the challenges they face on
a daily basis (see for example, Ellsworth, 1989). Furthermore, research
that addresses complex questions of language and power with respect to
inequities of race, class, gender, and sexual orientation raises many difficult questions regarding the relationship between the researcher and the
researched. What methodology is appropriate for exploring these questions? How can conclusions be validated? How can research ethics be
maintained?

With reference to the researchers themselves, the gendered division of
labour in mainstream educational research, in which theory construction
is often associated with male scholars and application is associated with
female scholars, has not escaped critical discourse research. By way of
example, in Caldas-Coulthard & Coulthard (1996), all the contributors to
the theory section of the collection, 'critical discourse theory,' are males
(Fowler, Kress, van Leeuwen, Fairclough, van Dijk) while the women

in the collection (Wodak, Ribeiro, Gough, Talbot, Caldas-Coulthard) are concentrated in the 'applications' section. Similarly, critical discourse researchers need to take up Wright's (1996) challenge to cultural studies that it not become Eurocentric and hegemonic, but a transnational, democratic field of study. This is a reminder that researchers need to be constantly on the alert for complicity in the perpetuation of unequal relations of power between the center and the periphery of academic power.

Finally – and this is ironical given my second point – critical discourse research has been unable to shake the hegemony of the English language in educational research internationally. While many of the leading theorists and researchers in this field are not anglophones (Bourdieu, Foucault, Wodak), their work has reached a wider audience only after being translated into English. In this respect, there is dramatic irony that the work of critical discourse researchers concerned with the hegemony of English internationally is published exclusively in English (see Peirce, 1989; Pennycook, 1994b; Phillipson, 1992; Tollefson, 1991). Critical discourse researchers cannot be complacent about complicity in the perpetuation of unequal relations of power in a variety of academic, social, and political relationships.

FUTURE DIRECTIONS

Because it is difficult to anticipate the future directions of critical discourse research in education, I conclude with a wish-list rather than a series of predictions. This wish-list must be understood in relation to the problems discussed in the previous section. First, I hope that critical discourse research will focus more directly on the interests, needs, and investments of learners and teachers, working collaboratively to address challenges and construct possibilities. As Connell et al. (1982, p. 29) found in their educational research in Australia, it was only when the researchers got close to the situations people found themselves in, and talked to them at length about their experiences, that they were able to make substantial progress in refining their research questions and in contributing to the development of theory. In a similar spirit, we need to be more explicit about the assumptions we bring to our research, the problems we have encountered, and the process whereby we have drawn conclusions. This will be invaluable to new generations of scholars and researchers.

Second, I hope that critical discourse researchers will continue to be responsive to broader developments in the humanities and social sciences. In this regard, we have much to learn from the innovative work of postmodern researchers grappling with questions of difference and marginalization. The work of Dei on anti-racist education (1997) is particularly noteworthy, and the collection edited by Bannerji (1993) is an important contribution to debates on racism, feminism and politics. In a similar spirit, the collection of articles edited by Ferguson, Gever, Minh-ha & West (1994) constitutes an insightful analysis of the way certain people and ideas are privileged over others at any given time. By entering into a dialogue with researchers in other disciplines, we can not only learn from them, but contribute to interdisciplinary debates on language, power, and social justice.

University of British Columbia
Canada

REFERENCES

Bakhtin, M.M.: 1981, *The Dialogic Imagination*, University of Texas Press, Austin.

Bannerji, H. (ed.): 1993, *Returning the Gaze: Essays on Racism, Feminism and Politics*, Sister Vision Press, Toronto.

Bourdieu, P.: 1977, 'The economics of linguistic exchanges', *Social Science Information* 16(6), 645–668.

Bourne, J.: 1988, ' "Natural acquisition" and a "masked pedagogy" ', *Applied Linguistics* 9(1), 83–99.

Caldas-Coulthard, R. & Coulthard, M. (eds.): 1996, *Texts and Practices: Readings in Critical Discourse Analysis*, Routledge, London.

Connell, R.W., Ashendon, D.J., Kessler, S. & Dowsett, G. W.: 1982, *Making the Difference: Schools, Families and Social Division*, George Allen & Unwin, Sydney.

Cope, B. & Kalantzis, M.: 1993, *The Powers of Literacy: A Genre Approach to Teaching of Writing*, University of Pittsburgh Press, Pittsburgh.

Corson, D.: 1993, *Language, Minority Education and Gender*, Multilingual Matters, Clevedon, Avon.

Corson, D.: 1997, 'Critical realism: An emancipatory philosophy for applied linguistics', *Applied Linguistics* 18, 166–188.

Cummins, J.: 1996, *Negotiating Identities: Education for Empowerment in a Diverse Society*, California Association for Bilingual Education, Ontario, CA.

Davies, B.: 1989, *Frogs and Snails and Feminist Tales: Preschool Children and Gender*, George Allen & Unwin, Sydney.

Delpit, L.: 1988, 'The silenced dialogue: Power and pedagogy in educating other people's children', *Harvard Educational Review* 58, 84–102.

Dei, G.J.S.: 1997, 'Race and the production of identity in the schooling experience of African-Canadian youth', *Discourse* 18(1), in press.

Edelsky, C.: 1996, *With Literacy and Justice for All: Rethinking the Social in Language and Education* (second edition), Taylor & Francis, London and Bristol, PA.

Ellsworth, E.: 1989, 'Why doesn't this feel empowering? Working through the repressive myths of critical pedagogy', *Harvard Educational Review* 59(3), 297–324.

Faircough, N.: 1992a, *Discourse and Social Change*, Polity Press, Cambridge.

Fairclough, N. (ed.): 1992b, *Critical Language Awareness*, Longman, London.

Ferguson, R., Gever, M., Minh-Ha, T. & West, C. (eds.): 1994, *Out There: Marginalization in Contemporary Cultures*, Massachusetts Institute of Technology, Boston.

Foucault, M.: 1980, *Power/Knowledge: Selected Interviews and Other Writings 1972–1977*, translated by C. Gordon, Pantheon Books, New York.

Fowler, R., Hodge, B. Kress, G. & Trew, T.: 1979, *Language and Control*, Routledge & Kegan Paul, London.

Freire, P.: 1970, *Pedagogy of the Oppressed*, Seabury Press, New York.
Gee, J.P.: 1990, *Social Linguistics and Literacies: Ideology in Discourses*, Falmer Press, Basingstoke.
Gilbert, P.: 1991, 'From voice to text: Reconsidering writing and reading in the English classroom', *English Education* 23(4), 195–211.
Giroux, H.: 1992, *Border Crossings: Cultural Workers and the Politics of Education*, Routledge, New York.
Goldstein, T.: 1997, *Two Languages at Work: Bilingual Life on the Production Floor*, Mouton de Gruyter, Berlin and New York.
Gumperz, J.: 1982, *Discourse Strategies*, Cambridge University Press, Cambridge.
Halliday, M.A.K.: 1978, *Language as Social Semiotic: The Social Interpretation of Language and Meaning*, Edward Arnold, London.
Hardcastle, J.: 1985, 'Classrooms as sites for cultural making', *English in Education* (Autumn), 8–22.
Harper, H.: 1995, *Danger at the Borders: The Response of High School Girls to Feminist Writing Practices*, unpublished PhD thesis, Ontario Institute for Studies in Education/University of Toronto, Toronto.
Heller, M.: 1987, 'The Role of language in the formation of ethnic identity', in J. Phinney & M. Rotheram (eds.), *Children's Ethnic Socialization*, Sage, Newbury Park, 180–200.
Heller, M.: 1994, *Crosswords: Language, Education and Ethnicity in French Ontario*, Mouton de Gruyter, Berlin.
Henriques, J., Hollway, W., Urwin, C., Venn, C. & Walkerdine, V.: 1984, *Changing the Subject: Psychology, Social Regulation, and Subjectivity*, Methuen, London and New York.
Holland, K., Bloome, D. & Solsken, J.: 1994, *Alternative Perspectives in Assessing Children's Language and Literacy*, Ablex, Norwood, N.J.
Hymes, D.: 1974, *Foundations in Sociolinguistics: An Ethnographic Approach*, University of Pennsylvania Press, Philadelphia.
Janks, H.: 1993, *Language, Identity and Power*, Hodder & Stoughton, Johannesburg.
Kress, G.: 1989, *Linguistic Processes in Sociocultural Practice*, Oxford University Press, Oxford.
Lantolf, J.: 1996, 'SLA theory building: "Letting all the flowers bloom!"', *Language Learning* 46(4), 713–749.
Lemke, J.: 1995, *Textual Politics: Discourse and Social Dynamics*, Taylor & Francis, Bristol, PA.
Luke, A.: 1988, *Literacy, Textbooks and Ideology*, Falmer Press, Basingstoke.
Martin-Jones, M. & Heller, M.: 1996, 'Introduction to the special issues on education in multilingual settings: Discourse, identities, and power', *Linguistics and Education* 8, 3–16.
May, S.: 1994, *Making Multicultural Education Work*, Multilingual Matters, Clevedon, Avon.
McKay, S.L. & Wong, S.C.: 1996, 'Multiple discourses, multiple identities: Investment and agency in second language learning among Chinese adolescent immigrant students', *Harvard Educational Review* 3, 577–608.
Mitchell, C. & Weiler, K.: 1991, *Rewriting Literacy: Culture and the Discourse of the Other*, OISE Press, Toronto.
Morgan, B.: 1996, ' Promoting and assessing critical language awareness', *TESOL Journal* 5(2), 10–14.
Morgan, R.: 1987, 'Three dreams of language', *College English* 49, 449–458.
Norton, B.: 1997, 'Language, identity, and the ownership of English', *TESOL Quarterly* 31(2), in press.
Peirce, B.N.: 1989, 'Toward a pedagogy of possibility in the teaching of english internationally: People's English in South Africa', *TESOL Quarterly* 23(3), 401–420.

Peirce, B.N.: 1995, 'Social identity, investment, and language learning', *TESOL Quarterly* 29(1), 9–31.

Peirce, B.N. & Stein, P.: 1995, 'Why the "monkeys passage" bombed: Tests, genres, and teaching', *Harvard Educational Review* 65(1), 50–65.

Pennycook, A.: 1994a, 'Incommensurable discourses?', *Applied Linguistics* 15(2), 115–138.

Pennycook, A.: 1994b, *The Cultural Politics of English as an International Language*, Longman, New York.

Pennycook, A.: 1996, 'Borrowing others' words: Text, ownership, memory and plagiarism', *TESOL Quarterly* 30(2), 201–230.

Phillipson, R.: 1992, *Linguistic Imperialism*, Oxford University Press, Oxford.

Rampton, B.: 1991, 'Second language learners in a stratified multilingual setting', *Applied Linguistics* 12(3), 229–248.

Saussure, F. de: 1959, *Course in General Linguistics* (W. Baskin, Trans.), McGraw-Hill, New York.

Schenke, A.: 1991, 'The "will to reciprocity" and the work of memory: Fictioning speaking out of silence in ESL and feminist pedagogy', *Resources for Feminist Research/ Documentation sur la recherche feministe* 20(3/4), 47–55.

Simon, R.: 1992, *Teaching Against the Grain: Texts for a Pedagogy of Possibility*, Bergin & Garvey, New York.

Sola, M. & Bennett, A.: 1985, 'The struggle for voice: Narrative, literacy and consciousness in an East Harlem school', *Journal of Education* 167(1), 88–110.

Starfield, S.: 1995, 'Academic literacy and social change: An ethnographic study', paper presented at the international TESOL conference in Long Beach, California.

Tollefson, J.: 1991, *Planning Language, Planning Inequality*, Longman, New York.

Van Dijk, T.: 1990, 'Discourse & society: A new journal for a new research focus', *Discourse & Society* 1(1), 5–16.

Walsh, C.A.: 1987, 'Language, meaning, and voice: Puerto Rican students' struggle for a speaking consciousness', *Language Arts* 64, 196–206.

Weedon, C.: 1987, *Feminist Practice and Poststructuralist Theory*, Blackwell, Longman.

Willinsky, J. & Hunniford, R.M.: 1986, 'Reading the romance Younger: The mirrors and fears of a preparatory literature', *Reading-Canada-Lecture* 4(1).

Wodak, R.: 1996, *Disorders of Discourse*, Longman, London and New York.

Wright, H.: 1996, 'Take Birmingham to the curb, here comes African cultural studies: An exercise in revisionist historiography', *University of Toronto Quarterly* 65(2), 355–365.

JAMES L. HEAP

CONVERSATION ANALYSIS METHODS IN RESEARCHING LANGUAGE AND EDUCATION

Conversation analysis (CA) developed within sociology in the 1960s as a variant of ethnomethodology (see Heritage, 1984). Studying, researching, and teaching within the University of California system, Harvey Sacks and his collaborators, Emanuel Schegloff and Gail Jefferson, initiated a distinct line of work using conversational materials to address questions of social order. These questions concern how speakers and hearers accomplish orderly and intelligible social interaction through the context-sensitive use of rules, procedures, and conventions for naturally occurring conversation (Zimmerman, 1988; Goodwin & Heritage, 1990). The central focus of this work has been the sequential organization of conversation as turns at talk. Researchers on language and education have used the methods and methodology of conversation analysis to advance understanding of classroom talk as a variant of naturally occurring conversation, and to explore and clarify a wide range of pedagogical, assessment, classroom management, and community relation issues in educational settings.

EARLY DEVELOPMENTS

First as a graduate student at the University of California, Berkeley, then as an instructor at UCLA and at the University of California, Irvine, Harvey Sacks worked with tapes and transcripts of calls to a suicide prevention center, and with additional conversation materials from many types of settings. Rather than treating these conversations as mere media for the delivery of messages, and coding the 'outcomes,' Sacks and his colleagues took up conversations as ordered phenomena, as objects for analysis. In line with ethnomethodology, the focus was on methods that members of a society use to produce talk recognizable to other members: recognizable as a certain type, achieving certain effects and functions in the context of the conversation. For example, 'hello' functions as a greeting when placed in the first slot of a conversation. Central to this focus on recognizability, or 'accountability' (Garfinkel, 1967; Heritage, 1984), was a concern with the consequentiality of action. In particular, talk came to be analyzed in terms of its sequential placement in the 'prior,' 'current,' or 'next' turn in a conversation.

N.H. Hornberger and D. Corson (eds), Encyclopedia of Language and Education,
Volume 8: Research Methods in Language and Education, 217–225.
© *1997 Kluwer Academic Publishers. Printed in the Netherlands.*

The early development of CA is largely available in the published lectures of Harvey Sacks, 1964–1972 (1995), and chronicled by Sacks' collaborator, Emanuel Schegloff, in excellent introductions to the two volumes of these remarkable lectures (1995). The classic article by Sacks, Schegloff, and Jefferson, 'A Simplest Systematics for the Organization of Turn-Taking for Conversation' (1974), lays out in considerable detail the analytic framework of conversation analysis.

MAJOR CONTRIBUTIONS

Button (1991) has formulated two different lines of work carried out under the banner of CA. The first produces fine-grained sequential analyses with the 'goal of describing and documenting the operation and organisation of stretches of sequences of conversation as activity in its own right, requiring no recourse to extra-conversational facets, and making no claims to be capturing wider sociological concerns.' Borrowing a jazz idiom, this first line can be called straight-ahead CA. The second line has an ethnographic dimension to it and is concerned with 'conversational organisation involved in the accomplishment of some interactional encounter' (quoted in Payne & Hustler, 1980, p. 53). This work can be called applied CA. The distinction between these two lines of work is merely heuristic and has not guided actual studies.

The major contribution to straight-ahead CA in education is Alex McHoul's 1978 piece titled 'The Organization of Turns at Formal Talk in the Classroom.' While the paper presented a concern with 'feelings' of 'formality,' its core framework reflected modifications which the rules of conversation underwent in classroom settings studied by McHoul in Liverpool, England and Canberra, Australia. Teachers were found to have exclusive access to the use of creative 'current speaker selects next' techniques; in McHoul's data, students were not allowed to self-select to speak.

Also falling, broadly, within straight-ahead CA in education would be McHoul's study of the organization of repair in classroom conversation (1990), French and MacLure's analysis of two types of strategies used by teachers to facilitate the 'successful' completion of question-answer sequences (1979), and Macbeth's explication of 'floors' as public structures-in-time of collective attention required if any teaching or learning is to occur (1992).

An important, early contribution related to the area of applied CA is Hugh Mehan's 1979 research study titled *Learning Lessons: Social Organization in the Classroom*. Mehan called his study a 'constitutive ethnography' and was heavily indebted to ethnomethodology, discourse analysis, and context analysis, but was influenced by conversation analysis. The third chapter focused on turn allocation, albeit without explicit use of the 'Simplest Systematics' framework.

In Mehan's detailed analysis of nine lessons in an elementary school classroom, attention was given both to the structure of lessons, in terms of relations between types of discourse moves (see Sinclair & Coulthard, 1975), and to the structuring of lessons, through teacher turn-allocation techniques and improvisational strategies used when students do not reply as expected. Of particular import in Mehan's study was the invocation of explicit criteria of adequacy (1979, pp. 19–24) concerned with retrievability of data, comprehensiveness of data treatment, convergence of analyst and members' perspectives, and an interactional level of analysis.

Within the corpus of work in applied CA in education only a few research reports can be mentioned. A number of studies have continued Mehan's focus on properties of initiation-response-feedback sequences. Heyman (1983) analyzed the use of IRF sequences in a science lesson. Farrar (1981) combined CA with speech act analysis and cognitive psychology to formulate what counts as instruction in classroom settings. Heap (1985) expanded Farrar's conception to analyze components of reading lessons, while Frieberg & Freebody (1996) analyzed reading and writing activities in classrooms and homes. Macbeth (1994) treats instruction as a course of affairs semantically, prosodically, and pragmatically achieved. Heyman (1986) has addressed how topics are formulated in classrooms, while Lerner (1995) has focused on turn design and its possible consequences for structuring subsequent literacy activities. Drawing from Sacks' early work on membership categorization (1995), McHoul & Watson (1984) analyze two axes along which commonsense and formal geographic knowledge are brought to bear in a high school lesson, Baker & Keogh (1995) show how 'school' and 'home' are talked into being over the course of accounting for student achievement in parent-teacher interviews, and Baker (1996) reveals how school staff 'find social order' in a system of 'ticketing rules' for managing student behavior.

METHODS

Methods and methodologies used in CA studies in educational settings depend on data collection, data representation, and analytic strategies which are relatively standardized across CA. There is heavy emphasis on the retrievability of data (Sacks, 1995; Mehan, 1979). Research cannot be done without high-quality audio, and where possible video, recording of talk-in-interaction. Invented talk is not acceptable as data. Coding systems which reduce data to analytic categories are avoided (see Heap, 1982). Data consists of audio/video recordings of everyday events in real time (Psathas & Anderson, 1990).

Methods of recording do not differ widely from those used in other qualitative, sociolinguistic approaches. Ethnographic fieldnotes in educational settings are of use primarily to identify speakers and to record any features of the setting which may be expected to bear on the adequacy of the description and resulting analyses, e.g., off-camera events to which speakers display an orientation. Fieldnotes are of no use for recording data. Information about research settings that is not available from the data themselves, e.g., speakers' mental states or scores on standardized tests, is not to be used by analysts, unless it can be shown that parties to an interaction apparently orient to this information (Schegloff, 1991; cf. Green & Meyer, 1991).

Data representation is achieved with some variant of the transcription protocols developed by Gail Jefferson (Psathas, 1995, pp. 70–78). The use and refinement of these protocols requires repeated listening and viewing of data. To this end, transcribers (who are usually analysts, not secretaries) depend on sophisticated playback technology, e.g., audio transcription machines and video units capable of undistorted, variable-speed playback functions. Since CA focuses closely on the sequential organization of utterances, the transcription system is designed to capture such things as simultaneous utterances, the onset and end of overlapping talk, latched or contiguous utterances.

The Jeffersonian system includes symbols to represent silences, pauses, and gaps in seconds and tenths of seconds. Since timing is quite important to the functions talk serves, transcribers use stopwatches, or, when working with videotaped data they depend on a time generator which overlays a running 'clock' on the tapes (depending on the technology, this will be done during the original taping, or added afterwards). In addition, untimed micro-intervals will be represented. Typically a dot appearing within parentheses denotes approximately a tenth of a second. The generic device for inserting transcriber comments is double parentheses, e.g., ((teacher leaves group)).

Punctuation marks are used to represent features of speech production, not grammatical units. A question mark represents a rising intonation, not a question. The system uses punctuation and diacritical marks to represent such things as sound stretches, cut-offs (of prior words), intonation, emphasis, pitch, and volume. As part of the system, aspirations – in-breaths and out-breaths – are also represented.

Transcription is not neutral (Psathas & Anderson, 1990). It involves a number of methodological and procedural decisions about what is worth representing (Baker, 1997). Transcription is the beginning of analysis, because it requires orientation to the problem of relevance: what features of talk-in-interaction are potentially germane to analysis? CA's transcription system addresses this problem by capturing features of talk which participants themselves can and do orient to over the course of interaction (Goodwin & Heritage, 1990). These features, e.g., pitch, intonation, aspirations, are potentially consequential for how a turn at talk projects an appropriate or desirable next turn, the turn to be taken by a current hearer. In that CA is primarily concerned with the sequential organization of talk, whether in classrooms or on the street, the transcription system is built to represent those features which hearers can and do analyze to produce next turns, or whole sequences of turns, as in instructional sequences (Mehan, 1979).

Consistent with the methodology of CA, the transcriber/analyst does not know before the work commences what will be germane to the completed analysis. Hence, it is an abiding feature of CA work that transcripts provide more detail than a published analysis may seem to require. Detailed transcripts, however, allow readers to generate alternative, or more refined, analyses of the interactions addressed by the analyst. To this end, it is a practice in CA to involve colleagues in transcription sessions to check and refine transcripts while analyses are being developed.

METHODOLOGY

In approaching data and their transcripted representation CA adopts a unique methodological stance, what can be called a *situated consociate perspective* (Heap, 1992). Along with interpretive sociologies (Weber, 1968), CA can be said to the take the point of view of the actor/speaker as a methodological standpoint for interpreting and analyzing data. However, interpretive sociologies overwhelmingly are concerned with the meaning, purpose, or intention of actors. The actor's self-understanding of action determines what the action "means," what it is.

CA eschews the subjectivist perspective of interpretive sociologies and instead follows the later Wittgenstein (1958) and Austin (1970), seeing the identity of action as dependent on community conventions and practices applied in ways sensitive to local settings of interaction. Action is viewed not in terms of what the speaker intended, but in terms of what anyone who witnessed the action could use as legitimate grounds for identifying the action. In conversation, such grounds are largely sequential, e.g., an utterance is to be heard as an answer because it follows what is hearable as a question.

A data strip can serve to illustrate differences in methodological perspectives. The data comes from a bilingual classroom observed by Lerner (1995). In the data strip 'side' refers to a page in an open book.

```
1  Teacher:   Do we know what this side is called?
2             (1.7) ((several students raise their hand))
3             Nolle.
```

4 Nolle: Ah its ah who you write it to,
5 Teacher: The dedication. ((with big nod))
(Lerner, 1995, p. 115)

Rather than trying to access the speakers' intentions, or invoking purely analytic criteria, e.g., syntax, for categorizing the functions of utterances, CA examines how each utterance can be heard by parties to the setting. The claims that the utterance on line 1 is hearable as a question, and that 'Nolle' (line 3) is hearable as a nomination, are supported by what is said on line 4.

In saying 'Ah its ah who you write it to' (line 4) Nolle produces an understanding, or analysis, of the teacher's prior turn at talk. This 'analysis,' as a set of presuppositions expressed through the content and placement of Nolle's turn, is hearable by parties to the setting, and by English speakers wishing to do Conversation Analysis. Nolle analyzes the teacher's turn as a question-with-nomination, with herself as the nominee. This analysis, in turn, is supported by what happens in the next turn. On line 5 the teacher utters 'The dedication' and nods affirmatively. This subsequent utterance and action publicly analyzes Nolle's prior turn as a correct, hearable answer, produced by a person who had a right to speak.

Proceeding in this way, CA is able to demonstrate, and depend upon, the sequential grounds which utterances provide for determining meaning and function, without recourse to what any speaker intends. A key assumption is that analysts share with members of society the competencies to recognize the sequential grounds of action. The analytic concern is how a consociate, whether member or analyst, could hear the talk, turn by turn, at any point in the conversation. In this sense, CA uses a situated consociate methodological perspective: the analysis is situated in the midst of talk-in-interaction as the conversation unfolds for persons who can witness it.

PROBLEMS, DIFFICULTIES, AND THE FUTURE

The two strains of CA introduced above (Major Contributions) establish between them the central issues of discussion amongst persons carrying out CA studies in education. There are two issues: the relation to education, and whether, when, and how information 'extraneous' to the data (audio or videotapes) is to be used.

The first issue concerns the connection between CA and the field of education. Should the study of talk-in-interaction in educational settings serve the interests primarily of CA, and its advancement as a discipline, or should such studies make use of CA methods, methodology, and findings in order to serve the field of education? The future direction many would like to see is one where, in exploring the link between sequential organization and task accomplishment, we learn more about talk-in-interaction while serving the needs of educators and education. This means taking both sequential organization and education equally seriously.

The second issue connects to the first and concerns whether, when, and how information 'external' to what can be seen and heard on tape can inform analyses of talk-in-interaction. Persons committed to the program of straight-ahead CA see no need to mention or feature information about the background or social-cultural characteristics of speakers. Hence, in discussions of turn taking systems and the organization of conversational repair in classrooms, one finds no mention of ethno-cultural heritage, class, gender, or sexual orientation.

Unless the identities of speakers can be discerned from interaction captured on audio or videotape, straight-ahead CA would not allow transcripts to list speakers as 'teacher' and 'pupil,' 'student,' or 'child.' To identify a speaker as a 'teacher' is to ascribe a role, which is an analytic imposition on the data. At every point in a transcript where someone is designated as 'teacher,' straight-ahead CA requires evidence that interactants display an orientation to that speaker *as* the teacher. If one 'is' a teacher, or student, that ought to be something visible, available, and oriented to by parties to the setting. This is to say that 'teacher' and 'student,' as roles, are accomplishments; that persons 'have' those roles cannot be taken for granted.

Persons doing applied CA recognize that roles are accomplishments, but for the analyses they wish to further, it is usually a side issue as to how such roles are accomplished. This stance reveals the root of the divide between straight-ahead and applied CA of education. The methodological constraint of straight-ahead CA, requiring evidence of public orientation by speakers to 'external' information, serves well the interest of CA in explicating any and all features of talk-in-interaction. This constraint has been more problematic in applied CA studies in education because the interest in talk-in-interaction is taken up on behalf of education. The very notion of education, especially as carried out in classrooms and schools, involving teachers, students, administrators, and parents, depends on a conception of education as an *institution*. An institution in sociological terms is a set of recurring, stable relations between persons serving some specified ends important to society. Institutions by their very nature transcend any particular setting. Hence, to do a CA study in or of education is to invoke the very sort of transcendent phenomena which straight-ahead CA forbids presupposing in analyses.

This difficulty should be thought of as a productive tension. Out of all the events captured on tape, applied CA committed to education tells us what to look at. Straight ahead CA tells us how to look, and what we must do in order to show how the features of institutions, like education, are produced *in situ*, in real time, interactionally. The future of conversation analysis in education will depend on how well the tension between the interests of straight-ahead CA and the commitments of applied CA are managed, explored, and made productive.

Ontario Institute for Studies in Education,
University of Toronto, Canada

REFERENCES

Austin, J.L.: 1970, *Philosophical Papers*, Oxford University Press, New York.
Baker, C.: 1996, 'Ticketing rules: Categorisation and moral ordering in a school staff meeting', in S. Hester & P. Eglin (eds.), *Culture in Action: Studies in Membership Categorization Analysis*, University Press of America, Boston.
Baker, C.: 1997, 'Transcription and representation in literacy research', in J. Flood, S.B. Heath & D. Lapp (eds.), *A Handbook for Literacy Educators: Research on Teaching the Communicative and Visual Arts*, Macmillan, New York.
Baker, C. & Keogh, J.: 1995, 'Accounting for achievement in parent-teacher interviews', *Human Studies* 18, 263–300.
Button, G.: 1991, *Ethnomethodology and the Human Sciences*, Cambridge University Press, New York.
Farrar, M. P.: 1981, 'Defining and examining instruction: An analysis of discourse in a literature lesson', Unpublished doctoral dissertation, Department of Educational Theory, University of Toronto.
French, P. & MacLure, M.: 1979, 'Getting the right answer and getting the answer right', *Research in Education* 22, 1–23.
Frieberg, J. & Freebody, P.: 1996, 'Analysing literacy events in classrooms and homes: Conversation-analytic approaches', in P. Freebody & C. Ludwig (eds.), *Everyday Literacy Practices in and out of Schools in Low Socio-Economic Urban Communities*, Vol. 1, Centre for Literacy Education Research, Brisbane, 185–369.
Garfinkel, H.: 1967, *Studies in Ethnomethodology*. Prentice-Hall, Inc, Toronto.
Goodwin, C. & Heritage, J.: 1990, 'Conversation analysis', *Annual Review of Anthropology* 19, 283–307.
Green, J. & Meyer, L.: 1991, 'The embeddedness of reading in classroom lfe: Reading as a situated process', in C. Baker & A. Luke (eds.), *Towards a Critical Sociology of Reading Pedagogy*, J. Benjamin Publishing Co., Philadelphia, 141–160.
Heap, J.L.: 1982, 'Understanding classroom events: A critique of Durkin, wth an alternative', *Journal of Reading Behavior* 14, 391–411.
Heap, J.L.: 1985, 'Discourse in the production of classroom knowledge: Reading lessons', *Curriculum Inquiry* 15, 245–279.
Heap, J.L.: 1992, 'Seeing snubs: An introduction to sequential analysis'. *The Journal of Classroom Interaction* 27, 23–28.
Heritage, J.: 1984, *Garfinkel and Ethnomethodology*, Polity Press, Cambridge.
Heyman, R.D.: 1986, 'Formulating topic in the classroom', *Discourse Processes* 9, 37–55.
Heyman, R.D.: 1983, 'Clarifying meaning through classroom talk', *Curriculum Inquiry* 13, 23–42.
Lerner, G.: 1995, 'Turn design and the organization of participation in instructional activities', *Discourse Processes* 19, 111–131.
Macbeth, D.: 1994, 'Classroom encounters with the unspeakable: "Do you see, Danelle?"', *Discourse Processes* 17, 311–335.
Macbeth, D.: 1992, 'Classroom "floors": Material organizations as a course of affairs', *Qualitative Sociology* 15, 123–150.
McHoul, A.W.: 1978, 'The organization of turns at formal talk in the classroom', *Language in Society* 7, 183–213.

McHoul, A.W.: 1990, 'The Organization of repair in classroom talk', *Language in Society* 19, 349–377.

McHoul, A.W. & Watson, D.R.: 1984, 'Two axes for the analysis of "commonsense" and "formal" geographical knowledge in classroom talk', *British Journal of Sociology of Education* 5, 281–302.

Mehan, H.: 1979, *Learning Lessons: Social Organization in the Classroom*, U.S.A., Harvard University Press, Cambridge.

Payne, G. & Hustler, D.: 1980, 'Teaching the class: The practical management of a cohort', *British Journal of Sociology of Education* 1, 49–66.

Psathas, G.: 1995, *Conversation Analysis: The Study of Talk-in-Interaction*, Thousand Oaks, Sage Publications.

Psathas, G. & Anderson, T.: 1990, 'The "practices" of transcription in conversation analysis', *Semiotica* 28, 75–99.

Sacks, H.: 1995, *Lectures on Conversation, Volumes One and Two*, Gail Jefferson (ed.), Blackwell, Cambridge, U.S.A.

Sacks, H., Schegloff, E.A. & Jefferson, G.: 1974, 'A simplest systematics for the organization of turn-taking for conversation', *Language* 50, 696–735.

Schegloff, E.A.: 1995, Introduction, *Lectures on Conversation, Volumes One and Two*, by Harvey Sacks. Blackwell, Cambridge, U.S.A.

Schegloff, E.A.: 1991, 'Reflections on talk and social structure', in D. Boden & D.H. Zimmerman (eds.), *Talk and Social Structure: Studies in Ethnomethodology and Conversation Analysis*, University of California Press, Berkeley and Los Angeles, 44–70.

Sinclair, J. & Coulthard, R. M.: 1975, *Towards an Analysis of Discourse: The English Used by Teachers and Pupils*, Oxford University Press, London.

Weber, M.: 1968, *Economy and Society*, Bedminster Press, New York.

Wittgenstein, L.: 1958, *Philosophical Investigations*, Macmillan, New York.

Zimmerman, D.: 1988, 'On conversation: The conversation analytic perspective', *Communication Yearbook/II* 10, 406–432.

TERESA L. MCCARTY

TEACHER RESEARCH METHODS IN LANGUAGE AND EDUCATION

In a poem entitled 'Inquiry,' Mary Harbage captures the substance and spirit of teacher research: 'To ease her disquietude,' Harbage writes, 'the teacher reached into the clutter of new ideas and untried ways ... asked a question,... and said,... "I will test and try, adjust and watch, and make of this something good and new" ' (1962, p. 391). The poem's publication date also suggests the enduring nature of concerns with teacher research. An offshoot of post-World War II action research, teacher research is 'systematic, intentional inquiry by teachers about their own school and classroom work' (Cochran-Smith & Lytle, 1993, p. 5). The primary participants in teacher research are K-12 teachers, working individually or collaboratively with other teachers and university-based researchers. Motivated by questions arising out of teachers' own practice – a 'disquietude' with the status quo, a dissatisfaction with existing theory – teacher researchers address questions of deep personal significance with an eye toward systemic change. Language and literacy have been of particular interest to teacher researchers and indeed, much of the current knowledge base in this area stems from teachers' classroom inquiries and their wider examinations of the sociocultural contexts of language learning. All recent teacher research utilizes a qualitative, case study or ethnographic approach; the aim, Nixon (1987, p. 24) insists, is not to generalize but to cultivate 'wisdom which will inform our strategic action.'

EARLY DEVELOPMENTS

Praxis as practical theory, or the dynamic interplay between reflection and action, is central to teacher research. In fact, the terms teacher research and action research are used synonymously throughout the literature. Kurt Lewin and the action research of the 1940s laid the foundation for the present teacher research movement. As early as 1904, however, Boone cited the need for 'a body of earnest teachers who are also students, and who are ready to make every day's undertakings an object of thoughtful, critical direction' (cited in McKernan, 1987, p. 8). Dewey's (1929) self-reflective science extended the concept of the researching teacher. But it was Lewin's work that brought concreteness to action research. Focusing on intergroup

N.H. Hornberger and D. Corson (eds), Encyclopedia of Language and Education,
Volume 8: Research Methods in Language and Education, 227–237.
© *1997 Kluwer Academic Publishers. Printed in the Netherlands.*

relations, Lewin (1946, p. 35) argued that research 'that produces nothing but books will not suffice,' and proposed an action research cycle of problem identification, planning, fact-finding, executing and evaluating the action(s) taken. An adherent of the 'scientific method,' Lewin nevertheless believed that law-like generalizations 'do not do the job of diagnosis which has to be done locally,' and called for a 'mood of relaxed objectivity' (1946, pp. 42, 44).

A decade later, Corey (1953) and Taba & Noel (1957) operationalized the action research paradigm in education, implementing versions of Lewin's action research cycle with cooperating teams of public school personnel. 'Our schools cannot keep up with the life they are supposed to sustain,' Corey (1953, p. viii) observed, 'unless teachers, pupils, [and] supervisors ... continuously examine what they are doing.' Presaging the calls of others, Corey also noted that pre-service teachers 'must accept greater responsibility for their own learning;' less emphasis, he said, 'should be placed on courses that require them to spend most of their time reading about ... what other people say they should do' (1953, p. 145; cf. Erickson, 1986, p. 157).

The 1960s and 1970s saw the 'eruption of the practical' (Carr & Kemmis, 1986, p. 17), as curriculum theorists such as Stenhouse (1975) argued for local curriculum decision-making. 'It is not enough that teachers' work should be studied,' Stenhouse claimed; 'they need to study it themselves' (1975, p. 143). Stenhouse made explicit the role of teacher-as-researcher and argued for a critically subjective methodology. Teacher research is not concerned with objectivity, he asserted, but 'with the development of a sensitive and self-critical perspective' (1975, p. 157).

MAJOR CONTRIBUTIONS

The decades since Stenhouse's 1975 publication witnessed the florescence of a world-wide teacher researcher movement. Until recently, however, that movement remained marginalized, even unnamed, as suggested by Britton's (1983) article, 'A Quiet Form of Research.' Yet throughout this time a significant body of data accumulated – naturalistic case studies by professional researchers and classroom teachers which qualitatively documented children's literacy development (see, e.g., Bissex & Bullock, 1987). 'Descriptive studies of writers' activity yield information that makes sense to classroom teachers,' Atwell (1982, p. 81) notes; 'it is a method that teachers can employ.' Atwell, Goodman (1978), Graves (1978), Clay (1982), Goswami & Stillman (1987) and others all directed attention to teachers' roles as participant observers, 'kid watchers,' and language and literacy theorists in the classroom. Such studies enhanced the visibility and credibility of teacher research in the wider teaching and research communities.

In the U.S., an emerging national network of writing projects officially validated teacher research. The National Council of Teachers of English, Office of Educational Research and Improvement, National Institute of Education, and International Reading Association made the teacher-as-scholar a funding priority in an effort to institutionalize teacher research at the school and district levels (Cochran-Smith & Lytle, 1993, p. 13). Atwell (1982, p. 85) states that such projects encouraged teachers to focus less on the narrow aspects of lesson planning and more on observing student learning. Moreover, she writes, 'We came to see ourselves as professionals, active in and central to the betterment of writing instruction, rather than as peripheral recipients of other's theories' (1982, p. 86).

Atwell's observations speak to the power of teacher research in documenting, interpreting and influencing children's literacy-in-process, but also to the personally and professionally transformative effects of such research. This latter emphasis and a parallel critique of the structural conditions in which teachers and students work, are at the heart of the critical action research carried out in the U.K. and Australia. Critical action research involves an investigatory cycle similar to Lewin's. While teachers' self-understandings are central to critical action research, it is distinguished by an explicit commitment to social critique and the involvement of teacher-participants in all phases of the research cycle (Tripp, 1990; Carr & Kemmis, 1986).

The epistemological framework for this approach lies in the Frankfurt School and in particular the work of Habermas (1974), who argued for a view of knowledge in which individuals are empowered 'through their own understandings and actions' (Carr & Kemmis, 1986, p. 130). This framework adds an emancipatory dimension to praxis. Like knowledge itself, praxis is not socially neutral; it is shaped by notions of social justice (Lather, 1986). Socially critical teacher research, then, is democratic and life-enhancing, both interpreting and acting upon the social context for practice 'to facilitate new forms of consciousness and practice' (Tripp, 1990, pp. 163–164; cf. Kincheloe, 1991; Stringer, 1996).

In sum, teacher/action research emerged as a means of bridging the gap between theory and practice by contextualizing research and involving educational practitioners in all stages of its execution. Originally experimental in design, teacher research has nonetheless recognized the need for flexible methods evaluated in light of their contributions to practice. Recent teacher research has emphasized interpretive case studies and the illumination of teachers' and students' emic understandings of language learning. At the same time, critical action researchers have called for broadening the interpretivist paradigm to include critique and reformulation of the social systems of which schooling is part.

Teacher research continues to be distinguished from 'research on teaching' or 'formal research' (Richardson, 1994). However, teacher research advocates argue that it is 'its own genre, not entirely different from other types of systematic inquiry into teaching yet with some quite distinctive features' (Cochran-Smith & Lytle, 1993, p. 10). Those features include strategies for transforming 'wonderings into research questions', data collection in which the most important tool 'is your eye and your view of classroom life,' and analysis involving 'seeing and seeing again' (Hubbard & Power, 1993, p. 2.10.65). Beyond its heuristic value for teachers, teacher research has a critical role to play in what we know about teaching. Toward that end, Lytle & Cochran-Smith propose a four-part typology which recognizes a range of teacher writing as research, including journals, essays, oral inquiry processes, and classroom studies (Lytle & Cochran-Smith, 1990). 'Taken seriously,' Lytle & Cochran-Smith (1990, p. 84) state, 'teacher research represents a radical challenge to assumptions about the relationships of theory and practice, school and university partnerships, and ... educational reform.' It is to a consideration of these most recent developments and their potentials that we now turn.

WORK IN PROGRESS

The presence of a professional journal devoted to teacher research (Teacher Research: The Journal of Classroom Inquiry), and the number of other theme issues on the subject, attest to its growing significance (see, e.g., *Peabody Journal of Education*, Winter 1987; *Theory Into Practice*, Summer 1990; *Educational Leadership*, October 1993; *English Journal*, October 1994, and *Practicing Anthropology*, Summer 1995). Many teacher researchers work alone, with little outside support, while others collaborate with other teachers or in school-university partnerships. This section considers both individual and group projects which illustrate a cross-section of cultural-linguistic, demographic, institutional, and content characteristics.

Individual Teacher Research. In addition to the journals above, Bissex & Bullock (1987), Goswami & Stillman (1987), and Patterson et al. (1993) provide rich descriptions by teachers of their research. For example, Crowell (1993), a teacher in a Spanish/English elementary classroom, began her research on literature, current events, and social studies in response to students' questions about the Persian Gulf War. Students, Crowell states, were her most important collaborators, patiently answering questions and editing transcripts of their conversations. Wood (1993), a seventh grade teacher, undertook a case study of a struggling adolescent writer in which in-depth interviews constituted the primary investigative tool. Awbrey (1987), a kindergarten teacher, spent a year examining the writing of four- and five-year olds; her methods were participant observation and the collection and analysis of students' writing. These and other individual projects represent the action research cycle in that they: (1) spring from teacher and student concerns; (2) involve action to elucidate that concern; (3) utilize multi-layered methods; (4) involve reflection; and (5) use knowledge to reframe practice.

Teacher-to-Teacher Collaboration. The Philadelphia Writing Project is a school-university partnership focusing on literacy learning and the nature of collaboration itself. Through the pairing of teacher-consultants with experienced K-12 teachers, participants visit each others' classrooms during the school day and engage in 'mutual observation, systematic reflection, and discussion of issues related to theory and practice' (Fecho & Lytle, 1993, p. 128). A key research question is, 'What does it mean for teachers to work together in the previously private spaces of each other's classrooms?' (Fecho & Lytle, 1993, p. 128). Participants found, first, that in the professional climate of autonomy and estrangement, cross-visitation bridges teachers' isolation but also exposes them to uncertainties that must be negotiated. Second, teachers' expectations of their partners also must be negotiated; teacher-consultants, for example, often are expected to possess 'magical teaching strategies' that will work in any setting (Fecho & Lytle, 1993, p. 132). Third, teacher-to-teacher collaboration requires revisioning staff development to include alternate schedules and other support. Finally, such collaboration necessitates rethinking teacher research methods themselves; strategies emerge spontaneously, the lines between researcher and researched are obscured, and researchers must take on multiple roles and tasks. Collaborative methods, Fecho & Lytle (1993, p. 136) note, are frequently 'messy and complex.'

Restructuring Preservice Teacher Education. Student Teachers as Researching Teachers (Project START) links preservice teachers and university mentors with cooperating teachers engaged in school reform. Through their classroom interactions and formal meetings over a year, participants engage in 'rich and complex discourse' that 'conventional supervisory structures are unlikely to generate' (Cochran-Smith, 1991, p. 304). Project START encourages novice teachers to construct their own theories of teaching and learning. This suggests an alternative model of teacher education that enables novice and experienced teachers to labor together to reform teaching and schools. The 'only way for beginners to learn to be both educators and activists,' Cochran-Smith (1991, p. 307) states, 'is to struggle over time in the company of experienced teachers who are themselves committed to collaboration and reform.

Indigenous Teacher Study Groups. For American Indians and Alaska Natives, the task of educational reform is unique. For nearly two centuries the U.S. government imposed a fierce English-only policy aimed at exterminating indigenous ethnolinguistic identities (McCarty, 1993; see the review by Corson in Volume 1 on policies for indigenous languages). As a result, indigenous communities in the U.S. are fighting for the very survival of their languages and cultures. In these communities, schools – historically sites of coercive assimilation – have emerged as primary agencies for local education control.

Indigenous teacher study groups are one proactive force in this struggle. Lipka & McCarty (1994) report on two such groups: bilingual teachers in the Rough Rock English-Navajo Language Arts Program (RRENLAP) in Arizona, and the Ciulistet Yup'ik Teacher Leader group in Alaska. Over more than a decade, both groups have engaged in sustained discussion and critique urged by the exchange of personal language and literacy histories, dialogue journals, classroom investigations, and learning from elders. These methods have been applied to the investigation and use of local knowledge to improve indigenous schooling. RRENLAP and Ciulistet have created 'zones of safety:' a space and place within teachers' work lives where conventional practices can be challenged, solidarity expressed, and new ideas scrutinized (Lipka & McCarty, 1994, p. 272). Though the groups remain marginalized, they have nonetheless reshaped school cultures according to local norms. Ciulistet founder Esther Ilutsik (1994, p. 12) describes the self-empowerment found in the groups: '[W]e continue to strengthen ourselves and our identity, and we hope that we can pass these values on to our students.'

Teachers as Ethnographers. The Funds of Knowledge Project is based on the assumption that Mexican-American households contain immense intellectual reserves that can be tapped as resources for classroom learning. The project involves a collaboration between teacher researchers and university researchers in anthropology and education. Four teachers were recruited to conduct ethnographic inquiries in Latino households. Unlike conventional home visits, these are 'research visits for the express purpose of identifying and documenting knowledge that exists in students' homes' (González et al., 1995, p. 444). Using field notes, journals, questionnaires, interviews, and monthly study group sessions, project participants analyzed household visits as a catalyst for developing new ideas about teaching. Those ideas led to the development of teachers as qualitative researchers, the formation of more trusting relationships between teachers and families, and the redefinition of local households as key resources for teaching (González et al., 1995). In addition, teachers created integrated curriculum units for language arts, mathematics, and science based on household funds of knowledge.

Teacher Research as Sustained Conversation: An Urban Literacy Project.
A six-year federally funded study on literacy education in urban environments, this project involves a university-based teacher educator, five
beginning elementary teachers, and two secondary teachers. The teachers
already had developed a theoretical foundation for literacy education; what
they did not know was how to teach literacy to children within the 'difficult environments of urban schools' (Hollingsworth et al., 1994, p. 19).
Teachers' individual classroom inquiries and their analysis of collaborative and sustained conversation led them to chart new ways of seeing and
assessing children's multiple literacies. 'Relational knowing,' or knowledge gained and enacted 'through a sense of care for self and others'
(Hollingsworth et al., 1994, p. 77), was central to these changes. 'While
we actually learned to teach literacy through its practice and research in our
classrooms,' participants state, 'conversations provided spaces or contexts
for becoming aware of and naming both what we'd learned and how we
learned it' (Hollingsworth et al., 1994, p. 35).

PROBLEMS AND DIFFICULTIES

Virtually all teacher researchers cite lack of time as an obstacle to their
work. Adding study groups, field journals, publishing, and community-
based ethnography to teachers' already full schedules is a costly investment. This is sometimes ameliorated by the provision of release time,
substitutes, and paid overtime. Yet teacher researchers still sacrifice to
conduct their work.

Beyond this, the institutional climate within schools alternatively constrains or enables teacher research. Teaching is an insular activity, carried
out within the bordered domain of the classroom. Teacher researchers who
publish or otherwise share their work risk being perceived as incompetent,
making teacher research 'a high-stakes game in which collaboration may
come at the price of exposure and loss of autonomy' (Cochran-Smith &
Lytle, 1992, p. 302). Moreover, teacher research is impacted by the larger
school power structure. RRENLAP exemplifies the democratization of
teacher-administrator relations; working as a co-learner with teachers, the
school principal demonstrated that what they invested their labor in, he
valued enough to do himself (Begay et al., 1995). Other teacher researchers
work under more oppressive conditions. Finally, funding also is a factor;
all collaborative projects described here received external funds in support
of their work.

These issues are nested in an array of social and political forces emanating from the wider academic community. Within that context, a paradox
exists: While teacher research has its genesis in the acknowledged irrele-

vance of much academic research to practice, teachers' socialization in academic institutions makes them likely to doubt whether theirs constitutes 'real research' (Page, 1994).

This highlights the lingering problems associated with the qualitative-quantitative paradigmatic debate. Concerns with procedural objectivity – eliminating the effects of the researcher on data – validity, reliability and generalizability, continue to haunt qualitative research in education. These concerns miss the point of teacher research entirely. As social inquiry and social practice, teacher research is inextricably bound with the world it seeks to study. 'Rather than engaging in futile attempts to eliminate the effects of the researcher,' Hammersley & Atkinson (1983, p. 17) note, 'we should set about understanding them.' To do that, teacher research emphasizes disciplined reflexivity, systematic documentation and analysis, and multi-faceted qualitative methods that permit the comparison of a variety of data. For teacher research, universal solutions do not suffice; 'the devil,' as Guba (1996, p. x) points out, 'is in the details.' Those details are not knowable in advance, or from a distance. They must be uncovered through long-term, systematic and subjective engagement.

FUTURE DIRECTIONS

Teacher research is a means of understanding the emic processes of language teaching and learning in the classroom, and of using those understandings to inform curriculum and practice. Ciulistet, RRENLAP, and the Funds of Knowledge Project further demonstrate how classroom research can be linked to community studies in ways that tap and validate diverse intellectual and social resources within multicultural environments. These forms of teacher research hold special promise for minority education, as they both reflect and generate fundamental shifts in power relations within historic contexts of domination and subordination.

Teacher research also is professional transformation and critique. Teachers who act and view themselves as researchers become more critical, confident, and willing to take risks; they acknowledge their roles as change agents (Allen & Shockley, 1996; Begay et al., 1995). Such change includes revisioning what counts as teaching – and as research. Duckworth (1986, pp. 494, 495) calls teaching the *sine qua non* of research; 'why should this be a separate research profession?,' she asks. Short (1993, p. 156) extends the possibilities by challenging college educators to engage as teacher researchers as a means of improving their own pedagogy. Working as extended professionals (Strickland, 1988), teacher researchers not only bridge the gap between theory and practice, they balance authority between those traditionally considered to be theorists, and those viewed as practitioners.

Teacher research thus opens new epistemological possibilities which have yet to be fully exploited. Teacher research represents a different way of knowing – through relationships, observation and assessment of practice, dialogue, reflection, engagement, and critique. It is research as social transaction. It *can become* research as social justice. Through its process and products, teacher research encourages us not only to challenge an unjust system, but to examine, confront, and transform the root causes of those injustices.

University of Arizona
USA

REFERENCES

Allen, J. & Shockley, B.: 1996, 'Conversations: composing a research dialogue: University and school research communities encountering a cultural shift', *Reading Research Quarterly* 32, 220–228,

Atwell, N.M.: 1982, 'Class-based writing research: Teachers learn from students', *English Journal* 71, 84–87.

Awbrey, M.J.: 1987, 'A teacher's action research study of writing in the kindergarten: Accepting the natural expression of children', *Peabody Journal of Education* 64, 33–64.

Begay, S., Dick, G.S., Estell, D.W., Estell, J., McCarty, T.L. & Sells, A.: 1995: 'Change from the inside out: A story of transformation in a Navajo community school', *Bilingual Research Journal* 19, 121–139.

Bissex, G.L. & Bullock, R.H.: 1987, *Seeing for Ourselves: Case-Study Research by Teachers of Writing*, Heinemann, Portsmouth, NH

Britton, J.: 1987, 'A quiet form of research', *English Journal* 72, 89–92.

Carr, W. & Kemmis, S.: 1986, *Becoming Critical: Education, Knowledge and Action Research*, The Falmer Press, London & Philadelphia.

Clay, M.: 1982, 'Looking and seeing in the classroom', *English Journal* 71, 90–92.

Cochran-Smith, M.: 1991, 'Learning to teach against the grain', *Harvard Educational Review* 61, 279–310.

Cochran-Smith, M. & Lytle, S.L.: 1992, 'Communities for teacher research: Fringe or forefront?', *American Journal of Education* 100, 298–324.

Cochran-Smith, M. & Lytle, S.L.: 1993, *Inside/Outside: Teacher Research and Knowledge*, Teachers College Press, New York & London.

Corey, S.M.: 1953, *Action Research to Improve School Practices*, Teachers College, Columbia University, New York.

Crowell, C.G.: 1993, 'Living through war vicariously with literature', in L. Patterson et al. (eds.), *Teachers are Researchers: Reflection and Action*, International Reading Association, Newark, DE, 51–59.

Dewey, J.: 1929, *The Sources of a Science of Education*, Liveright Publishing Corporation, New York.

Duckworth, E.: 1986, 'Teaching as research', *Harvard Educational Review* 56, 481–495.

Fecho, B. & Lytle, S.L.: 1993, 'Working it out: Collaboration as subject and method', in S.J. Hudelson & J.W. Lindfors (eds.), *Delicate Balances: Collaborative Research in Language Education*, National Council of Teachers of English, Urbana, IL.

Erickson, F.: 1986, 'Qualitative methods in research on teaching', in M. Wittrock (ed.),

The Handbook of Research on Teaching (third edition), Macmillan, New York, NY, 119–162.

González, N., Moll, L.C., Floyd-Tenery, M., Rivera, A., Rendon, P., González, R. & Amanti, C.: 1995, 'Funds of knowledge for teaching in Latino households', *Urban Education* 29, 443–470.

Goodman, Y.: 1978, 'Kid-watching: An alternative to testing', *National Elementary Principal* 57, 41–45.

Goswami, D. & Stillman, P. (eds.): 1987, *Reclaiming the Classroom: Teacher Research as an Agency for Change*, Boynton/Cook, Upper Montclair, NJ.

Graves, D.H.: 1978, 'We can end the energy crisis', *Language Arts* 55, 795–796.

Guba, E.G.: 1996, 'Foreword', in E.T. Stringer (ed.), *Action Research: A Handbook for Practitioners*, Sage, Thousand Oaks, ix–xiii.

Habermas, J.: 1974, *Theory and Practice*, tr. T. McCarthy, Beacon Press, Boston.

Hammersley, M. & Atkinson, P.: 1983, *Ethnography: Principles in Practice*, Routledge, London & New York.

Harbage, M.: 1962, 'Inquiry', *Educational Researcher* 19, 391–393.

Hollingsworth, S., with Cody, A., Davis-Smallwood, J., Dybdahl, M., Gallagher, P., Gallego, M., Maestre, T., Minarik, L.T., Raffel, L., Standerford, N.S. & Teel, K.M.: 1994, *Teacher Research and Urban Literacy Education: Lessons and Conversations in a Feminist Key*, Teachers College Press, New York & London.

Hubbard, R.S. & Power, B.M.: 1993, *The Art of Classroom Inquiry: A Handbook for Teacher-Researchers*, Heinemann, Portsmouth, NH.

Ilutsik, E.: 1994, 'The founding of Ciulistet: One teacher's journey', *Journal of American Indian Education* 33, 6–13.

Kincheloe, J.: 1991, *Teachers as Researchers: Qualitative Inquiry as a Path to Empowerment*, Falmer, London.

Lather, P.: 1986, 'Research as praxis', *Harvard Educational Review* 56, 257–277.

Lewin, K.: 1946, 'Action research and minority problems', *Journal of Social Issues* 2, 34–46.

Lipka, J. & McCarty, T.L.: 1994, 'Changing the culture of schooling: Navajo and Yup'ik cases', *Anthropology & Education Quarterly* 25, 266–284.

Lytle, S.L. & Cochran-Smith, M.: 1990, 'Learning from teacher research: A working typology', *Teachers College Record* 92, 83–103.

McCarty, T.L.: 1993, 'Language, literacy, and the image of the child in American Indian classrooms', *Language Arts* 70, 182–192.

McKernan, J.: 1987, 'Action research and curriculum development', *Peabody Journal of Education* 64, 6–19.

Nixon, J.: 1987, 'The teacher as researcher: Contradictions and continuities', *Peabody Journal of Education* 64, 20–32.

Page, E.: 1994, 'Does real research mean teacher research?', *English Journal* 83, 51–54.

Patterson, L., Santa, C.M., Short, K.G. & Smith, K. (eds.): 1993, *Teachers are Researchers: Reflection and Action*, International Reading Association, Newark, DE.

Richardson, V.: 1994, 'Conducting research on practice', *Educational Researcher* 23, 5–10.

Short, K.G., 1993: 'Teacher research for teacher educators', in L. Patterson et al. (eds.), *Teachers are Researchers: Reflection and Action*, International Reading Association, Newark, DE, 155–159.

Stenhouse, L.: 1975, *An Introduction to Curriculum Research and Development*, Heinemann, London.

Strickland, D.S.: 1988, 'The teacher as researcher: toward the extended professional', *Language Arts* 65, 754–764.

Stringer, E.T.: 1996, *Action Research: A Handbook for Practitioners*, Sage, Thousand Oaks, CA.

Taba, H. & Noel, E.: 1957, *Action Research: A Case Study*, Association for Supervision and Curriculum Development, Washington, DC.

Tripp, D.H.: 1990, 'Socially critical action research', *Theory Into Practice* 29, 158–166.

Wood, K.: 1993, 'A case study of a writer', in L. Patterson et al. (eds.), *Teachers are Researchers: Reflection and Action*, International Reading Association, Newark, DE, 106–114.

ILANA SNYDER

RESEARCH METHODS FOR STUDYING THE USE OF COMPUTERS IN LITERACY CLASSROOMS

This review's broad concern is the complex connections between literacy practices and electronic technologies. More specifically, it looks at research methods, taken to be a set of practices and discourses, for studying the use of computers in language and literacy classrooms.

Different methods for investigating computers in literacy contexts reflect distinctive ways of doing research: academics working in universities; researchers and practitioners forming partnerships; teacher-led research; and small-scale classroom studies, based on teachers' experience and their informal observations. All are represented here.

Literacy is defined as the uses of reading and writing to achieve social purposes in contexts of use. The idea that there is one monolithic type of literacy is questioned; instead, there are literacies (Gee, 1990). When computers are used for literacy purposes, the notion of 'computer-mediated literacies' is preferred, explained as both social *and* technical practices (Cochran-Smith, 1991). By contrast, the meaning of the phrase 'computer literacy' is coloured by its colloquial usage (also see the review by Abbott in Volume 2).

EARLY DEVELOPMENTS

The history of research methods in this emerging field parallels the trajectory of the wider area of composition studies, but in a condensed timeframe. The first computer-writing studies were most often quantitative, experimental in conception and design. There was a gradual shift to qualitative methods with an emphasis on the socially constructed nature of reality, the intimate relationship between the researcher and what is studied, and the situational constraints that shape inquiry. More recent studies have adopted multiple perspectives which draw on methods from both traditions, while others examine computer-mediated literacies through a particular ideological lens.

It would be a mistake, however, to represent the two decades of research in this area as a process of evolution. Each of the earlier waves are still operating in the present as a set of practices that researchers follow or argue against. An array of choices now characterises the field with no

N.H. Hornberger and D. Corson (eds), Encyclopedia of Language and Education,
Volume 8: Research Methods in Language and Education, 239–248.
© *1997 Kluwer Academic Publishers. Printed in the Netherlands.*

single approach privileged. Of course, there are no fewer problems and difficulties, particularly in studies which attempt to blend methods from different paradigms. Inevitable are tensions between the relativist, doubting, postmodern sensibility and the more certain, traditional, positivist conceptions of research in this area.

There are a number of useful overviews of the research, extending in their coverage almost to the present (Cochran-Smith, 1991; Bangert-Drowns, 1993; Hawisher, LeBlanc, Moran & Selfe, 1996). Together they establish what we already know about students and their computer-mediated literacy practices as well as suggesting what we still need to find out. Moreover, they address the difficulties of interpreting studies that reflect contrasting conceptual frameworks and which differ in design, methods of data collection, variables examined and modes of analysis.

MAJOR CONTRIBUTIONS

The first studies coincided with the availability of micro-computers and word processing software (Gould, 1978). Investigators asked the classic question in educational research (Does this innovation improve things?) and chose the traditional method of exploring it (empirical), although case study was also used. Experimental and quasi-experimental studies assessed whether the quality of texts produced with computers was better than those produced with pens. Chiefly through the perspective of cognitive psychology, early research also examined the effects of the use of computers on composing processes, particularly prewriting and revising. Implicit was the conviction that if students planned carefully and revised more with computers, their texts would be better (Collier, 1981; Bridwell, Sirc & Brooke, 1985; Daiute, 1986).

Surveys examined students' attitudes to computers (Bridwell, Sirc & Brooke, 1985) and case studies explored the responses of individuals and groups to their use (Catano, 1985). By the mid-80s, there emerged a shift in focus from the isolated writer to the writer in context. With this increased sensitivity to the sociocultural setting in which the computers were used, studies became more distinctly ethnographic (Dickinson, 1986; Herrmann, 1987).

This variation in method was accompanied by a new teaching emphasis. Still interested in the effects of word processing on writing quality, revision and attitudes, studies concentrated on the writing pedagogy, often a process approach, that teachers adopted when introducing the technology. The computer was investigated as a potentially felicitous tool that might both facilitate and enhance a process approach (Sommers, 1985).

The research, like composition studies, was in transition: some researchers were operating in the current-traditional paradigm, concerned with correctness and error; many were operating in the writing-process paradigm; and a few were beginning to adopt the social view (Hawisher, LeBlanc, Moran & Selfe, 1996). However, no matter which paradigm was adopted, classroom studies, based on teachers' experience and their informal observations of the use of computers, reflected themes similar to the more formal research reports (Sommers, 1985).

Although the emphasis in this review is on the methods used by researchers to study computers in literacy contexts, it is also relevant to consider the studies' findings. This is because we know that how researchers carry out research influences what is likely to be learned. Not surprisingly, the results of the quality-focused studies were equivocal. There is probably a short answer to the question: Do students write better with computers? It depends – on the writer's preferred writing and revising strategies, keyboarding skill, prior computer experience, supplementary teaching interventions, the teacher's goals and strategies, the social organisation of the learning context and the school culture (Bangert-Drowns, 1993). Nevertheless, one group, developing writers, seemed to benefit more than other students in a word-processing environment (Cirello, 1986).

A number of related methodological issues probably affected these findings. First, the subjects were often required to write a minimal number of essays over just a few weeks, yet conclusions were drawn. Second, some studies required subjects to use computers to transcribe after initial composing with pens, making it difficult to discern the effects of a machine used for only part of the development of the text. Third, subjects were sometimes expected to acquire word-processing skills at the same time as they produced computer texts for comparison with their pen texts. Fourth, the operating complexity and relative lack of sophistication of the technology possibly influenced findings (Gould, 1978; Collier, 1981).

Studies which examined the effects of word processing on revision strategies mainly reported an increase in the frequency. Daiute (1986), however, reported more only when a prompting program incorporated in the word-processing software encouraged students to revise. Other studies examined the kinds of revisions writers made. Distinguishing between meaning level and surface-level changes (Faigley & Witte, 1981), studies found that students made more surface-level revisions when using computers (Bridwell, Sirc & Brooke, 1985).

Research which looked at attitudes reported both positive and negative responses. Students asserted that writing on the computer was more fun, easier and that they wrote better. Other studies connected negative attitudes to mechanical and classroom management problems (Selfe, 1985). However, once students felt comfortable with the technology attitudes improved (Bridwell, Sirc & Brooke, 1985).

Studies in which word processing was combined with effective writing pedagogy produced uniformly positive findings: when instruction involved teaching students strategies aimed at improving their writing skills, writers using word processing achieved at a higher level than similar writers not using computers (Sommers, 1985; Daiute, 1986).

When computers were considered by researchers as part of a dynamic, integrated classroom environment (Dickinson, 1986; Herrmann, 1987), the findings were consistently positive. Computer-produced writing achieved higher ratings (Herrmann, 1987); collaboration and writing-focused talk were facilitated (Dickinson, 1986); classrooms were less teacher-centred (Herrmann, 1987); and writing was transformed from a private to a public activity.

The mid-80s marked the end of the first generation of research and the beginning of a second. From 1986–1988, the research consolidated but researchers also began to explore the possibilities of the computer as a site for the social construction of knowledge. Shifts in interests and methods can be identified: feminist criticism, cultural criticism and critical pedagogy were all invoked to frame and inform research; the war between quantitative and qualitative approaches abated; and the researcher was increasingly understood as implicated in research processes.

The first description of a paperless writing class was published in which all student and teacher contributions occurred over a network (Jennings, 1987). The contextual approach to computers and their use (Kramarae, 1988) made gender issues central to discussion of technology and there was the growing recognition that computers in classrooms appear 'unlikely to negate the powerful influence of the differential socialisation of students by social class and its effects on their success or failure in school' (Herrmann, 1987, p. 86). In fact, the contrary seems to be the case. Computers in classrooms may make the impact of students' differential socialisation and enculturation experiences more severe. Indeed, a Scandinavian study (Staberg, 1994) shows that adolescent girls are rejecting computers in disproportionate numbers, presumably because of their lack of sympathy for the control ideology that drives the construction and invention of computers, and because of the obstacle to quality interaction between people that they often erect.

As researchers were no longer simply concerned whether the use of technology makes things better, they asked different kinds of questions which, of course, affected the methods they used. Researchers argued that we cannot understand how electronic technologies affect students' literacy practices 'apart from the ways these are embedded within, and mediated by, the social systems of [particular] classrooms' over time (Cochran-Smith, 1991, p. 107). Qualitative methods, including observation and interviews, seemed the best way to investigate their questions: Cochran-Smith, Paris & Kahn (1991) worked with teachers and students in five elementary classrooms over two years to explore how computers made learning to read and write different; in a case study that involved active participant observation, Miller & Olson (1994) found that the existence of innovative practice associated with the introduction of computers in the classroom has less to do with the advent of technology than with the teacher's pre-existing conception of practice.

However, at the same time, some researchers continued to investigate the influence of word processing on writing quality and revision strategies, while attempting to avoid problems encountered in earlier studies. The findings were correspondingly more persuasive: when the student subjects were experienced users, papers written on computer were rated higher (Owston, Murphy & Wideman, 1992); when students with different writing abilities were observed, the effects of word processing interacted with individual student differences (Joram, Woodruff, Bryson & Lindsay, 1992); when similar groups of student writers were compared, the group which received unsolicited metacognitive guidance from a specially designed computer tool wrote better essays (Zellermayer, Salomon, Globerson & Givon, 1991).

Increasingly, researchers examined what is now widely known as computer-mediated communication (CMC). This form of interaction is made possible when computers are used to create electronic forums on local-area networks (LANs) and wide-area networks (WANs). It has been noted that these electronic spaces in which writers and readers can create, exchange, and comment on texts have the potential for supporting student-centred learning and discursive practices that can be different in form, and, some claim, more engaging and democratic than those in traditional classrooms (Batson, 1988).

Most of the studies of CMC are with post-secondary students, however, the findings still have implications for school-based research. Researchers have undertaken comparative observational studies of college students engaged in both face-to-face discussions and electronic exchanges about their writing (Palmquist, 1993; Geest & Remmers, 1994). Palmquist concluded that the use of networked-based communication both shaped and was shaped by the curricula and that the interaction between networked-based communication and face-to-face may lead to better academic performance. By contrast, Geest and Remmers concluded that computer-mediated peer review had many of the drawbacks of 'distance learning'.

Experimental design has also been used to examine the effects of a computer-mediated networked learning environment on writing (Allen & Thompson, 1995). Fifth-grade students in the treatment group used word processing to write texts collaboratively then sent them electronically to readers who responded to their writing. When the students knew they would be sending their writing to an outside reader and when they received prompt response, there was a positive effect on the quality of their writing.

The Internet has become a site for research, and hypertext, fully electronic non-sequential reading and writing, a particular focus of interest. However, there is much hype and little systematic research investigating these new structures and modes of communication. Writing about hypertext is dominated by explications of the technology's convergence with contemporary literary theories (Snyder, 1996). Claims are also made for hypertext's educational potential. These include the promotion of more independent and active learning, changes to teaching and curriculum practices, and challenges to our assumptions about literacy and literary education (Snyder, 1996).

Common assertions made on behalf of hypertext in the teaching of writing include the possibility for promoting associative thinking, collaborative learning, synthesis writing, distributing traditional authority in texts and classrooms and facilitating deconstructive reading and writing. The use of hypertext in literary studies is not as yet widespread but advocates argue that its impact cannot be ignored when it is integrated into a literature program. Accounts of literary courses that use hypertext technology in creative ways are beginning to appear. But for the present, information about the connections between hypertext and the development of reading and writing abilities remains largely dependent on anecdote and prediction.

WORK IN PROGRESS

In Australia, a literacy and technology study is examining teacher education, exemplary classroom practices and curriculum initiatives, using document analysis, case study and observational 'snapshots' of good practice (Lankshear, Bigum, Durrant, Green, Morgan, Murray, Snyder & Wild, 1996). Also originating in Australia, but including accounts of current research in the US, the UK and Australia, a group is working on a book which aims to contribute to our theoretical understandings of computer-mediated literacy practices (Snyder, 1997). The following paragraphs summarise some of this work.

Hawisher and Selfe are extending their history of literacy and technology studies. Knobel, Lankshear, Honan and Crawford are investigating the new technologies in the context of second-language learning. Kress has turned his attention to the future of writing in an age when the visual has assumed new importance. Concerned with the changes electronic technologies portend for reading and writing practices, Burbules is exploring the emergence of new rhetorics and literacies. Also interested in changes to textual practices, Moran and Hawisher are examining the uses and impact of electronic mail. Douglas, Joyce and Snyder are taking further their work on hypertext. Douglas is considering the implications of hypertext for argumentative writing, Joyce continues to explicate constructive hypertext and its connections with new narrative forms, while Snyder looks at the limitations of polarised responses to the use of hypertext.

Concentrating on the changes to the cultures of teaching and learning in computer-mediated educational sites, Smith and Curtin are conducting a study of the social implications for schooling of students' out-of-school computer activities. Beavis is considering the influences of new media forms, in particular computer games, for schools and curriculum. Johnson-Eilola is examining learning in the age of global communication networks. These examples represent just some of the many important projects undertaken by researchers across the globe working in the area of computer-mediated literacies.

PROBLEMS AND DIFFICULTIES

To some extent, the research findings are inconclusive and our knowledge in this area partial. What we have learned is that the field is volatile and the political, social and cultural influences complex. One explanation is that reading and writing with electronic technologies are processes simply too new and dynamic to be thoroughly investigated. But it also may be that reading and writing are such complex cognitive, social and cultural practices that we may never fully understand the influences of these technologies.

A difficulty with research in this area is that technological determinism – the assumption that qualities inherent in the computer medium itself are responsible for changes in social and cultural practices – permeates the academic discourse. Technologies such as hypertext are credited with transforming education systems, democratising schools and promoting the breakdown of artificial divisions between the disciplines. Computer-supported forums are represented as democratic spaces in which issues related to gender, race and socioeconomic status are minimised; students speak without interruption; and marginalised individuals can acquire more central voices. Such claims need to be interrogated as they overlook the human agency integral to all technological innovation. Researchers need to assume a critical perspective to explore the cultural and ideological characteristics of technology and the implications of these characteristics in educational settings.

This field is characterised by rapid change. As new sites for research emerge, 'sites' that are virtual and boundless, researchers are faced with the challenge of how to investigate them effectively. To continue to meet the demands of the new research contexts in this chameleon field, we need to be wary of nominating as necessarily better or more desirable particular research approaches. We should also avoid naturalising whatever is the current favoured methodological approach as the most progressive. Researchers require flexible, sensitive frameworks for understanding and portraying the complex phenomena of computer-mediated literacy settings.

FUTURE DIRECTIONS

We have reached what could be called a maturing of the field of literacy and technology research. The growth of a multi-method approach has strengthened our understanding that different perspectives give us different truths and that future research can be enriched by hearing multiple voices. We are in the process of developing ways of understanding the connections between literacy practices and the uses of the new electronic technologies that are both 'structured *and* dynamic' (Snyder, 1995, p. 57).

The research agenda is fertile with possibilities. In the first instance, researchers should build on previous investigations, adding to the growing knowledge base about the connections between literacy, technology, curriculum and culture. It would be salutary to concentrate on students who have grown up with the technologies. A longitudinal approach to the study of young people immersed in computer culture will yield new understandings of computer-mediated literacy practices. As students represent a different generation, one with a different relationship than ours to computers and to print text, we must observe them, ask them questions and listen to their answers. They should be our co-researchers.

We know that the introduction of computers into literacy curricula is a contextual change that encourages alterations in the political, social and educational structures of systems, but we need to look more closely at how. There needs to be more research into how language and literacy teachers integrate computers into curricula and how computers interact with the whole school curriculum. How does pedagogy change? Do teachers' expectations alter? What are the implications for teachers' professional development and for the training of preservice teachers?

We need more research on patterns of resistance to the new technologies. We need to explore further why teachers who work in environments that have computer facilities remain wary of the use of the technology in their classrooms, despite (or perhaps because) of the fact that we face a future dominated by computer culture. We should also be careful in ascribing to the technology powers it does not possess. If we see computers used in innovative ways we want to be cautious about inferring that there is a cause-and-effect relationship between adopting computers and effective teacher practice (Miller & Olson, 1994).

Confronted by the largely uncharted territories of cyberspace in which our students are increasingly the navigators, messier, less certain, more reflexive, multivoiced research texts seem to be a useful way to respond. It is likely, however, that the problem of representation will continue to be complicated by the fluid, metamorphosing, unpredictable nature of the electronic spaces themselves.

Monash University
Australia

REFERENCES

Allen, G. & Thompson, A.: 1995, 'Analysis of the effect of networking on computer-assisted collaborative writing in a fifth grade classroom', *Journal of Educational Computing Research* 12(1), 65–75.

Bangert-Drowns, R.L.: 1993, 'The word processor as an instructional tool: A meta-analysis of word processing in writing instruction', *Review of Educational Research* 63(1), 69–93.

Batson, T.: 1988, 'The ENFI project: A networked classroom approach to writing instruction', *Academic Computing* 2(32–322), 55–56.

Bridwell, L.S., Sirc, G. & Brooke, R.: 1985, 'Revising and computing: Case studies of student writers', in S. Freedman (ed.), *The Acquisition of Written Language: Revision and Response*, Ablex, New Jersey, 172–194.

Catano, J.: 1985, 'Computer-based writing: Navigating the fluid text', *College Composition and Communication*, 36(3), 309–316.

Cirello, V.J.: 1986, 'The effect of word processing on the writing abilities of tenth grade remedial writing students', *Dissertation Abstracts International*, 47(2531A) (University Microfilms No. 86 14, 353).

Cochran-Smith, M.: 1991, 'Word processing and writing in elementary classrooms: A critical review of related literature', *Review of Educational Research* 61(1), 107–155.

Cochran-Smith, M., Paris, C.L. & Kahn, J.L.: 1991, *Learning to Write Differently: Beginning Writers and Word Processing*, Ablex Publishing Corporation, Norwood, New Jersey.

Collier, R.M.: 1981, 'The influence of computer-based text editors on the revision strategies of inexperienced writers', Paper presented at Annual Meeting of Pacific North-West Conference on English in the Two Year College, Calgary, Canada, ERIC Document Reproduction Service No. 211 998.

Daiute, C.: 1986, 'Physical and cognitive factors in revising: Insights from studies with computers', *Research in the Teaching of English* 20(2), 141–159.

Dickinson, D.K.: 1986, 'Cooperation, collaboration and computers: Integrating a computer into a second grade writing program', *Research in the Teaching of English* 20(4), 357–378.

Faigley, L.L. & Witte, S.: 1981, 'Analysing revisions', *College Composition and Communication* 32, 400–414.

Gee, J.: 1990, *Social Linguistics and Literacies: Ideology in Discourses*, Falmer Press, London.

Geest, van der, T. & Remmers, T.: 1994, 'The computer as means of communication for peer-review groups', *Computers and Composition* 11(3), 237–250.

Gould, J.D.: 1978, 'Experiments on composing letters: some facts, some myths and some observations', in L. Gregg & I. Steinberg (eds.), *Cognitive Processes in Writing*, Lawrence Erlbaum, New Jersey, 97–127.

Hawisher, G.E., LeBlanc, P., Moran, C. & Selfe, C.L.: 1996, *Computers and the Teaching of Writing in American Higher Education, 1979–1994: A History*, Ablex, Norwood, New Jersey.

Herrmann, A.: 1987, 'Ethnographic study of a high school writing class using computers: Marginal, technically proficient and productive learners', in L. Gerrard (ed.), *Writing at Century's End: Essays on Computer-Assisted Instruction*, Random, New York, 79–91.

Jennings, E.M.: 1987, 'Paperless writing: Boundary conditions and their implications', in L. Gerrard (ed.), *Writing at Century's End: Essays on Computer-Assisted Composition*, Random, New York, 11–20.

Joram, E., Woodruff, E., Bryson, M. & Lindsay, P.H.: 1992, 'The effects of revising with a word processor on written composition', *Research in the Teaching of English* 26(2), 167–193.

Kramarae, C.: 1988, *Technology and Women's Voices: Keeping in Touch*, Routledge & Kegan Paul, New York.

Lankshear, C., Bigum, C., Durrant, C., Green, B., Morgan, W., Murray, J., Snyder, I. & Wild, M.: 1996, 'Literacy, technology and education: A project report', *The Australian Journal of Language and Literacy* 19(4), 345–59.

Miller, L. & Olson, J.: 1994, 'Putting the computer in its place: A study of teaching with technology', *Journal of Curriculum Studies* 26(2), 121–141.

Owston, R.D., Murphy, S. & Wideman, H.H.: 1992, 'The effects of word processing on students' writing quality and revision strategies', *Research in the Teaching of English* 26(3), 249–276.

Palmquist, M.E.: 1993, 'Network-supported interaction in two writing classrooms', *Computers and Composition* 10(4), 25–58.

Selfe, C.L.: 1985, 'The electronic pen: Computers and the composing process', in J.L. Collins & E.A. Sommers (eds.), *Writing On-Line: Using Computers in the Teaching of Writing*, Boynton/Cook, New Jersey, 55–66.

Sommers, E.A.: 1985, 'The effects of word processing and writing instruction on the writing processes and products of college writers', ERIC Reproduction Service No. 269 762.

Snyder, I.A.: 1995, 'Multiple perspectives in literacy research: Integrating the quantitative and qualitative', *Language and Education* 9(1), 45–59.

Snyder, I.: 1996, *Hypertext: The Electronic Labyrinth*, Melbourne University Press, Melbourne.

Snyder, I.: 1997, (ed.), *Page to Screen: Taking Literacy into the Electronic Era*, Allen & Unwin, Sydney.

Staberg, E.M.: 1994, 'Gender and science in the Swedish compulsory school', *Gender and Education* 6(1), 35–45.

Zellermayer, M., Salomon, G., Globerson, T. & Givon, H.: 1991, 'Enhancing writing-related metacognitions through a computerised writing partner', *American Educational Research Journal* 28(2), 373–91.

MARILYN MARTIN-JONES

BILINGUAL CLASSROOM DISCOURSE: CHANGING RESEARCH APPROACHES AND DIVERSIFICATION OF RESEARCH SITES

Classroom-based research in bilingual and multilingual settings is now entering its third decade. Its origins lie in studies carried out in bilingual education programmes in the United States in the 1970s. During the last twenty years or so, research in this area has taken a number of significant theoretical and methodological turns. These developments have been partly due to the interdisciplinarity of the work undertaken and to intersecting currents of influence. They are also due to the gradual diversification of research sites. As research began to be taken in different historical locations and in different educational contexts in Africa, Europe, North America (including Canada), South America, South and South East Asia, we began to see different concerns being addressed (also see Volume 5).

EARLY DEVELOPMENTS

The first significant breakthroughs were made when researchers began to work with audio recordings of classroom interactions and when analyses took a linguistic turn. Researchers such as Milk (1981, 1982) and Guthrie (1984) were among the first to adopt a linguistic approach in their work. Milk focused on the Spanish/English discourse of a Mexican-American teacher in a twelfth grade class in San Jose, California. Guthrie conducted a comparative study of two teachers (one bilingual and one monolingual) working with Chinese learners in a Californian elementary school. These researchers gave particular prominence to the analysis of classroom discourse functions. Their aim was to throw light on the ways in which teachers and learners were getting things done bilingually. In their analyses of their audio-recorded data, they drew on descriptive frameworks developed by those who were working on monolingual discourse. For instance, Milk (1981) used an adapted version of the classroom discourse model proposed by Sinclair & Coulthard (1975). The original inventory of 22 classroom discourse acts compiled by Sinclair and Coulthard was adapted so as to focus on the patterns of code-switching.

I discussed the methodology of these studies (along with some of the research findings) in an earlier research review (Martin-Jones, 1995), so I will not replicate this here. I will just note that this work was constrained

N.H. Hornberger and D. Corson (eds), Encyclopedia of Language and Education,
Volume 8: Research Methods in Language and Education, 249–258.
© *1997 Kluwer Academic Publishers. Printed in the Netherlands.*

by the approach adopted to discourse analysis. Analyses were oriented toward cataloguing and quantifying. The focus was still on individual acts rather than on the sequential flow of classroom discourse. The main preoccupation was with teacher talk and the analysts' interpretations of the functions of teachers' utterances tended to be privileged.

In monolingual and bilingual classrooms, teachers and learners exchange meanings with each other in intricate and highly routinised sequences of interaction. They attend to each others' contributions to the interaction and, in a bilingual setting, they also attend to each others' proficiency in the languages involved in the interaction. What was still lacking in the early studies of bilingual classroom talk was an account of what Mehan has called: "the mutual synchronization of behaviour" (1981, p. 40).

THE INTERACTIONAL TURN: MAJOR CONTRIBUTIONS

The late 1970s saw a surge of interest in the dynamics of spoken interaction. The impetus for this was the seminal work by Erving Goffman (1967) and the development of ethnomethodology (Garfinkel, 1972), conversational analysis (Sacks, Schegloff & Jefferson, 1974), interactional sociolinguistics (Gumperz, 1982) and microethnography (Erickson & Shultz, 1981). The impact of these approaches to the analysis of talk was already evident in studies of bilingual classroom discourse conducted in the early 1980s (see, for example, Cazden et al., 1980; Zentella, 1981; Mohatt & Erickson, 1981; Erickson & Mohatt, 1982; Moll et al., 1985). Attention shifted away from the communicative functions of individual utterances to the sequential structures of classroom discourse. The focus was now on the joint enactment of teaching and learning by bilingual teachers *and* learners rather than just on teacher talk. The contexts for teaching/learning were no longer seen as given but as constituted through interaction and therefore continually open to change and negotiation.

This concern with the situated and sequential nature of classroom discourse has continued to be a central feature of most research carried out in bilingual settings. With the diversification of research sites in the late 1980s and early 1990s and with the refinement of approaches to the study of bilingual codeswitching (Auer, 1984; Heller, 1988), considerable advances were made. In the first section below, I will give examples of studies which have foregrounded the situated nature of bilingual classroom talk, drawing attention to the ways in which meanings are negotiated moment by moment in bilingual classroom interactions. In the second section, I will look at research which focused on timing and synchrony in classroom interactions, and, in particular, on the accomplishment of cultural congruence. In the third section, I will turn to research which has identified patterns of codeswitching which recur across sequential structures of classroom discourse and I will show that this led researchers to look for explanations beyond the immediate context of the interaction, and beyond the school, in the wider social and political context.

My decision to organise this part of my review into three separate sections does not imply that these dimensions of bilingual classroom discourse are unrelated. In fact, most of the studies referred to below have taken account of all three dimensions of bilingual discourse: its situatedness, synchrony and sequentiality. Some have also aimed to gain insights into the impact of language policies and ideologies and the construction of asymmetrical social relations through the lens of bilingual discourse practices. Unfortunately, because of the scope of this review, I am unable to provide a full account of each of the studies mentioned or to give examples of real classroom discourse practices. I therefore refer my readers to the researchers' own accounts. I have also had to be selective in the range of studies mentioned. The field is growing rapidly and the range and quality of the work undertaken to date is impressive. I have tried to capture some of this range in the studies selected.

Foregrounding the Situated Nature of Bilingual Classroom Talk

The interactional sociolinguistic approach developed by John Gumperz (1982) has been particularly influential in studies of bilingual classroom discourse, especially his notion of "contextualization cue" (1982, p. 131). According to Gumperz, contextualization cues are any choices of verbal or non-verbal forms within a communicative encounter which interlocutors recognise as 'marked', that is, choices which depart from an established or expected pattern of communication. Contextualization cues range from lexical and syntactic choices to different types of codeswitching and style shifting. They also operate at the prosodic, paralinguistic, kinesic and gestural level. An interactional sociolinguistic approach to classroom discourse analysis foregrounds the ways in which teachers and learners draw on contextualization cues and on the background knowledge that they bring to different communicative encounters. (Background knowledge is also characterised in this research literature as frames, scripts, schemata, structures of expectation or members' resources.) Contextualization cues and knowledge resources are seen as the key means by which participants in teaching/learning encounters negotiate their way through an interaction, make situated inferences as to what is going on and work out their respective discourse roles.

We now have ample examples in the research literature of teachers using code contrast as a resource for demarcating different kinds of discourse: to signal the transition between preparing for a lesson and the start of the lesson; to specify a particular addressee; to distinguish 'doing a lesson' from talk about it; to change footing or make an aside; to distinguish quotations from a written text from talk about them; to bring out the voices of different characters in a narrative; to distinguish classroom management utterances from talk related to the lesson content.

When codeswitching occurs in classrooms, it frequently co-occurs with other contextualization cues, particularly prosodic cues or non-verbal cues, such as a change in eye gaze direction or gestures. This may well be a distinctive feature of bilingual *classroom* discourse, particularly in situations where teacher talk predominates.

Teachers codeswitch to get their points across but they also attend to the language proficiencies and preferences of the learner(s). Auer (1984) has provided a useful distinction between two kinds of codeswitching which enables us to take account of this. He has identified two main orientations to the use of code contrast as a contextualization cue: one being discourse-related and the other being participant-related. Discourse-related switching (or, language alternation, in Auer's terms) is speaker-oriented: it serves as a resource for demarcating different kinds of utterances within an interactional sequence. Participant-related switching is hearer-oriented: it takes account of the hearer's linguistic preferences or competences. Although this distinction was first formulated in community-based research on bilingualism, it is particularly relevant to the analysis of bilingual classroom discourse and has been taken up by researchers in different educational settings (Arthur, 1996; Nussbaum, 1990).

Participant-related codeswitching predominates in some bilingual classrooms. It occurs when teachers provide translations, reformulations and clarifications. It also occurs when teachers "negotiate the cultural relevance" of lesson content to learners' life-worlds outside the classroom (Canagarajah, 1995, p. 188). Or, it can be manifested in occasional switches in teachers' discourse (e.g. on question tags) aimed at encouraging contributions from learners or checking on understanding (Arthur, 1996).

As Nussbaum (1990) shows, teachers *and* learners engage in participant-related codeswitching. But, because most of the research so far has been done in classroom contexts where teacher-led discourse predominates, the evidence of spontaneous switching by learners is still scanty. Certainly, teachers' attitudes to learner switching vary considerably: some studies describe classrooms where learners' persistent use of L1 is accepted by teachers because this enables learners to make contributions (see Lin, 1990, 1996). In other classrooms, learner codeswitching is either discouraged or proscribed (Arthur, 1996). In yet another context, Canagarajah (1995) reports that learners in English classes in Jaffna switched into Tamil in secretive exchanges when their teacher was not paying attention. In this way, they helped each other make sense of the lesson content.

Some uses of code-switching do recur in diverse bilingual learning environments. However, as Auer (1984) points out, it is impossible to compile a comprehensive inventory of the functions of codeswitching. The number of possible functions is infinite. Speakers continually create new ways of drawing on code contrast as a communicative resource.

Because of the fine-grained nature of the interactional sociolinguistic approach to the study of bilingual classroom interaction, extensive use is made of audio-recording. Particular teaching/learning events are transcribed and analysed in detail. Care is taken not to privilege the analyst's interpretation of the meanings generated by codeswitching. Researchers check their interpretations with the participants in the events by playing back the audio-recordings. The aim is to achieve as much convergence as possible between the participants' understandings of what was going on in the event and those of the analyst.

Investigating the Accomplishment of Synchrony in Bilingual Interactions

The microethnographic approach to social interaction (Erickson & Shultz, 1981) was developed alongside the early work in interactional sociolinguistics (see the review by Garcez in this volume). There is a similar emphasis on the situated and sequential nature of classroom discourse. By the early 1980s, recommendations were being made about how this approach might be applied to studies in bilingual classrooms (Mehan, 1981; Moll, 1981; Trueba & Wright, 1981).

Microethnographic studies focus especially on rhythm, timing and synchrony. Particular attention is given to the ways in which non-verbal cues co-occur with verbal ones and to the manner in which these constellations of cues are interpreted. As Hornberger (1995) has noted in a recent review of ethnographic and sociolinguistic research in educational settings, microethnography preserves some of the elements of earlier work in the ethnography of communication (Hymes, 1968; see also the review by Farah in this volume). The focus of the descriptive and analytic work is still on key events and the participant structures within them. However, microethnography aims for detailed analysis of the face-to-face interactional processes involved in a communicative event whilst the ethnography of communication entails a full description of the constituent components of an event.

The methodology of microethnographic studies overlaps with that developed in interactional sociolinguistic work. However, microethnography involves more use of video-recording, because of the emphasis given to capturing the full range of non-verbal contextualization cues which co-occur with verbal cues at particular moments of the interaction. The transcription work is also more detailed because of the need to take account of non-verbal cues.

Microethnographic work in classrooms has been particularly successful in documenting congruences (or incongruences) which emerge in interactions between teachers and learners. I will briefly mention here one illustrative study carried out by Erickson, Cazden, Carrasco and Maldonado-Guzman in two first grade classes of a bilingual education programme in Chicago (see Cazden et al., 1980). The teachers and learners in this study were all Mexican-Americans. The aim was to provide a detailed microethnographic account of the interactional styles of two successful bilingual teachers. (The classes were positively evaluated by parents who opted for bilingual provision for their children whenever possible). Whilst there were differences between the teachers in their approach to classroom organisation, there were also similarities in the ways in which they interacted with the children, especially in the manner in which they achieved classroom control. According to Cazden et al. (1980), the teachers had a culturally-specific style which was manifested in particular constellations of verbal and non-verbal cues in the teacher-learner interactions that were video-recorded. These included: codeswitching, use of terms of address which were familiar to the children, frequent use of diminutives, regular reminders to the children that they should observe community norms of *respeto* (respect), references to the families known to the teacher and non-verbal expressions of *cariño*.

Identifying and Explaining Patterns of Codeswitching Across the Sequential Structures of Classroom Discourse

In an early paper on ethnographic research in bilingual education classrooms, Mehan (1981) emphasised the contingent nature of classroom discourse. He noted that young learners not only learn lessons but also have to learn the complex interactional routines of each classroom. These vary across and even within teaching/learning events. Different teachers may also engage in different practices. Mehan also noted that, in bilingual classrooms, learners have the additional challenge of working out the local codeswitching practices. He therefore stressed the need to take account of learners' contributions to teaching/learning exchanges, even when the talk is heavily teacher-dominated, in order to gauge how well bilingual children are faring with the communicative challenges of bilingual classroom life.

Since this paper by Mehan (1981), there has been considerable interest in the accomplishment of reciprocity in bilingual classroom exchanges. The main focus has been on the management of turn-taking in more than one language. The methodology differs from that involved in analysing local codeswitches or clusters of contextualization cues. It involves tracking codeswitching across the sequential structures (e.g. Initiation-Response-Evaluation (IRE) exchanges) which recur in particular classroom events to establish if any patterns of codeswitching predominate.

Some of the patterns documented so far have been particularly telling. This has led researchers to seek explanations beyond the parameters of the bilingual interactions themselves: in the life histories, attitudes and ideologies of the teachers; in the circumstances of the institutions where the teaching and learning is taking place; in policies and wider educational discourses about the education of bilingual children and in the social and political conditions which have shaped educational practices and forms of provision in each historical location. What we have seen emerging in the 1990s is research of a more critical nature in which links are made between local discourse practices, ideologies about legitimate forms of bilingual and monolingual language use in the classroom and the role of schooling in the reproduction of asymmetrical relations of power between social groups with different languages and forms of cultural capital (see, for example, a collection of papers edited by Martin-Jones & Heller, 1996; see also the reviews by May and Norton in this volume).

Here I will give just one example of bilingual classrom research which has documented recurring patterns of codeswitching across classroom routines and which has also incorporated a critical perspective. This was based in Hong Kong, in Anglo-Chinese secondary schools, where English is still the medium of instruction. Lin (1990) investigated patterns of code-switching in English language lessons. She also did a follow-up study of five content lessons where English was supposed to be the medium of instruction (Lin, 1996). In the English lessons, Lin observed that the teachers made ample use of Cantonese in teaching English vocabulary and grammar and noted that they did so "in highly ordered patterns of alternation between English and Cantonese" (Lin, 1990, p. 115): the teacher first introduced a grammar point in English, then repeated the point and/or elaborated on it in Cantonese. Then, key elements were reiterated in English.

In the content lessons, the following pattern predominated:
Teacher – Initiation (English–Cantonese)
Students – Response (Cantonese)
Teacher – Evaluation (Cantonese–English)
(Adapted from Lin, 1996, p. 72)

The teachers' acceptance of responses from students in Cantonese served as a means of enabling the students to contribute to the coproduction of the body of knowledge officially sanctioned for that lesson. But, at the same time, the pattern of codeswitching between English and Cantonese in the teachers' contributions to these exchanges gave clear messages to the learners about the relative value of English and Cantonese as languages of learning. Lin dubbed this type of bilingual classroom communication: "Cantonese-annotated English academic monolingualism" (1996, p. 70). She argued that: "the main purpose of using Cantonese (L1) is not to establish bilingual knowledge of academic terms but to expediently annotate English (L2) key terms, key statements, or texts to students who have limited English linguistic resources" (Ibid).

A further pattern of codeswitching identified by Lin (1996) within the IRE exchanges in this corpus was frequent codeswitching into English on single lexical items, usually key terms for the lessons recorded. There was no parallel pattern of switching into Cantonese in stretches of English discourse. Lin argued that this provided further evidence of the dominance of English as the language of academic learning.This pattern of switching into the dominant language on single lexical items or key terms has been documented in many studies of bilingual classroom interaction, especially in locations where there is a sharp differentiation in status between the languages or where most of the texts used and produced are in the dominant language.

FUTURE DIRECTIONS

Since the interactional turn in research in bilingual classrooms, we have developed a much better understanding of the range and complexity of the cultural and communicative processes at work in these settings. We also have powerful analytic tools for investigating teaching/learning events that are accomplished bilingually (or, indeed, with more than two languages or language varieties). As research sites have diversified, we have had broader and richer insights into the ways in which bilingual teachers and learners draw on the verbal and non-verbal resources available to them within the communicative cycles of classroom life.

Future studies in this area are likely to move in one of two broad directions. There will be research which continues to refine the analytic tools developed so far, probing yet further the dynamics of bilingual classroom interaction and perhaps throwing more light on the way in which codeswitching contributes to the scaffolding of joint knowledge construction. There will also be research which builds on the attempts that have already been made to incorporate a critical perspective, grounding micro-analyses of bilingual discourse practices within wider social and historical accounts.

Reviewing trends in research on codeswitching, Gal (1992) drew a distinction between two broad research goals: (1) Aiming for universalising explanations which "focus on the perspective of the speaker and listener" (1992, p. 135); (2) Aiming for historically contextualised explanations. In the first kind of research, codeswitching is assumed to be more or less the 'same' everywhere: "a salient example of broader processes of interpretation and production which characterise all of human interaction" (1992, p. 139). Studies which pursue the second goal take account of the perspectives of the speaker and listener but *also* aim to interpret and explain the specific bilingual discourse practices documented with reference to their social and historical location. Research in bilingual classrooms appears to be moving along these two broad trajectories: with some researchers concentrating on providing fine-tuned analyses of *how* teachers and learners accomplish lessons in two languages; while others also try to explain *why* the codeswitching practices observed in particular historical locations are the way they are.

Lancaster University
England

REFERENCES

Arthur, J.: 1996, 'Codeswitching and collusion: Classroom interaction in Botswana primary schools', *Linguistics and Education* 8(1), 17–34.

Auer, P.: 1984, *Bilingual Conversation*, John Benjamins, Amsterdam.

Canagarajah, A.S.: 1995, 'Functions of codeswitching in ESL classrooms: Socialising bilingualism in Jaffna', *Journal of Multilingual and Multicultural Development* 16(3), 173–195.

Cazden, C.B., Carrasco, R., Maldonado-Guzman, A.A. & Erickson, F.: 1980, 'The contribution of ethnographic research to bicultural bilingual education', in J.E. Alatis (ed.), *Current Issues in Bilingual Education: Georgetown University Round Table on Languages and Linguistics*, Georgetown University Press, Washington, DC.

Erickson, F. & Mohatt, G.: 1982, 'Cultural organization of participant structures in two classrooms of Indian students', in G.D. Spindler (ed.), *Doing the Ethnography of Schooling: Educational Anthropology in Action*, Holt, Rinehart and Winston, New York.

Erickson, F. & Shultz, J.: 1981, 'When is a context? Some issues and methods in the analysis of social competence' in J.L. Green & C. Wallat (eds.), *Ethnography and Language in Educational Settings*, Ablex, Norwood, NJ, 147–160.

Gal, S.: 1992, 'Concepts of power in the research on codeswitching', *Papers from the Codeswitching Summer School, Pavia (Italy), September 9–12 (European Science Foundation Network on Codeswitching and Language Contact*, European Science Foundation, Strasbourg, France, 135–151.

Garfinkel, H.: 1972, 'Remarks on ethnomethodology', in J. Gumperz & D. Hymes (eds.), *Directions in Sociolinguistics: the Ethnography of Communication*, Holt, Rinehart and Winston, New York.

Goffman, E.: 1967, *Interaction Ritual: Essays on Face-to-Face Behaviour*, Garden City, New York.

Gumperz, J.J.: 1982, *Discourse Strategies*, Cambridge University Press, Cambridge.

Guthrie, L.F.: 1984, 'Contrasts in teachers' language use in a Chinese-English bilingual classroom', in J. Handscombe, R.A. Orem & B.P. Taylor (eds.), *On TESOL 1983: The Question of Control*, TESOL, Washington, DC.

Heller, M. (ed.): 1988, *Codeswitching: Anthropological and Sociolinguistic Perspectives*, Mouton de Gruyter, Berlin.

Hornberger, N.: 1995, 'Ethnography in linguistic perspective: Understanding school processes', *Language and Education* 9(4), 233–248.

Hymes, D.: 1968, 'The ethnography of speaking', in J. Fishman (ed.), *Readings in the Sociology of Language*, Mouton De Gruyter, The Hague, 99–139

Lin, A.: 1990, *Teaching in Two Tongues: Language Alternation in Foreign Language Classrooms* (Research Report No. 3), City Polytechnic of Hong Kong, Hong Kong.

——: 1996, 'Bilingualism or linguistic segregation? Symbolic domination, resistance and codeswitching', *Linguistics and Education* 8(1), 49–84.

Martin-Jones, M.: 1995, 'Codeswitching in the classroom: Two decades of research', in L. Milroy & P. Muysken (eds.), *One Speaker, Two Languages: Cross-Disciplinary Perspectives on Codeswitching*, Cambridge University Press, Cambridge, 90–111.

Martin-Jones, M. & Heller, M. (eds.): 1996, *Linguistics and Education* 8(1&2), two Special Issues on 'Education in multilingual settings: Discourse, identities and power', 1–228.

Mehan, H.: 1981, 'Ethnography of bilingual education', in H.T. Trueba, G.P. Guthrie & K.H. Au (eds.), 36–55.

Milk, R.: 1981, 'An analysis of the functional allocation of Spanish and English in a bilingual classroom', *California Association for Bilingual Education: Research Journal* 2(2), 11–26.

——: 1982, 'Language use in bilingual classrooms: Two case studies', in M. Hines & W. Rutherford (eds.), *On TESOL '81*, Teachers of English to Speakers of Other Languages (TESOL), Washington, DC, 181–191.

Mohatt, G. & Erickson, F.: 1981, 'Cultural differences in teaching styles in an Odawa school: A sociolinguistic approach', in H.T. Trueba, G.P. Guthrie & K.H. Au (eds.).

Moll, L.E.: 1981, 'The micro-ethnographic study of bilingual schooling', in R.V. Padilla (ed.), *Ethnoperspectives in Bilingual Education Research III*, Eastern Michigan University, Ipsilanti.

Moll, L.E., Diaz, E., Estrada, E. & Lopez, L.: 1985, 'Making contexts: The social construction of lessons in two languages', in M. Saravia-Shore & S. Arvizu (eds.), *Cross Cultural and Communicative Competencies: Ethnographies of Educational Programs for Language Minority Students*, Council on Anthropology and Education, Washington, DC.

Nussbaum, L.: 1990, 'Plurilingualism in foreign language classes in Catalonia', *Papers from the Workshop on the Impact and Consequences of Codeswitching. (European Science Foundation Network on Codeswitching and Language Contact)*, European Science Foundation, Strasbourg, France, 141–163.

Sacks, H., Schegloff, E. & Jefferson, G.: 1974, 'A simplest systematics for the organisation of turn-taking in conversation', *Language* 50, 696–735.

Sinclair, J.M. & Coulthard, R.M.: 1975, *Towards an Analysis of Discourse: The English Used by Teachers and Pupils*, Oxford University Press: Oxford.

Trueba, H.T., Guthrie, G.P. & Au, K.H. (eds.): 1981, *Culture and the Bilingual Classroom: Studies in Classroom Ethnography*, Newbury House, Rowley, Mass.

Trueba, H.T. & Wright, P.: 1981, 'A challenge for ethnographic researchers in bilingual settings: Analyzing Spanish-English classroom interaction', *Journal of Multilingual and Multicultural Development* 2, 243–57.

Zentella, A.C.: 1981, '*Ta Bien*, you could answer me *En Cualquier Idioma*: Puerto Rican codeswitching in bilingual classrooms', in R. Duran (ed.), *Latino Language and Communicative Behavior*, Ablex Publishing Corporation, Norwood, NJ, 109–132.

SUBJECT INDEX

NAME INDEX

CUMULATIVE SUBJECT INDEX

CUMULATIVE NAME INDEX

TABLE OF CONTENTS

VOLUME 1: LANGUAGE POLICY AND POLITICAL ISSUES IN EDUCATION

TABLE OF CONTENTS

TABLE OF CONTENTS

VOLUME 2: LITERACY

TABLE OF CONTENTS

TABLE OF CONTENTS

VOLUME 3: ORAL DISCOURSE AND EDUCATION

TABLE OF CONTENTS

TABLE OF CONTENTS

VOLUME 4: SECOND LANGUAGE EDUCATION

TABLE OF CONTENTS

TABLE OF CONTENTS

VOLUME 5: BILINGUAL EDUCATION

TABLE OF CONTENTS

TABLE OF CONTENTS

VOLUME 6: KNOWLEDGE ABOUT LANGUAGE

TABLE OF CONTENTS

TABLE OF CONTENTS

VOLUME 7: LANGUAGE TESTING AND ASSESSMENT

TABLE OF CONTENTS

Section 2: Methods of Testing and Assessment

Section 3: The Quantitative and Qualitative Validation of Tests

Section 4: The Ethics and Effects of Testing and Assessment

Encyclopedia of Language and Education

Set ISBN Hb 0-7923-4596-7; Pb 0-7923-4936-9

1. R. Wodak and D. Corson (eds.): *Language Policy and Political Issues in Education.*
   1997
   ISBN Hb 0-7923-4713-7
   ISBN Pb 0-7923-4928-8

2. V. Edwards and D. Corson (eds.): *Literacy.* 1997
   ISBN Hb 0-7923-4595-0
   ISBN Pb 0-7923-4929-6

3. B. Davies and D. Corson (eds.): *Oral Discourse and Education.* 1997
   ISBN Hb 0-7923-4639-4
   ISBN Pb 0-7923-4930-X

4. G.R. Tucker and D. Corson (eds.): *Second Language Education.* 1997
   ISBN Hb 0-7923-4640-8
   ISBN Pb 0-7923-4931-8

5. J. Cummins and D. Corson (eds.): *Bilingual Education.* 1997
   ISBN Hb 0-7923-4806-0
   ISBN Pb 0-7923-4932-6

6. L. van Lier and D. Corson (eds.): *Knowledge about Language.* 1997
   ISBN Hb 0-7923-4641-6
   ISBN Pb 0-7923-4933-4

7. C. Clapham and D. Corson (eds.): *Language Testing and Assessment.* 1997
   ISBN Hb 0-7923-4702-1
   ISBN Pb 0-7923-4934-2

8. N.H. Hornberger and D. Corson (eds.): *Research Methods in Language and Educa-*
   tion. 1997
   ISBN Hb 0-7923-4642-4
   ISBN Pb 0-7923-4935-0

KLUWER ACADEMIC PUBLISHERS – DORDRECHT / BOSTON / LONDON